Western Sahara

As the Spanish were preparing to leave colonized Western Sahara in 1975, Morocco invaded, sparking a war with the Western Saharan Polisario Front. About 70% of Western Sahara was occupied by Morocco, which stations up to 140,000 soldiers in the territory, primarily along a 1700 kilometre long sand berm that is protected by one of the world's largest fields of landmines. In 1991, Morocco and the Polisario Front agreed to a truce ahead of a referendum on Western Sahara's future. However, Morocco has since refused to allow the referendum to take place, and has begun the extensive exploitation of Western Sahara's non-renewable natural resources. This has both highlighted the plight of the Saharawi people who live in refugee camps in Algeria and in occupied Western Sahara, and pushed the Polisario Front back to a position where it is openly canvassing for a return to war.

This book was originally published as a special issue of *Global Change, Peace & Security*.

Damien Kingsbury holds a Personal Chair and is Professor of International Politics in the School of Humanities and Social Sciences at Deakin University, Melbourne, Australia. His research interests include assertions of self-determination, the role of the military in politics, post-colonial political structures, and nation formation. He is the author of *Sri Lanka and the Responsibility to Protect: politics, ethnicity and genocide* (2012), and *East Timor: the price of liberty* (2009).

Western Sahara
International law, justice and natural resources

Edited by
Damien Kingsbury

LONDON AND NEW YORK

First published 2016
by Routledge

2 Park Square, Milton Park, Abingdon, Oxfordshire OX14 4RN
711 Third Avenue, New York, NY 10017

Routledge is an imprint of the Taylor & Francis Group, an informa business

First issued in paperback 2017

Copyright © 2016 Taylor & Francis

All rights reserved. No part of this book may be reprinted or reproduced
or utilised in any form or by any electronic, mechanical, or other means,
now known or hereafter invented, including photocopying and recording,
or in any information storage or retrieval system, without permission in
writing from the publishers.

Notice:
Product or corporate names may be trademarks or registered trademarks,
and are used only for identification and explanation without intent to infringe.

British Library Cataloguing in Publication Data
A catalogue record for this book is available from the British Library

ISBN 13: 978-1-138-95892-0 (hbk)
ISBN 13: 978-1-138-50261-1 (pbk)

Typeset in Times New Roman
by RefineCatch Limited, Bungay, Suffolk

Publisher's Note
The publisher accepts responsibility for any inconsistencies that may have
arisen during the conversion of this book from journal articles to book chapters,
namely the possible inclusion of journal terminology.

Disclaimer
Every effort has been made to contact copyright holders for their permission to
reprint material in this book. The publishers would be grateful to hear from any
copyright holder who is not here acknowledged and will undertake to rectify
any errors or omissions in future editions of this book.

Contents

Citation Information		vii
Notes on Contributors		ix
1.	The role of resources in the resolution of the Western Sahara issue *Damien Kingsbury*	1
2.	The taking of the Sahara: the role of natural resources in the continuing occupation of Western Sahara *Jeffrey J. Smith*	11
3.	Western Sahara, resources, and international accountability *Stephen Zunes*	32
4.	The status of Western Sahara as occupied territory under international humanitarian law and the exploitation of natural resources *Ben Saul*	47
5.	The hidden cost of phosphate fertilizers: mapping multi-stakeholder supply chain risks and impacts from mine to fork *Dana Cordell, Andrea Turner and Joanne Chong*	69
6.	The role of natural resources in the building of an independent Western Sahara *Fadel Kamal*	89
7.	Independence by *fiat*: a way out of the impasse – the self-determination of Western Sahara, with lessons from Timor-Leste *Pedro Pinto Leite*	104
8.	Saharawi conflict phosphates and the Australian dinner table *Erik Hagen*	120
	Index	137

Citation Information

The chapters in this book were originally published in *Global Change, Peace & Security*, volume 27, issue 3 (October 2015). When citing this material, please use the original page numbering for each article, as follows:

Chapter 1
The role of resources in the resolution of the Western Sahara issue
Damien Kingsbury
Global Change, Peace & Security, volume 27, issue 3 (October 2015), pp. 253–262

Chapter 2
The taking of the Sahara: the role of natural resources in the continuing occupation of Western Sahara
Jeffrey J. Smith
Global Change, Peace & Security, volume 27, issue 3 (October 2015), pp. 263–284

Chapter 3
Western Sahara, resources, and international accountability
Stephen Zunes
Global Change, Peace & Security, volume 27, issue 3 (October 2015), pp. 285–299

Chapter 4
The status of Western Sahara as occupied territory under international humanitarian law and the exploitation of natural resources
Ben Saul
Global Change, Peace & Security, volume 27, issue 3 (October 2015), pp. 301–322

Chapter 5
The hidden cost of phosphate fertilizers: mapping multi-stakeholder supply chain risks and impacts from mine to fork
Dana Cordell, Andrea Turner and Joanne Chong
Global Change, Peace & Security, volume 27, issue 3 (October 2015), pp. 323–344

Chapter 6
The role of natural resources in the building of an independent Western Sahara
Fadel Kamal
Global Change, Peace & Security, volume 27, issue 3 (October 2015), pp. 345–359

CITATION INFORMATION

Chapter 7
Independence by fiat: *a way out of the impasse – the self-determination of Western Sahara, with lessons from Timor-Leste*
Pedro Pinto Leite
Global Change, Peace & Security, volume 27, issue 3 (October 2015), pp. 361–376

Chapter 8
Saharawi conflict phosphates and the Australian dinner table
Erik Hagen
Global Change, Peace & Security, volume 27, issue 3 (October 2015), pp. 377–393

For any permission-related enquiries please visit:
http://www.tandfonline.com/page/help/permissions

Notes on Contributors

Damien Kingsbury holds a Personal Chair in the Faculty of Arts and Education at Deakin University, Melbourne, and is Professor of International Politics in the School of Social Sciences and Humanities. Professor Kingsbury is author or editor of more than two dozen books and numerous book chapters and journal articles on political and security issues and has acted as adviser to a number of non-state military organizations seeking settlement of outstanding political claims. His primary research focuses on conflict resolution and political transitions in authoritarian and post-conflict environments.

Jeffrey J. Smith is a Canadian law professor (Carleton University), lawyer, and doctoral fellow (McGill University). He was previously counsel for the United Nations Transitional Administration in East Timor, engaged in the international law dimensions of that country's preparation for independence in 2002. Jeffrey has written extensively about Western Sahara, including its fisheries and environmental protection challenges, and the history and status of the Saharawi state-in-exile. His present areas of research include the development of international environmental law within the law of the sea, climate change regulation, human migration, and governance of the Arctic Ocean area. Jeffrey resides in Montreal and Ottawa.

Stephen Zunes is a prominent specialist on US Middle East policy. Professor Zunes has presented numerous lectures and conference papers in the United States and over a dozen foreign countries. He has traveled frequently to the Middle East and other conflict regions, meeting with prominent government officials, scholars, and dissidents. He has served as a political analyst for local, national, and international radio and television, and as a columnist for the *National Catholic Reporter*, *Huffington Post*, *Truthout*, *Alternet*, and *Common Dreams*. He has published scores of articles in academic journals, anthologies, magazines, and newspaper op-ed pages on such topics as US foreign policy, Middle Eastern politics, Latin American politics, African politics, human rights, arms control, social movements, and nonviolent action.

Ben Saul is Professor of International Law at the University of Sydney and an Australian Research Council Future Fellow. Ben has expertise in general public international law (particularly terrorism, human rights, the law of war, the use of force, international criminal law, environmental law, and the United Nations). He has published 11 books, over 80 scholarly articles, made hundreds of scholarly presentations, been awarded numerous research grants, and his research has been used in international and national courts. His book *Defining Terrorism in International Law* (Oxford, 2006) is the leading work on the subject, and he is lead author of the *Oxford Commentary on the International Covenant on Economic, Social and Cultural Rights* (2014), awarded the 2015 Certificate of Merit by the American Society of International Law. Ben has taught law at Oxford, the Hague Academy of International Law, and in China, India, Nepal, and Cambodia, and has been a Visiting Professor at Harvard. He has a doctorate

NOTES ON CONTRIBUTORS

in law from Oxford and honours degrees in Arts and Law from Sydney. Ben practises as a barrister in international, regional, and national courts, and was counsel in the largest successful case against Australia before the United Nations Human Rights Committee, *FKAG v Australia* and *MMM v Australia* (2013), involving the illegal indefinite detention of over 50 refugees. Ben has advised or consulted to various international organisations, governments, and NGOs and delivered technical assistance projects in developing countries. He has served on various professional and international bodies, including the International Law Association's International Committee for the Compensation of Victims of War. Ben often appears in the national and international media, including writing opinion in *The New York Times*.

Dana Cordell is a Research Principal at the Institute for Sustainable Futures, University of Technology Sydney. Dr Cordell leads and undertakes transdisciplinary research projects on sustainable food and resource futures at the Institute for Sustainable Futures. Many projects involve high-level stakeholder engagement to improve the research relevance, impact, and foster mutual learning. In 2008 Dr Cordell co-founded the Global Phosphorus Research Initiative – the first global platform to undertake research, facilitate networking and debate among policy-makers, industry, scientists, and the public to ensure food systems are resilient to the emerging global challenge of phosphorus scarcity. As a food security expert, Dr Cordell also provides expert advice and commentary to UNEP, the UK Parliament, and Australia's Chief Scientist.

Andrea Turner is a Research Director at the Institute for Sustainable Futures, University of Technology Sydney. She is a charted civil engineer with a postgraduate degree in environmental engineering and over 20 years experience in the water industry. She has led numerous water efficiency, drought, and resource planning research projects from city to regional scale for utilities and government agencies in Australia and internationally. She has worked extensively with organisations such as the International Water Association, EU Switch, US based Alliance for Water Efficiency, and Australian based National Water Commission and Water Services Association of Australia to develop resources, guides, training, and tools to aid best practice water management and planning.

Joanne Chong is a Research Director at the Institute for Sustainable Futures, University of Technology Sydney. Joanne leads cross-sectoral, multi-disciplinary applied research working in collaboration with governments, civil society, donors industry, enterprise, and community stakeholders to build and enhance policy, governance, and practices for sustainable resource outcomes. Joanne is a water resource sector specialist and has undertaken risk, vulnerability and capacity assessment, scenario analysis, strategic planning and monitoring and evaluation in urban and rural contexts in Australia and in Asia Pacific countries.

Fadel Kamal, a Saharawi lawyer, is a senior executive in the Saharawi Republic (SADR) Petroleum and Mines Authority. He currently serves as the Frente Polisario representative in Australia and New Zealand.

Pedro Pinto Leite is a Portuguese/Dutch international jurist who lives in Leiden. He studied at the Law Faculty of the University of Lisbon and obtained a masters degree in international law from the Leiden University. Since November 1991 he is the secretary of the International Platform of Jurists for East Timor (IPJET). He is also a member of the International Council of the International Association of Jurists for the Western Sahara (IAJUWS). He is the editor of two collective works, *International Law and the Question of East Timor* (1995) and *The East Timor Problem and the Role of Europe* (1998), co-editor of *International Law and the Question of Western Sahara* (2007), *Le droit international et la question du Sahara occidental* (2009) and *El Derecho Internacional y la Cuestión del Sáhara Occiden*tal (2012), and wrote many monographs, chapters in other books and articles on self-determination questions.

Erik Hagen is board member of Western Sahara Resource Watch and director of the Norwegian Support Committee for Western Sahara. He has followed the issue of the plundering of Western Sahara's resources since 2002, as both an investigative journalist and a civil society activist.

The role of resources in the resolution of the Western Sahara issue

Damien Kingsbury

Faculty of Arts and Education, Deakin University, Melbourne, Australia

The westernmost corner of Algeria, near the border with Morocco, Western Sahara and Mauritania, is a desolate and unforgiving place, where summer temperatures reach and sometimes exceed 50 degrees C. This barren plateau type of desert is known as *hammada* and has historically been referred to as 'the Devil's Garden'. It is an apt name for an environment where sustaining life is impossible without complete reliance on external support.

It is in this area, near the Algerian town of Tindouf, that the Popular Front for the Liberation of Saguia el-Hamra and Rio de Oro (Frente Popular de Liberación de Saguía el Hamra y Rio de Oro, or Polisario Front) administers refugee camps for Saharawi people displaced by Morocco's 1975 invasion of Spanish Sahara (later known as Western Sahara). Between around 100,000 and 165,000 people live in the six camps in the area,[1] surviving on aid from Algeria, South Africa and the wider international community. The Polisario Front also administers the 'liberated' territory of Western Sahara, known as the Saharawi Arab Democratic Republic (SADR).[2]

It is in this all but forgotten place that the four-decades-old claim to Western Saharan independence was again building towards armed conflict. A growing young population, educated but with very few jobs, almost no opportunities and little future, was pushing for its administration to reclaim their land from Moroccan occupation. As the Saharawi refugees wait in these remote and desolate camps, their compatriots in occupied Western Sahara are regularly subjected to abuse and oppression; dissent is not allowed in occupied Western Sahara and is dealt with harshly, often through extra-judicial means.

Meanwhile the relative wealth that the Saharawi people regard as their birthright and which might provide a basis for them to build more complete lives in a future independent state is being sold off to foreign companies, in return for which they receive nothing. Almost all of these resources are finite and such financial legacy as might have been available to the SADR is being depleted by Morocco as a colonial occupier.[3] Faced with being locked into an indefinite and futile future in 'the Devil's Garden' or pressing the issue militarily, with some hope of breaking the current deadlock, the latter was increasingly the preferred option.

The papers in the collection consider aspects of the role of Western Sahara's resources in finding a resolution to the status of Saharawi refugees and Morocco's illegal military occupation of Western Sahara. In part, Western Sahara's natural resources might provide an avenue for finding a way towards a resolution of this issue but, probably more so, the lack of access to

---

1 Population figures are disputed, but the Algerian government claims 165,000, possibly for reasons of greater foreign aid. The camps are named after towns in occupied Western Sahara, including Dakhla, El-Aaiun, Smara and Awserd, as well as Boujdour and the administrative camp of Rabouni.

2 Arabic: al-Jumhūrīyah al-'Arabīyah aṣ-Ṣaḥrāwīyah ad-Dīmuqrāṭīyah, Spanish: República Árabe Saharaui Democrática.

3 WSRW, *P is for Plunder: Morocco's Export of Phosphates from Occupied Western Sahara 2012, 2013* (Melbourne: Western Sahara Resource Watch, 2014).

those resources by the Saharawi people, and their being plundered under Moroccan administration, is an increasing source of conflict. There is, therefore, an increasing likelihood that, should the issue of Morocco's occupation of Western Sahara not be settled, there will be a return to war in north-west Africa.

This potential and increasingly likely return to war will destabilize north-west Africa at a time when much of North Africa is already in turmoil. The costs to the Saharawi, and perhaps to Morocco, Algeria and the region, will be high.

Background to the conflict

The oasis of Tindouf, in the middle of this otherwise uninhabitable land, had been settled in 1852 by one of the Saharan tribes, the Tajakant, which, along with other regional tribes, was descended from the Arabic Beni Hassan tribe that had conquered the north of Africa in the eleventh century and which blended with local Berber and Tuareg tribes. As a result of tribal conflict, 43 years later, the Tajakant were displaced by the Reguibat tribe, which continues to dominate not just this town but has become the dominant tribe in the region, including in Western Sahara. The colonial French did not reach Tindouf until 1934, when they established it as an outpost of French Algeria.

Although Morocco claims historical ownership of a much greater region than it now occupies, historical maps show that, for example, in 1595 it was divided into two provinces, together being smaller than current Morocco. The following century, an expansionist Morocco seized territory as far south as Senegal, but in 1765 signed a peace treaty with Spain recognizing it did not have authority over Tekna tribes in the border area between Morocco and Western Sahara. While the Tekna continued to acknowledge Moroccan sovereignty, their territory marked the boundary of the Moroccan state.

The Spanish had, since the seventeenth century, used ports in what was to become Western Sahara to facilitate the slave trade from Mauritania. When the French occupied Algeria and imposed a protectorate over Morocco, they set the southern limit at the Draa River (just north of the current southern border). The French did not delineate the southern land border in the desert on the basis that it was uninhabitable. Growing tensions between Spain and France over regional control resulted, in the 1884 Berlin Conference at which the region was divided between colonial powers, with, Spain controlling the north of Morocco and what was to become Spanish Sahara between just south of the Draa River in Morocco and Mauritania. The Reguibat resisted Spanish colonialism, not being subdued in what was Spanish Sahara until 1934, a half a century after Spain's colonial takeover.

Following its independence from France in 1956, Morocco had claimed the oasis of Tindouf, but so had the recently independent Algeria. In the 1963 'Sand War', Algeria ensured that Tindouf remained as part of Algeria and thus set the international boundaries of the new state.[4] However, Tindouf is in an otherwise inhospitable region, and the area to the south of it is perhaps even more so. This is the area of six self-administered Saharawi refugee camps, administered independently by the Polisario Front which claims to be the legitimate representative of the Saharawi people of former Spanish Sahara.

Morocco's invasion

From the dying days of European colonialism, the position of the United Nations had been that there should be a referendum among the indigenous population of Spanish Sahara in order to

---

4 'Simply – Western Sahara', *New Internationalist*, no. 297; 'A Brief History of the Territory and its People', http://www.arso.org/05-1.htm (accessed August 15, 2015); Janos Besenyo, *Western Sahara* (Budapest: Publikon Publishers, 2009).

settle the status of the Spanish colony. With the growth of a new national consciousness among still colonized peoples, in 1971 a group of Saharawi students formed a political organization that, two years later, would become the Polisario Front. The intention of the Polisario Front was to end Spanish colonialism in what was then Spanish Sahara, to which end the organization initiated a guerrilla campaign against the colonial administration.

The Polisario Front grew quickly, especially with the defection of Saharawi Spanish troops. Spain backed the National Saharawi Union Party (Partido de Union Nacional Saharaui – PUNS), privileging ties with Spain, Morocco moved to claim Spanish Sahara on the basis of claimed historical links between its royal family and the Saharawi people, while Mauritania claimed Spanish Sahara based on a common ethnicity. In June 1975, a visiting UN envoy, Simeon Ake, noted that there was 'overwhelming consensus' in Spanish Sahara for independence.[5]

However, Morocco had claimed the territory since its own independence and had won and lost territory to the colonial Spanish in the late 1950s. In response to this move towards decolonization, the Moroccan army began attacks from early October 1975 and the following month initiated its 'Green March' of about 350,000 militarily supported civilians to occupy Spanish Sahara. Under pressure from Morocco, in mid-November 1975, Spain signed the 'Madrid Accords' which divided the colony between Morocco and Mauritania (not published by the Official State Bulletin and hence not formalized), just four days later ratifying the contradictory 'Law on the Decolonization of Sahara'.

As Morocco and Mauritania invaded, war with the Polisario Front ensued. In February 1976, the Polisario Front declared the Saharawi Arab Democratic Republic. With war raging, Saharawi refugees flooded across the border to what were to become the camps near Tindouf. Though severely outnumbered, the Algerian-backed Polisario Front had initial military successes to the extent that, in 1978, the understaffed and divided Mauritanian army had to withdraw. The following year, Mauritania formally recognized SADR. By August 1979, however, Morocco had annexed that southern part of Western Sahara abandoned by Mauritania. Between 1982 and 1987, Morocco built a series of six walls, each further consolidating its territorial control over Western Sahara, the last partitioning Western Sahara with around 70% of the territory inside the 'useful' zone and the arid and resource-poor outer region ('liberated zones') remaining under SADR control.

Under international law, Morocco's invasion of Spanish Sahara remains illegal.[6] However, the functional military stalemate created by the construction of the 1987 wall meant that, as the Cold War was drawing to an end, the parties agreed to an internationally monitored referendum on self-determination for the Saharawi people in 1988, ratified in 1991.[7] This was to be implemented and monitored by the United Nations Mission for Referendum in Western Sahara (MINURSO), which has continued to have its mandate renewed by the UN Security Council, despite its inability to implement most of its originally stated agenda. Morocco has since refused to allow the ballot. Initial disputes were over who would be eligible to vote, with the Polisario Front arguing in favour of those included in the last Spanish census and their descendants, and Morocco claiming the right to vote by settlers since then.

There have been a number of attempts to find a settlement to the Western Sahara problem but, despite no progress, the 1988 ceasefire between the Polisario Front and Morocco (ratified by the UN in 1991) has held. Morocco's rejection of a vote has led to a stalemate. There have been

---

5   T. Shelley, *Endgame in the Western Sahara: What Future for Africa's Last Colony?* (London: Zed Books, 2004), 171–2.

6   *Western Sahara, Advisory Opinion*, ICJ Reports 1975, 12; Hans Corell, 'Western Sahara: UN Legal Counsel Renders Opinion on Oil Prospecting Contracts', UN News Centre, February 5, 2002; Hans Corell, 'Letter dated 29 January 2002 from the Under-Secretary-General for Legal Affairs, the Legal Counsel, addressed to the President of the Security Council', S/2002/161, United Nations, February 12, 2002.

7   United Nations Security Council Resolution 690: The Situation Concerning Western Sahara, New York, 1991.

further attempts to find a resolution, including the Houston Agreement of 1997 for a referendum in 1998 and the subsequent Moroccan-drafted 'Baker Plan I' of 2001[8] and 'Baker Plan II' of 2003, which was endorsed by the United Nations Security Council (UNSC)[9] but which Morocco refused to accept. The Baker Plans were followed by the Manhasset Negotiations of 2007–8, which similarly failed to find a solution to the deadlock.

This, however, could change. Morocco has put forward an 'autonomy' proposal for Western Sahara, in which the territory could be self-administering within the state of Morocco. However, there is little faith among the Saharawi in that autonomy being genuine, and it does not include an alternative to autonomy. The Polisario Front has, however, said it will accept the autonomy proposal if the Saharawi people are allowed to vote on it. They expect the proposal would be rejected, thereby further establishing grounds for the alternative of independence. Hans Corell, meanwhile, has written that the UNSC should simply declare Western Sahara independent. Corell also noted that companies were entering into illegal contracts with the government of Morocco for exploitation of Western Sahara's natural resources.[10]

Western Sahara continues to be listed by the UN as a non-self-governing territory, with Spain as its *de jure* administering authority, which Spain refuses to accept.[11] For Spain to represent Western Sahara in the UN would raise questions of remaining colonialism at Ceuta, which Spain is reluctant to give up. Ceuta controls the Straits of Gibraltar and provides a control point for African immigration. The UN also acknowledges Morocco as the de facto administering authority for 80% of the territory and SADR as the de facto administering authority for the other 20% of the territory).[12]

Return to war?

Two generations of Saharawis have grown up either in the refugee camps or under often brutal Moroccan occupation. Based on informal responses from younger Saharawis in the SADR-run camps, there is a strong and growing sense of frustration among them that they are trapped, while the resources of their homeland are being exploited by Morocco. Many seem to believe that returning to war with Morocco to reclaim their land is now the only option.

The Polisario Front has also expressed frustration with Morocco and the failure of an internationally mediated settlement that allows a democratic vote.[13] There is now explicit recognition within the SADR administration that returning to war is possible. The decision about whether SADR will return to war was intended to be made at its four-yearly General Popular Congress in November 2015. There was a growing sense that if SADR does not escalate the situation, the Saharawis will remain doomed to being a people divided by occupation; half repressed, half exiled, with a view increasingly being expressed in conversation with Polisario leaders that the resources upon which they intend to build the economic future of their state are being exploited and depleted by Morocco.

The view that the Polisario Front may return to war followed comments by SADR Foreign Minister Mohammed Salem in 2014 when, in response to a pledge by Morocco's King Moham-

---

8 J. Mundy, 'Seized of the Matter: The UN and the Western Sahara Dispute', *Mediterranean Quarterly* 15, no. 3 (2004): 130–48.

9 United Nations Security Council Resolution 1495, New York, 2003.

10 Hans Corell, 'The Responsibility of the UN Security Council in the Case of Western Sahara', *International Judicial Monitor* (Winter 2015).

11 United Nations General Assembly, Article 73e of the UN Charter; also see: A/5446/Rev.1, annex 1; UN Security Council S/2002/161, 'Letter dated 29 January 2002 from the Under-Secretary-General for Legal Affairs, the Legal Counsel, addressed to the President of the Security Council'.

12 UN Security Council A/RES/68/91 of 11 December 2013, also United Nations Annual Working Paper on Western Sahara, A/AC.109/2014/1.

13 See 'Polisario Urges UN to Press for Western Sahara Referendum', Agence France Presse, February 16, 2016.

mad to maintain its presence in Western Sahara 'until the end of time', he said: 'We will have no other choice but to return to armed struggle'.[14]

Should SADR return to war, it will at least require the tacit agreement of its host country, Algeria. This will then escalate tensions between Algeria and Morocco which, despite recently more normalized relations, have a history of antagonism dating back to the 'Sand War' of 1963, in particular over the territory around Tindouf.[15] The conflict could also spill over into the conflict in neighbouring Mali, where Islamist fighters from North African jihadi groups have descended. Such conflict could also involve Mauritania, which had initially also invaded southern Western Sahara.

With conflict across the Arab world, from Libya to Iraq to Yemen, war between SADR and Morocco, perhaps involving Algeria and other regional states, would very likely further destabilize an already deeply unstable part of the world. There is, then, a desire by many, both within the region and beyond it to avoid such an outcome. But Moroccan intransigence in the face of international law and its continued exploitation of Western Sahara's natural resources appears to be making such an outcome increasingly inevitable. As one Saharawi leader said,[16] it would now take only a small incident for the situation to descend into war.

According to SADR Prime Minister Abd Alkadar Taleb Omar, the Polisario Front did not wish to return to war if that was avoidable. 'We will consider all options for the future at the Congress later this year', he said. 'We have been very patient and waited many years. We have the support of many friends, especially in the African Union. But France and Spain are blocking progress [towards the referendum].' Prime Minister Omar said that diplomacy, politics and war were all along the same spectrum of possibilities, meaning that where one failed it would lead to another along that spectrum. 'There is much conflict in this region', he noted, 'and we wish to avoid adding to that if we are able to do so.'[17]

The Governor of Awserd[18] camp and member of Polisario Front Secretariat, Salek Baba Hasana, was more blunt:

> We prefer a peaceful solution in accordance with international law and UN Security Council resolutions. But there has been a weakness of the UN to impose a solution. Morocco's affiliation with France, as a permanent member [with power of veto] has blocked a resolution through the UN Security Council. But we have not lost hope in an international solution. But if it fails, all other choices are on the table, including armed struggle.[19]

Governor Hasana noted that 'If there is conflict, we have the permission from Algeria, which has stood by us as good friends. The main thing depends on the will of our people and the will of friendly countries, which adopt the principles of freedom and justice'.

Despite a slight thaw in Algerian–Moroccan relations, the bilateral relationship remains tense.[20] However, Algeria faces some threat to its east from Islamist insurgents stemming from the civil war in Libya, and would be unlikely to want to open up a new war on its western front. Having noted that, it is possible that it could remain passive in the face of a Polisario

---

14 'Polisario Threatens War with Morocco after Speech by King', *World Tribune.com*, November 12, 2014, http://www.worldtribune.com/2014/11/12/polisario-threatens-war-morocco-speech-king/ (accessed May 5, 2015).

15 Michael Jacobs, 'Hegemonic Rivalry in the Maghreb: Algeria and Morocco in the Western Sahara Conflict', University of South Florida, January 2012; 'Morocco and Algeria: The Impossible Reconciliation?', *Al Monitor*, July 7, 2013, http://www.al-monitor.com/pulse/politics/2013/07/reconciliation-between-morocco-and-algeria-possible.html# (accessed August 15, 2015).

16 Informal discussion with the author, Rabouni camp, April 10, 2015.

17 Informal Interview with the author, Rabouni camp, April 12, 2015.

18 Also spelled Aousserd.

19 Interview with the author, Awserd camp, April 11, 2015.

20 'Morocco–Algeria Relations Tense Despite Breakthrough Periods', *Middle East Monitor*, 2014, https://www.middleeastmonitor.com/news/africa/15984-morocco-algeria-relations-tense-despite-breakthrough-periods (accessed May 4, 2015).

Front return to war, supporting it by not engaging in the conflict. Morocco would be similarly reluctant to try to punish Algeria for its support for the Polisario Front, given it would be unlikely to achieve any positive outcomes but would draw away from its significant military presence in Western Sahara of about 140,000.

'No-one wants to go to war', Governor Hasana said, 'but we may be forced. It is already 16 years. Our army is better than before and we can certainly defend our people and get back our land. In 1976, we just had militias and Morocco was considered one of the strongest African armies. We have trust in our people [to decide the issue].' Governor Hasana's view of the Saharawi people's options appeared to be less diplomatic than those of the Prime Minister but more in line with those expressed informally by others. 'We have been here [in the camps] for 40 years, but our presence here is only temporary', he said. 'We have in our minds that we came yesterday and will go tomorrow. We continue to resist and are able to continue to resist.'[21]

When asked about the option of Saharawi autonomy within Morocco, he replied:

> There is only the democratic solution in accordance with international law. There are three choices; integration, autonomy or independence. Integration is in contradiction with international law. So we are just talking about autonomy or independence. There cannot be a solution without respect for the right of self-determination. The presence of Morocco [in Western Sahara] is colonial and illegal. This is a decolonization case. There is no state that acknowledges the sovereignty of Morocco over Western Sahara.

While it is technically correct that no country recognizes Morocco's legal sovereignty over Western Sahara, more than 20 countries either support Morocco's territorial claim over Western Sahara or support an autonomy proposal under Moroccan sovereignty. However, SADR is recognized by 84 countries, the African Union (of which it is a member) and the UN Security Council has approved more than 100 resolutions in favour of self-determination for Western Sahara.[22] Of international organizations, only the Organization of Islamic Cooperation recognizes Morocco's sovereignty over Western Sahara.

The SADR Minister Delegate for Asia and former ambassador to the UN and Washington, Mouloud Said, argued that France has primarily been behind the impasse which has led to the Polisario Front again considering returning to war.

> There were several attempts under James Baker to find a resolution to the problem, but the French stopped him [in the UN Security Council]. So the situation depends more on than the Moroccan position, but the French position. The French like to see this part of the world as their back yard.[23]

Minister Mouloud acknowledged that diplomatic pressure had to date not been sufficient and that there might need to be a crisis that paralleled that in relation to Timor-Leste, with which SADR sees itself most closely aligned in terms of the characteristics of its struggle.[24] He noted that the Santa Cruz Massacre of 1991 galvanized world attention on Timor-Leste, after which the EU shifted its position to one of more strongly seeking a final resolution to the territory's status. This was followed, in 1998, by Indonesia's economic crisis, the resignation of President Suharto, the differing approach to occupation by his successor, President Habibie, which led to a referendum and, finally, Australian-led military intervention to quell post-referendum violence by the Indonesia military and its proxy militias.

The view of SADR's Minister for Education, Mariam Salek Hmada, was that the Polisario Front's commitment to education had led to growing frustration and an increasing desire for a

---

21 Interview with the author, Awserd camp, April 11, 2015.
22 44 resolutions since 1991 are listed at MINURSO, United Nations Mission for the Referendum in Western Sahara, http://www.un.org/en/peacekeeping/missions/minurso/resolutions.shtmla (accessed August 15, 2015).
23 Interview with the author, Awserd camp, April 11, 2015.
24 Indonesia invaded what was then Portuguese Timor in late 1975 following moves for its Portuguese colonial masters to withdraw, and the occupation was not recognized by the UN.

final resolution. 'The path to freedom is knowledge. If you don't have education you don't know the meaning of freedom', she said.

> But there are no markets and no jobs for our youth. The UN can't solve the problem of the referendum or of the plundering of resources without any benefit to the indigenous people. This has created frustration among the youth in particular. The youth have been pressing Polisario to go back to war as the talks between the UN and Morocco are just a waste of time.[25]

'The youth are therefore angry. Eventually Polisario will be forced to follow the will of the people', according to Ms Hmada.

> We know what war means. We know the challenges faced by the region, in Libya and Mali. Any movement will take the region to the brink. Yet the last thing to be given by the UN is human rights monitoring and to stop plundering of Saharawi resources. The UN says to the Saharawi people to stay where we are and does not give anything in return, which is not possible.

Ms Hmada also expressed concern that if the Polisario Front leadership did not act, some youth would be attracted away by radical Islamist agendas. 'We are not extremists, but the lack of progress for the youth means we cannot always be an exception [to Islamist extremism].'

In all discussions in the SADR camps, there was recognition that change was only likely to come about through there being an event that acted as a catalyst for growing tensions among the Saharawi population. Such a catalyst, or critical juncture, might involve a radical shift in Morocco's economic or political circumstances, such as an economic embargo or the death, abdication or forced removal of not just the king but also his immediate successors, or the creation of an opportunity cost that becomes too high for Morocco to bear. For this to be the case, the cost would have to be borne by Morocco's elite rather than its citizens, if it is to have any likely impact on perceptions about viability.

However, the Moroccan economy is stable and growing, its political environment is also stable and effectively set (if with a lack of tolerance for dissent). Despite Western Sahara's similarity with Timor-Leste's position under international law, its practical similarities have more in common with West Papua, in that regardless of the moral or legal claims, there is little likelihood of resolution under the current circumstances.

Should Polisario return to war, it will at least require the tacit agreement of its host country, Algeria. This will then escalate tensions between Algeria and Morocco which, despite recently more normalized relations, have a history of antagonism dating back to the 'Sand War' of 1963, over the territory around Tindouf. There could also be spill-over into the conflict in neighbouring Mali, where Islamist fighters from northern jihadi groups have descended. Such conflict could also involve Mauritania, which had initially also invaded southern Western Sahara. The essays presented here each look at what is driving this conflict and what might need to be addressed, including a recognition of the basic rights of the Saharawi people, for it to be avoided.

Jeffrey Smith opens the discussion by looking at the role of natural resources in the continuing issue of Western Sahara's occupation by Morocco. Aspects of the development of the territory's resources have featured in the United Nations and efforts to arrive at self-determination for the Saharawi people. Misconceptions about the effect of resources development continue, however, because of a lack of credible information and analysis of the causal connection of resources to the stalled process of self-determination and the territory's occupation. Smith begins with Spain's colonial establishment of Western Sahara and resource development and then considers how the revenue accruing since 1975 from resource extraction compares to the cost of occupying Western Sahara. He concludes that taking resources from occupied Western Sahara has never been profitable relative to the costs of occupation. He argues that exploitation of natural resources is pursued as a basis for the settlement of Moroccan nationals in the

---

25 Interview with the author, Rabouni camp, April 12, 2015.

territory to help generate acceptance for its territorial acquisition among the international community.

Stephen Zunes follows this discussion by considering the established illegality of facilitating the exploitation of natural resources by an occupying power in a non-self-governing territory. Yet, as he notes, as in the cases as Namibia and East Timor, this illegality has often been overlooked by foreign corporations and governments. The resource-rich territory of Western Sahara is no exception, as European, North American and Australian companies have sought to take advantage of lucrative fishing grounds or mineral deposits. While some have tried to claim that such resource extraction is legal since Morocco reinvests the money it receives into the territory through ambitious development programmes, the benefits of such 'development' have largely gone to Moroccan settlers and occupation authorities, rather than the indigenous population. As with Namibia and East Timor, it has fallen to global civil society to pressure such companies, through boycotts and divestment campaigns, to end their illegal exploitation of Western Sahara's natural resources.

Ben Saul similarly explores international law on occupation and its implications on natural resources in Western Sahara. He argues that much of the international legal analysis of dealings in natural resources in Western Sahara has focused on its status as a non-self-governing territory, as well as the right of self-determination of the Saharawi people. What he says is overlooked in the legal debates is a close examination of the application of the international law of occupation under international humanitarian law (IHL). Saul's paper therefore considers whether and how Western Sahara constitutes an 'occupied territory' under IHL, discussing some of the unique peculiarities that complicate the legal answer. He then considers issues of state and individual criminal responsibility under international law for illegal dealings with natural resources and property in Western Sahara by Moroccan and foreign companies, including under Australian federal criminal law implementing international obligations.

Dana Cordell et al. follow this exposition of international law by identifying the larger social and environmental burden of phosphate mining in Western Sahara. She notes that without phosphorus, many foods would not be produced, as farmers need access to phosphate fertilizers to ensure high crop yields. Yet the world largely relies on non-renewable phosphate rock that is mined in only a few countries. Growing global demand for phosphorus could surpass supply in the coming decades, while Morocco alone controls 75% of the remaining reserves, including those in Western Sahara. The market price of phosphate fertilizers also hides a far deeper burden, with consequences as far-ranging as the exploitation and displacement of the Saharawi people, to nutrient pollution with the result that some aquatic ecosystems have been classified as 'dead zones', along with jeopardizing future generations' ability to produce food. The full cost of phosphate rock might indicate that it should be used more sparingly, to extend the availability of high-quality rock for future generations, to diversify phosphorus sources to include those with lower societal costs, and to share responsibility for these costs and consequences.

Exploitation of Western Sahara's natural resources do, however, have an important role in nation building, according to SADR representative Fadel Kamal. He claims the SADR government believes that its significant natural resources will play an important part in the development of a viable, self-reliant and democratic nation which will contribute to the peace, stability and progress of the entire Maghreb region. His paper examines the SADR's efforts to manage its natural resources through the establishment of the SADR Petroleum and Mines Authority, the launch of licensing rounds, its claim to an exclusive economic zone in the Atlantic Ocean and the recent enactment of a Mining Code. The paper draws on the SADR's efforts to protect its natural resources and examines the SADR oil and gas licensing rounds as an example of SADR's assertion of sovereignty. The SADR natural resources strategy has, Fadel says, two basic goals: to deter Morocco's efforts to exploit the SADR natural resources and to prepare for the recovery of full sovereignty.

It is not enough, of course, to identify a problem; it is also necessary to consider possible ways forward. Pedro Pinto Leite does this by moving beyond the impasse that existed at the time of writing, and which was threatening a dire outcome, to how Western Sahara's independence could be achieved. In doing this, Leite contrasts Western Sahara with the example of East Timor (Timor-Leste), identifying the International Commission of Jurists' common position on the right to self-determination of both Sahrawis and East Timorese.

Leite notes that East Timor is now independent, but that most of Western Sahara remains under foreign occupation, subject to serious human rights violations, with its natural resources pillaged. Morocco refuses to hold a promised referendum, as noted above, while the UN Security Council has been unable to take suitable action due to the use or threat of veto by France and the US. Leite asserts that it is therefore time to recall that the Sahrawi Republic (SADR) was proclaimed and that its government controls the majority of the people and a part of the territory. In that respect, SADR qualifies as a state, and is recognized as such by more than 80 countries. The UN, he argues, should follow the example of the African Union and welcome SADR into its fold. In order to reach that goal, the UN General Assembly should 'consider the matter immediately', recognize SADR and force a breakthrough.

These papers are followed by a 'communication' from Erik Hagen, tracing what he calls the 'Saharawi conflict phosphates' and their link to the Australian dinner table. Hagen notes that companies in Australia and New Zealand have been large importers of phosphate rock from Western Sahara for many years. A report launched by Western Sahara Resource Watch (WSRW), for which Hagen works, showed that companies in New Zealand and Australia accounted for a fifth of the purchases from Western Sahara for the year 2014. WSRW estimates that the total exports from the occupied territory last year was around 2.1 million tonnes, at a value of US$230 million, carried on board 44 bulk vessels. These exports took place, he noted, even though the Saharawi people objected to it, and despite its clear violation of international law. Several international investors have also deemed such trade unethical, while a handful of previously importing companies have ceased importing from the occupied territory due to legal and ethical concerns. Hagen elaborates on the global phosphate trade of the Saharawi phosphate rock, and the research and international campaigning done by Western Sahara Resource Watch in halting the controversial trade.

According to Minister Mouloud:

> The UN has lost all credibility it had with the people. That leaves the leadership up against the wall. There is frustration and disappointment. Some people say we should have not stopped the war in '91. This frustration makes people more upset than they were in 1975. They are more ready for war. The people are more committed to the issue. In the occupied territories, they hate Morocco more than we do, they are more radical than us.

As a result, he said, 'We are in an area of the unknown, where anything can happen at any time. A small incident can restart a war'.[26].

It is important to note, following Leite's suggestion, that there remains time for a resolution to this growing threat of a new Sahara war but, with Morocco appearing to harden its stance on not allowing a popular vote, this is looking increasingly remote. From the perspective of Polisario, if Morocco does not move soon, many Saharawi believe it will be left with little choice but to return to war. With conflict across the Arab world, from Libya to Iraq to Yemen, war between Polisario and Morocco, perhaps involving Algeria and other regional states, can only further destabilize an already deeply unstable part of the world. There is, then, a desire by many, both within the region and beyond it to avoid such an outcome.

---

26   Informal interview, Rabouni camp, April 12, 2015.

Disclosure statement

No potential conflict of interest was reported by the author.

The taking of the Sahara: the role of natural resources in the continuing occupation of Western Sahara

Jeffrey J. Smith

Faculty of Law, McGill University, Canada

The role of natural resources in the continuing 'question' of Western Sahara is not fully understood. In recent years, the development of the territory's resources has been at issue in efforts to arrive at self-determination for the Saharawi people. Misconceptions about the effect of such development persist, however, because of a lack of credible information and limited analysis of the connection of resources to the stalled process of self-determination and the territory's occupation. The present analysis surveys the history, problems resulting from and consequences of the exploitation of resources in a Western Sahara that has for 40 years been under armed occupation. It begins with Spain's colonizing of Western Sahara and involvement with its resources before turning to the territory's abandonment to Morocco and Mauritania following which Spain retained some resource rights. Revenue from extraction of the two primary resources since 1975 is then assessed and compared to the costs to occupy Western Sahara. The relevant international law is considered, including the right of non-self-governing peoples to sovereignty over natural resources, and the application of international humanitarian law. Rationales for Morocco's extraction of resources are examined, the evidence revealing that the activity is pursued as a basis for the settlement of Moroccan nationals in the territory to better serve an ostensible annexation project, and generate acceptance for territorial acquisition in the organized international community. The prospects for application of the law and the place of natural resources in the resolution of the question of Western Sahara are finally contemplated.

> The restraints which are implicit in the non-recognition of South Africa's presence in Namibia ... impose on member States the obligation to abstain from entering into economic and other forms of relationship or dealings with South Africa on behalf of or concerning Namibia which may entrench its authority over the Territory.[1]

In the final months of 2015 the pillage of resources from Western Sahara continued uninterrupted while the people of the territory marked 40 years of occupation. The taking has been constant: fish from the richest coastal area in Africa, the Canary Current Large Marine Ecosystem, along with the large-scale export of phosphate mineral rock. The year had, for a time, brought the start of seabed petroleum drilling on the territory's Atlantic coast. These and other resources continue to be removed despite the protests of the territory's original inhabitants, the Saharawi people, who insist such acts violate their sovereign right of ownership to the resources. For their part, the United Nations and the states most interested in Western Sahara have remained silent.

Only in recent years has the question of resources in Western Sahara received attention. There has been little analysis of how the production and export of resources may contribute to Morocco's annexation of the territory. When it comes to ensuring for the Saharawi people their right to

---

1 International Court of Justice, *Namibia Advisory Opinion*, 1971 ICJ Reports 16, para. 124.

self-determination – the obligation of all states and collectively the organized international community – the implications of exporting resources from the territory have featured infrequently even as the Saharawi have been emphatic in their opposition. As with the right of sovereignty over natural resources for a non-self-governing people, so has the requirement of international humanitarian law (IHL) that prohibits the plunder of natural resources gone unremarked.[2] Under occupation, the exploitation of Western Sahara's resources has been substantial and occasionally revealed as unsustainable, with some fish stocks in the territory's coastal waters near collapse in the late 1990s.[3] Equally serious, the exploitation of fish, phosphate, and production of minor agricultural resources, together with salt and sand, has impeded the prospect of self-determination for the Saharawi people, entrenching the status quo of occupation.

The 'question' of Western Sahara, as the United Nations describes it, is one about the right of the Saharawi people to exercise their choice of self-determination as the inhabitants of the former colony of Spanish Sahara. A long delayed self-determination referendum and the active conflict between the Frente Polisario and Morocco from 1975 until 1991 (which included Mauritania until 1979) have been the principal features of such a question. However, serious human rights abuses (including the maltreatment of the Saharawi population in Moroccan-occupied areas, forced disappearances and the introduction of settlers into the territory) remain significant. That there has been comparatively limited concern about the territory's resources and what the taking of them entails for an occupation and the stalled self-determination of the Saharawi people should not be surprising.

Western Sahara's principal natural resources are phosphate mineral rock from the Bu Craa mine and fish from a highly productive area of the Atlantic Ocean.[4] Possible land and seabed petroleum reserves may yet add to this. In the 30 years after invasion, the fishery was the most highly valued. After 2008 phosphate became the leading resource as a result of its sudden increase and then a sustained historically high market price. It has become apparent that, as with earlier decolonization cases such as Namibia and East Timor, the exploitation of natural resources perpetuates the occupation of Western Sahara and thereby delays its people's self-determination. In light of the territory's increasing potential for mineral resources and petroleum, there is a greater need to understand how the exploitation of resources is part of the 'question' of Western Sahara.

The present analysis surveys the history, problems resulting from, and consequences of the exploitation of resources in a Western Sahara that has for 40 years been under armed occupation. It begins with Spain's colonizing of Western Sahara and involvement with its resources before turning to the territory's abandonment to Morocco and Mauritania, following which Spain retained some resource rights. Revenue from extraction of the two primary resources since 1975 is then assessed and compared to the costs of occupying Western Sahara. The relevant international law is considered, including the right of non-self-governing peoples to sovereignty

---

2   Morocco occupies three-quarters of Western Sahara which has an area of 266,000 km²within colonial frontiers established by France and Spain. Mauritania and Morocco partitioned Western Sahara in April 1976. Mauritania quit the territory in 1979 upon concluding a peace treaty with the Saharawi national liberation movement, the Frente Polisario (the Popular Front for the Liberation of Saguia el-Hamra and Río de Oro). Morocco then occupied the area left by Mauritania.The term 'occupation' is used in its ordinary meaning in international affairs and law, noting the UN General Assembly's declaratory use of it in the case of Western Sahara and the conclusion of the International Court of Justice in 1975, discussed below, that Morocco did not have any legal basis for a claim to the territory.

3   The Canary Current Large Marine Ecosystem on the coast of northwest Africa is the third most globally productive fishery. UNFAO, 'Protection of the Canary Current Large Marine Ecosystem' (undated), http://www.canarycurrent. org/resources/publications (accessed December 1, 2014).

4   Phosphate rock exports from the Bu Craa (Bou Craa; بوكراع) site by the Moroccan state-owned Office Chérifien des Phosphates (OCP SA) through its subsidiary operating entity, PhosBouCraa, are planned to continue at 2.6 million tonnes/year, averaging 2.2 million tonnes in recent years, with a notable peak of 2.78 million tonnes in 2011, OCP SA *Prospectus – 17 April 2014* (a debt-financing prospectus issued on the Irish Stock Exchange), 95 [OCP 2014 *Prospectus*] (unpublished, copy on file with author). The coastal fishery is carried out by Moroccan, European Union member state, Russian and Japanese vessels, the latter joining for a seasonal tuna fishery in October 2014.

over natural resources, and the application of international humanitarian law. Rationales for Morocco's extraction of resources are examined, the evidence revealing that the activity is pursued as a basis for the settlement of Moroccan nationals in the territory to better serve an ostensible annexation project, and generate acceptance for territorial acquisition in the organized international community. Finally, the prospects for application of the law and the place of natural resources in the resolution of the question of Western Sahara are contemplated.

I. Natural resources in Africa's last colony

The history of foreign involvement in Western Sahara's resources is one of appropriation by outsiders. From the time the Saharawi were colonized, they never enjoyed the entire benefit of the coastal fishery or the later mining of phosphate rock, even as the two commodities came to be exploited at industrial levels. The year 1885 marked Spain's formal establishment of the colony, ostensibly for a Canary Islands fleet which had fished the coast for centuries. Spain's early concern for a territory it obtained by Europe's division of Africa at the Conference of Berlin was negligible. Only after 1895 did it build settlements, in the north at el Aauin (Laayoune) and mid-coast at Dakhla (Villa Cisneros), and it would not consolidate possession of the territory until the 1930s.[5] Geological surveys in the 1940s revealed promising phosphate deposits at Bu Craa in the northern part of the territory. In 1962 Spain decided they should be developed, enacting the necessary legislation and constructing a 100-kilometer conveyor belt to transport the phosphate to a loading facility at the coast near el Aauin.[6] By the time Spain decided to leave Western Sahara, Bu Craa was producing 2.7 million tonnes per year after it started operation in 1973. Long after it gave up the territory, the Spanish government would retain a 35% share in the enterprise.[7]

To understand why Western Sahara's natural resources have received little attention, the means by which Spain abandoned its colony must be recalled.[8] The formal pretext was the November 1975 Madrid Accords.[9] That treaty allowed Mauritania and Morocco to occupy the territory (something that was by then already underway) and noted that the three states would assure the Saharawi people their right to self-determination. The Accords were meant to give Spain legitimacy in quitting the Sahara, and an acceptance that its colony could be annexed by two neighboring states, whatever provision was made or not for the rights of the Saharawi people. The Accords were contrary to international law, for Spain did not have the right to transfer away the Saharawi people's territory or delegate the conduct of their self-determination to

---

5   The territory's frontiers were established by the *Convention pour la délimitation des possessions françaises et espagnoles dans l'Afrique occidentale,* 1900, 92 BFSP 1014; the *Convention between France and Spain respecting Morocco,* 1904, 102 BFSP 432; and the *Treaty between France and Spain regarding Morocco,* 1912 (1913) AJIL 7 at Supplement 81.

6   'The phosphate mined at Boucraa is sedimentary [i.e. is apatite] and consists of two layers of phosphate ... Mining of the second layer, which is less rich [in phosphoric content] and contains more silica, is expected to commence in 2014, following the completion of the necessary processing infrastructure.' No part of the Bu Craa enterprise appears set for capital improvement or expansion in coming years. See OCP 2014 *Prospectus,* 81–2.

7   The government of Spain divested its ownership in 2002. The entire corporate interest is now held by OCP SA, which became an incorporate entity in 2008, assuming control of all phosphate extraction and export activities in Morocco from the government agency of the same name.

8   Western Sahara is a case of unique dualities in its factual and legal setting. It (its people) are characterized as non-self-governing, and so Western Sahara in law and by UN declaration is a colony. But is also a place under armed occupation, given the absence of a legal claim to the territory by the occupying state. The territory proper has two present de facto sovereigns, a 'government in exile' that is the Saharawi Republic and Morocco. It has a divided original population, one part under occupation, the other self-governing refugees. And, as discussed below, two bodies of law apply to the development and export of its resources.

9   *Declaration of Principles (Tripartite (Madrid) Accords (Mauritania/Spain/Morocco))* (November 14, 1975), 14 ILM 1512.

others.[10] The tragedy of Western Sahara resulted out of Spain's failure to act consistently with international law and what were by then the many successful decolonization cases.

The Madrid Accords accomplished more than simply a territorial cession. The treaty created the basis for exploitation of the territory's resources, if unwittingly, up to the present. With the Accords were protocols revealed only after 2009. The first allowed Spain continued access to the Saharan fishery, an arrangement that continued until Spain joined the European Economic Community (the EEC) in 1986. (Control of member state fishing was and is through the Common Fisheries Policy that began with the 1957 Treaty of Rome.) Morocco agreed that Spain could have 20 years of fishing for as many as 800 vessels in 'Saharan waters' with fine-tuning to be done in specific treaties after 1976.[11] A second protocol ratified Spain's ownership share in the Phosboucraa enterprise and detailed arrangements for Morocco to receive assistance with geological exploration, the building of vessels to transport phosphate (*roca fosfatos*), tourism and agriculture. The third protocol continued arrangements for fishing in Mauritanian waters, which had been open to Spanish vessels after the country's independence in 1964.[12] The division of the territory's ocean resources has been discussed by Driss Dahak, a Moroccan law of the sea advisor and UNCLOS (UN Convention on the Law of the Sea) negotiator. He describes how Spanish–Moroccan fisheries cooperation was made part of the Accords because Morocco considered itself obliged to accept Spain's demands given the 'particular political circumstances' of the time.[13] Subsequent fishery treaties between the two states were short-lived, revisited in June 1979, December 1979, April 1981, December 1982 and August 1983. The last provided for reciprocal commitments, with Spain to continue with access and Morocco to receive 'assistance in the technical domain and the financing of projects'.[14] A similar arrangement continues under the present 2006–07 European–Morocco fisheries treaty.

After Spain joined the EEC, the first Brussels-directed treaty came into operation in 1988.[15] It had a four-year term, during which Morocco was to be paid 282 million European Currency Units (ECU). Subsequent treaties were agreed upon in 1992 (310 million ECU) and 1995 (500 million ECU). The treaties with Morocco ended for a time in 1999 when no agreement for renewal could be reached because of concerns over the sustainability of fish stocks.[16] In retrospect, the amounts paid were remarkable; more than 1 billion ECU for 11 years of access to the Saharan fishery. This is explained in part by the volumes of fish taken, the redistributionist and developmental goals of the EEC/EU common fisheries policy, and perceptions of the importance of the Saharan fishery to the Canary Islands economy.

Morocco and Spain also reportedly considered dividing the continental shelf between the Canary Islands and the Saharan coast. (Mauritania and Morocco did so through their April 1976 treaty, above.) However, the two states did not apparently begin to negotiate maritime

---

10 The *Madrid Accords* arguably lapsed on February 26, 1976 when Spain withdrew its remaining presence in Western Sahara. They were undoubtedly abrogated when Mauritania and Morocco partitioned the territory that April under the *Convention concerning the State Frontier Line established between the Islamic Republic of Mauritania and the Kingdom of Morocco*, April 14, 1976, 1977 UNTS 117 (in force November 10, 1976).

11 *Madrid Accords* first protocol, 1975. The protocol provided for joint oversight with a review five years into its 20-year term and compensation for Spanish government property connected to the fishing industry left in the territory.

12 Respectively, the second and third protocols to the Madrid Accords.

13 D. Dahak, *Les Etats Arabes et le Droit de la Mer*, Tomes I et II (Rabat: Les Editions Maghrébines, 1986), 409. Dahak notes that a 1977 fishing agreement was not ratified by Morocco in response to 'Spain declaring after 1976 that it had only ceded administration of the territory, and not its sovereignty'. Ibid., 410, translation.

14 Ibid., 411 (footnote omitted). The 1983 agreement prescribed a first annual catch limit of 136,602 tonnes, to be reduced for conservation reasons in following years by 5%, 10% and 14%.

15   *Agreement on Relations in the Sea Fisheries Sector between the European Community and the Kingdom of Morocco*, OJ L181 (June 23, 1988).

16 T. Shelley, *Endgame in the Western Sahara: What Future for Africa's Last Colony?* (New York: Zed Books, 2004), 74. During these years, the ECU exchange rate averaged US$0.84. On the 1995 treaty see G. White, 'Too Many Boats, Not Enough Fish: The Political Economy of Morocco's 1995 Fishing Accord with the European Union', *Journal of Developing Areas* 31 (1997): 313.

boundaries in the area. The concept of extended maritime jurisdictional areas was only then emerging, with many states awaiting the result of the UN Law of the Sea Conference in the middle of developmental meetings.[17] The issue is of renewed interest in recent years, with both states authorizing seabed petroleum exploration in waters south and east of the Canary Islands in 2014 and 2015.

Today, the direct involvement of third states in Western Sahara's natural resources remains limited to the fishery. Mauritania has no connection with the territory's resources except indirectly by an extended continental shelf claim that appears to encroach on the Saharan seabed.[18] The government of Spain has relinquished its interest in Phosboucraa, the local operating subsidiary of Morocco's Office Chérifien des Phosphates (OCP SA), the government phosphate mining, marketing and export entity recreated as a corporation in 2008. No other state is involved with production or commercial trade of the territory's phosphate. After 2000, petroleum development in Western Sahara had been limited to exploration, including seismic surveys. This changed in December 2014 with the American firm Kosmos Energy Ltd. starting seabed drilling northwest of Dakhla at the Gargaa (El-Khayr, or CB-1) deepwater site.[19] Commercial involvement with the Saharan fishery is through a 2013 Morocco–Russia treaty (a renewal of earlier ones dating from 2006) and the resumed[20] EU–Morocco Fisheries Partnership Agreement (the FPA) that first operated from 2007 until December 2011.[21]

The Frente Polisario, as the national liberation movement for the Saharawi people and government of the Saharawi Arab Democratic Republic, constantly protests at the taking of the territory's natural resources. It does so in matters large and small. The Frente Polisario condemned the FPA to the European Commission when its first protocol was set to expire in February 2011. A November 2010 letter from Mohamed Sidati, the Frente Polisario's EU delegate, to the then EC Fisheries Commissioner Maria Damanaki is typical:

---

17 '[T]he negotiations for the Madrid Accord ... provided that "The experts of the two countries will meet prior to 31 December 1975 for the purpose of mapping the median line between the coasts of the two countries' and that the government of Spain had expressed reservations about petroleum exploration permits issued by the government of Morocco in 1971 in areas between Morocco and the Canary Islands, considered by Spain as having exceeded an equidistance line between the coasts of the two countries"'. Dahak, *Les Etats Arabes et le Droit de la Mer*, 239 (translation, footnote omitted).

18 The claim to an extended continental shelf (ECS) was first defined in a preliminary submission to the UN Commission on the Limits of the Continental Shelf (CLCS) in May 2009, and further detailed in September 2014. The claim most likely encroaches into Western Sahara's seabed area as there is not yet a territorial sea boundary or an exclusive economic zone (EEZ) boundary between the two states at Cape Blanc. In December of the same year, Spain delivered to the CLCS its ECS claim for the seabed west of the Canary Islands that also appears to overlap with a presumptive Saharan seabed. Morocco has protested at the claim, and the government of the Saharawi Republic has, in turn, protested at Morocco's protest on the basis that it could only be advanced with Morocco in (the illegal) possession of the relevant Saharan coastline. See Letter of Ahmed Boukhari, Frente Polisario representative to the UN at New York to the UN Secretary-General (April 12, 2015) (unpublished, copy on file with the author).

19 Kosmos Energy Ltd. undertook extensive seabed surveys in 2012–14, and has suggested to investors that up to 1 billion equivalent-to-petroleum barrels may be present in its Boujdour Offshore block. In completing test well assessment in March 2015, the company noted petroleum was present but not economically viable for the time being, http://www.kosmosenergy.com (accessed March 20, 2015).

20 In September 2014.

21 See the *Agreement between the Government of Russian Federation and the Government of The Kingdom of Morocco for a Marine Fisheries Partnership*, 2010 (unpublished, copy on file with the author) and *Fisheries Partnership Agreement between the European Communities and the Kingdom of Morocco*, July 28, 2005 (entered into force March 7, 2007) (the FPA), http://eur-lex.europa.eu (accessed December 1, 2014). The operative protocol to the FPA was extended in February 2011 as its four-year term was about to expire. That December, the European Parliament ended the extension. In 2013, a new protocol was reached, entering into force in July 2014 with fishing beginning that September. It has a term of four years and will see Morocco annually paid €30 million. EU fishing in Saharan waters – not geographically defined under the FPA's protocols – has been criticized. See J. Smith, 'Fishing for Self-determination: European Fisheries and Western Sahara – The Case of Ocean Resources in Africa's Last Colony', *Ocean Yearbook* 27 (2013): 267.

WESTERN SAHARA

[We] repeat our previous communications to the Commission that *fishing by European vessels in Western Sahara's waters pursuant to an arrangement with the Kingdom of Morocco is contrary to the interests and wishes of the people of Western Sahara, and is therefore contrary to international law.*[22]

In June 2014 the SADR (Saharawi Arab Democratic Republic) government wrote to the government of New Zealand with a request that it prohibit the import of phosphate rock by two companies.[23] In January 2015, the president of the SADR wrote to UN Secretary-General Ban Ki-moon to protest at seabed oil drilling, calling for intervention by the UN Security Council:

The Saharawi government concludes that the present petroleum activity is illegal and impedes progress toward the conduct of a 'free and fair referendum' as that has been accepted by the parties. (See report of Secretary-General 18 June 1990, UN document S/21360, paragraph 47(g).) The activity underscores to the Saharawi people that a violation of well settled, universally [accepted] rules of international law is allowed to continue. That suggests the organized international community is unwilling to ensure the paramount obligation of self-determination flowing from Article 73 of the UN Charter.[24]

II. The plunder of the Sahara

A starting point to assess what has resulted from 40 years of resource extraction in an occupied Western Sahara is to consider the value of what has been taken, and assess that in light of the economic cost of annexing the territory. To this end, a survey of how the two originally occupying states dealt with resources is useful before turning to the matter of the resources' value. For its part, Mauritania realized virtually no resource income, having garrisoned and fought for its part of the territory at great financial and political cost. Assessing the economic rents taken by Morocco reveals little better result for that country. The kingdom has incurred significant direct cost to maintain an occupation which, even in recent years of high phosphate market prices and assured foreign flag fishing, has been a demand on its state treasury.

The more consequential impact, however, has been that of creating a semblance of normalcy to what is a project of annexation. Resource exports allow Morocco to foster the international community's acceptance that it is legitimately in possession of the territory. That a majority of the population in the occupied part of the territory are now Moroccan settlers who benefit most from the resources is overlooked. In some respects, the issue can only be discounted by states and the UN, because to engage it as the law requires would demand addressing the legality of an occupation itself. The significance of Western Sahara's resources for Morocco has been far-ranging, on a parallel with resource exploitation in South African-occupied Namibia and Indonesian-annexed East Timor.

---

22   Emphasis in original. The 2010 letter added: 'The waters adjacent to the coast of Western Sahara are NOT Morocco's, as confirmed by the declaration by the Saharawi Arab Democratic Republic (SADR) of an Exclusive Economic Zone on 21 January 2009 ... Exploitation by EU vessels of Western Sahara's fisheries resources, without the prior consultation and consent of the representatives of the Saharawi people, is in direct conflict with the non-derogable right of the Saharawi people to exercise sovereignty over their natural resources, and is therefore in violation of international law, including international human rights law and the relevant principles of the Charter of the United Nations' (unpublished, copy on file with the author). On the history of the Frente Polisario and development of the Saharawi state, see S. Zunes and J. Mundy, *Western Sahara: War, Nationalism, and Conflict Irresolution* (Syracuse, NY: Syracuse University Press, 2010).

23   Letter of SADR Minister of Foreign Affairs to the New Zealand Minister of Foreign Affairs, 'The import to New Zealand of phosphate from occupied Western Sahara', June 12, 2014. Morocco responded with a June 16 letter to New Zealand, requesting the SADR's letter be disregarded. Morocco's letter was disclosed through a Twitter account in November 2014 by someone with access to its ministry of foreign affairs diplomatic cables, 'Le Makhzen'. (The correspondence is unpublished, copies on file with the author.)

24   Letter of SADR president Md. Abdelaziz to UN Secretary-General Ban Ki-moon, January 26, 2015, http://www. spsrasd.info (accessed April 1, 2015). The Secretary-General noted the letter in his annual report to the UN Security Council, 'Report of the Secretary-General on the Situation Concerning Western Sahara' (April 10, 2015) UN doc. S/2015/246, para. 62.

The activities to support resource extraction have been manifested in several ways, including a substantial military presence and the construction of civil and military works, such as port facilities at el Aauin and Dakhla. Morocco does not hold the territory by force alone. Rather, it has introduced an ever-larger population of settlers into Western Sahara who partly rely on resource development for employment and to create a local production economy.[25] Morocco's capacity to support its settlers in Western Sahara, to be clear, does not turn only on the exploitation of natural resources. But given the lack of industry, manufacturing, higher education facilities and market services for a largely urbanized population of what is now about 400,000 people (including the Saharawi), resources have a central role in the pursuit of a seemingly viable local economy.

Allowing, if not promoting, the settlement of Moroccan nationals, arguably the most acute 'problem on the ground', does two things to delay Saharawi self-determination. The first has been to confuse the demographic of those properly entitled to vote in a self-determination referendum. The second is to introduce a population, a part of which might prefer or be compelled to be relocated should Saharawi independence result. The result has been paralysis, with the ability of the UN to ensure a proper referendum now seriously doubted. An increasing Moroccan population coupled with a denial of self-determination, founded in part on the exploitation of natural resources, is clearly a valuable result for Morocco.

A calculation of the value of resources taken from Western Sahara since 1975 is possible. Some gaps in the data exist, because they are not available on the public record or because they cannot be sufficiently assessed to be credible. Export volumes of phosphate rock, also checked against the decline in reserves at the Bu Craa mine site, together with known market values for the commodity, allow a ready calculation. The value of the fishery from 1975 through 1988 is more obscure. After 1988, that value can be derived from the payments under the EC/EU–Morocco fisheries treaties and later the Russia–Morocco treaties. Of course, allowance has to be made for fisheries other than those under the EU and Russian treaties, for example by locally operated vessels (with some registered in flag of convenience states) after the first FPA protocol was ended in 2011 and a brief tuna fishery conducted by Japan in late 2014.[26] It should be noted that little European and no recorded Russian fishery since 1975 has taken place in waters immediately adjacent to those of Western Sahara, that is, to the north in the area between Spain's Fuerteventura Island and the mainland of Morocco. Fisheries 'with Morocco' take place in the highly productive waters of the Canary Current area on the mid-coast of Western Sahara and to the south.

Therefore, the following calculation is proposed in order to arrive at a net present value resulting from the exploitation of the Saharan fishery since 1975, as of 1 October 2015. There are four sources (or categories) of revenue to assess, namely: (i) the Spanish fishery until 1988; (ii) payments by the EEC/EU from 1988 until the present; (iii) the Russian fishery, notably the payments under 2010 and 2013 agreements; and (iv) a local commercial fishery based in Dakhla using Moroccan and flag of convenience vessels which increased after the temporary end of EU fisheries in late 2011. Periodic fisheries by other states, such as a 2014 tuna fishery by Japanese

---

25 Even less about natural resources has been the organized international community's response to Morocco introducing its nationals as settlers into Western Sahara. 'The Occupying Power shall not deport or transfer parts of its own civilian population into the territory it occupies.' Article 49, *Fourth Geneva Convention: Convention (IV) relative to the Protection of Civilian Persons in Time of War*, August 12, 1949, 75 UNTS 287 (entered into force October 21, 1950).

26 In October 2014 four or possibly five Japanese flag longliners operated southwest of Dakhla in a seasonal tuna fishery, landing their catch in Las Palmas. It is estimated that the four-week activity resulted in a total catch of 1600 tonnes at a market value of $12 million. The vessels were detected by Saharawi authorities and a protest at their presence was made by the Western Sahara Resource Watch NGO to the government of Japan. (Personal conversations of the author with SADR officials and Western Sahara Resource Watch (WSRW) managers, October 2014). The calculation of the value of the catch is the author's from a variety of stated market prices for yellowfin tuna in October 2014 following an estimate of the capacity and likely catch taken by the four vessels. For fisheries market prices, see the UN Food & Agriculture Organization (UNFAO) seafood pricing website: http://www.globefish.org (accessed April 15, 2015).

flag vessels, together with permit fee revenue realized by Morocco for local (artisanal) fishing, are discounted.[27] Fishing revenues from the period after 1999 until resumption of EU fishing in early 2007, from all states, are also discounted because of the lack of credible figures. A base date of 1 October 2015 for the valuation was chosen to allow for a full 40-year analysis.

To begin with, data for Spain's payments to Morocco from 1975 until 1988 is difficult to obtain. Accurate figures in what few records are publicly available are obscure and not always directly connected to the Saharan fishery. For this analysis the present value of Spain's payment during that period is dismissed. The present value of EEC/EU-era payments from 1988 through 1999 is straightforward; taking the 1.1 billion ECU paid until 1999 and calculating its value on 1 October 2015 results in a Figures of $1.072 billion.[28] Figures for Russia's actual payments from January 2010 through mid-2015 are not publicly available, although from the presence of Russian vessels on the Saharan coast, their patterns of activity, transshipment of catches to freezer ships, and prices stated for various species such as mackerel and sardines an annual catch-of 50,000 tonnes is indicated. Under its 2010 treaty with Morocco, Russia was to pay 17.5% of a stated value of all species caught of $255 per tonne, to an annual maximum of 120,000 tonnes. In the 2013 successor treaty that operated through 2015, Russia was required to pay 17.5% of a stated value of $497 per tonne for up to 100,000 tonnes and a lump sum payment of $5 million annually.[29] A realistic (i.e. one supported by observation) annual catch of 50,000 tonnes, as noted, is applied here. From 2010 through 1 October 2015, therefore, a present value of $27 million results.[30]

Payments by the European Commission under the 2006–07 FPA can next be calculated. Such payments were nominally €36.1 million annually for the first four years of the treaty starting in 2007 with an additional €30 million during the extension of its protocol until December 2011 and then, under a second four-year protocol agreed in 2013, €30 million annually.[31] (European flag vessels returned to Saharan waters in September 2014.) Morocco did not actually seek

---

27 Such occasional and local fisheries are discounted because of the entire lack of credible data about catches and market earnings from them. A crude estimate is that they may be worth $10 million annually.The author's personal observation (and from discussions with expatriate Saharawi fishers from Dakhla) is that there is little third state or otherwise IUU (illegal, unregulated, unreported) fishing in Saharan coastal waters (i.e. a presumptive exclusive economic zone). In July 2015 the SADR government protested to the government of the Faroe Islands about the presence of a vessel suspected of IUU fishing west of Cape Blanc. (Unpublished letter dated July 7, 2015, copy on file with the author.)

28 A conservative approach to calculating the present value of the 1.1 billion ECU is used: an exchange rate figure of $800 million; a benchmark date of December 31, 1999 for the 2015 present value; and inflation compounded at 2.00% per annum. If accurately known, historic inflation in Morocco could be the better determinant of present value, but it is not used in the present analysis.

29 The best figure for comparative purposes is present value; the current value of annual revenues remaining after capital, operation and maintenance costs. Under its 2010 three-year agreement with Morocco, Russia was obligated to pay 17.5% of $255/tonne for most species, with an allowable catch of up to 120,000 tonnes in the first year (and a further 80,000 tonnes shared jointly with Morocco). Russia is now required to annually pay $5 million and 17.5% of the caught value of fish (at $497 per tonne for frozen fish) for up to 10 vessels and a maximum of 100,000 tonnes under its 2013 treaty. Payments under the first three-year 2006 agreement are disregarded in the present analysis because of a lack of accurate catch data. A copy of the 2013 agreement can be found at WSRW's website, http://www.wsrw.org (accessed January 15, 2015).

30 The size (capacity) and fishing patterns of Russian flag vessels in Saharan waters suggests a higher value catch. The trawler *Oleg Naydenov* was one such vessel observed by Saharawi authorities after 2010, which had a capacity of 3372 tonnes. In April 2015 the vessel caught fire in Las Palmas and, after being towed out to sea, sank south of Gran Canaria where it began to release fuel oil. Saharawi authorities monitor fishing using several methods, including at-sea observation, vessel port visit reconciliations, satellite tracking and publicly available records such as catch landing by EU member state fishing vessels. (Personal conversations with SADR officials 2014–15.)

31 The second protocol, 'Protocol between the European Union and the Kingdom of Morocco setting out the fishing opportunities and financial contribution provided for in the Fisheries Partnership Agreement between the European Union and the Kingdom of Morocco', OJ L328/2 (July 12, 2013), was concluded in 2013 and entered into force in 2014. The second protocol and the Fisheries Partnership Agreement are stated to form an integral part of the 1996 EU–Morocco Association Agreement; Article 1 of the second protocol. Article 2 provides that €16 million is payment for the annual catch by EU permitted vessels and €14 million is 'support for the fisheries sector in Morocco'.

payment of a sector resource development component of the €36.1 million first protocol overall annual rent in at least one of its five years. Therefore, the present value (as at 1 October 2015) of annual FPA payments is €190 million, or $240 million. Finally, no value is assigned to the catch payments made by commercial vessels operating locally from Dakhla. This reduces the present value of the overall catch, of course, as such vessels work in relatively rich waters and are capable of week-long voyages to obtain 400 tonnes of fish. Accordingly, a *conservative* present value of the Saharan fishery under 40 years of occupation is $1.34 billion.

The *indirect* economic result of the Saharan fishery during this period has been considerable, although in the absence of accurate data, no attempt is made here to calculate it. But some discussion is useful. The commercial fishery is largely based at Dakhla. The port experiences continual activity associated with vessel provisioning and repair, and catch processing. Employment in primary fisheries and secondary support services in Dakhla may account for more than 10,000 persons. Assigning a *present* annual value of $60 million for direct rent of the Saharan fishery under treaties with other states and the EU, as well as local vessel fees, and a further $60 million from resulting economic activity yields a current total annual return of $120 million.

Calculating the value of extracted phosphate is straightforward, although there is little credible information about the cost of operating the Bu Craa enterprise.[32] Even during the long period from 1975 through 2006 when the market price of phosphate remained stable at $30 per tonne and production averaged 1.1 million tonnes, Phosboucraa may conceivably have been profitable, although that seems unlikely if the capital cost of the infrastructure (including the long conveyor belt and loading dock facilities) is accounted for. In recent years, the relative values of the fishery and phosphate have become reversed, starting with an unexpected price spike for phosphate in 2008. During 2011 the market price for phosphate again increased before stabilizing at $200/tonne, a figure it would hold through 2012 before declining through 2013 and leveling at about $110 per tonne through 2015.[33] The value of phosphate exports in recent years has been as much as six times that of the fishery and much greater than agricultural production, and sand and salt exports.

From an annual 1.1 million tonnes average in each of 31 complete years from 1976 through 2006 at $30 per tonne, there results a net present value of $1.81 billion as at 1 October 2015.[34] figures from 2007 through to 1 October 2015 can be adjusted for value of the latter date, $2.46 billion, and added to the to-2006 present value total, for an overall total of $4.27 billion.[35]

---

32 See *OCP-Bou Craa Production 1975–2006* (unpublished, copy on file with the author). In 1975 production was 2.7 million tonnes. In 1980, 1981 and 1982, there was no production. Annual production did not exceed 1 million tonnes until 1989. It would not return to the 1975 level until 2006. Less than 1 million tonnes per year was produced at Bu Craa during much of the 1980s, exceeding 2 million tonnes only after 1998. In 2011, exports reached a high of 2.78 million tonnes: OCP 2014 *Prospectus*, 95. In 2012, 2013 and 2014, production and exported annually averaged 2.1–2.2 million tonnes. In late 2014 and early 2015 exports were delayed because of reported structural problems at the el Aauin phosphate loading dock.

33 See 'OCP SA Note d'Information: Emission d'un Emprunt Obligatoire', http://www.ocpgroup.ma (accessed January 5, 2015), which details two bond offerings of 2 billion Dirhams each, opened for subscription September 22, 2011, with interest at 4.46\% on a seven-year term. Bo Craa is discussed at pages 104, 126 and 149–50. No data is given in the 2011 prospectus about the volume of reserves or production at the site.

34 Present value is calculated here on the basis of annual production of 1.1. million tonnes (1976–2006, inclusive), $30/tonne (idem), and average annual inflation rate of 2.50% from 1976 until 1986, and 2.00% thereafter, compounded annually, not in advance, and known production, export and market value figures for the years 2007–15 (until October 1, 2015), inclusive. Again, the better rate of inflation may be local figures, that in Morocco perhaps averaging 5% in these years. See also figures available from the US Geological Survey at its website, http://minerals.usgs.gov/minerals (accessed December 1, 2014).

35 This figure does not include phosphate rock exports in 2015, the known value of which, until July 15, 2015, was $80 million from 700,000 tonnes shipped. It is expected that 1.4 to 1.8 million tonnes will be exported in the year, with a total value of $160 to $200 million. (Conversations of the author with SADR officials and WSRW managers, July 2015.)

WESTERN SAHARA

Table 1. Value of natural resources exported from Western Sahara, 1976–2015

Resource	Present value at 1 October 2015
Fishery	$1.34 billion
Phosphate rock	$4.27 billion
Petroleum	$0 (single well production December 2014–March 2015)
Other	$40 million(estimated: sand and salt, excluding agricultural products)
Total	$5.65 billion

2250 persons are reported employed in the Bu Craa enterprise, 10% of OCP SA's overall work-force.[36]

These figures can be compared to the sums Morocco claims to have spent in developing the territory. In 2011 and 2015 the figures were made public. The former was a total of $900 million (€600 million) said to have been spent from 2004 through 2009, and 20 billion Dirhams ($2.5 billion at 2011 exchange rates) since 1975.[37] These amounts, ostensibly spent until 2015, were made available by the Kingdom of Morocco through its embassy in Australia in March 2015. They also appear to include the 2011 figures, above. The document notes that:

> Concretely, an important budget has been developed, since 1976, to the development of the region. *This effort that surpasses, by far, the income generated by the exploitation of natural resources,* comes as follows:
>
> -For the period 2001/2005, an average annual amount of 9.5 billion Dirhams was devoted to the Southern Provinces (Western Sahara) (1 AUD = 8 MAD)
> -Since the creation of the Agency for the Development of the Southern Provinces, the state spent more than 7.7 billion Dirhams for the period of 2006–2009.[38]

The declared investment (i.e. its present value for comparative purposes), whether as stated in 2011 or in 2015, is about 90% of the present value of the two principal resources taken from Western Sahara during the years of occupation. (It should be recalled that, until 2009, less than half the $4.27 billion present value of phosphate rock had by then been realized.) Generally after 2000 and until 2009, therefore, Morocco's stated civil expenditures exceeded the gross market value of the territory's principal resources. Making good an annexation project, however, is a continuing task. What counts is the revenue from resources from year to year, and an overall calculation or estimate of all that has gone before is useful only to illustrate the relative cost of the occupation, something discussed below, and to assess an idealized eventual

---

36 OCP 2014 *Prospectus*, 110. Some 400 Saharawi persons are said to be employed in this workforce, a figure the author arrived at after interviews with persons living in the occupied part of Western Sahara and SADR government officials from October 2012 until February 2015. In an undated document titled 'Allegations regarding exploitation of natural resources' made available in March 2015 by Morocco's embassy in Australia, Morocco notes 'the basis of [OCP's] exploitation is motivated, above all, by social considerations imposed by the necessity to preserve the jobs of the Western Sahara workers who support more than 700 families' (unpublished, copy on file with the author).

37 See e.g. submissions made in October 2011 to the UN General Assembly Special Political and Decolonization Committee at New York, http://www.un.org/en/ga/fourth (accessed February 1, 2015). Morocco did not provide data to support its figures. It is not clear if the figures include costs to construct and maintain public infrastructure in the territory.

38 'Allegations regarding exploitation of natural resources', a document issued by the Embassy of the Kingdom of Morocco in March 2015 (undated) (unpublished, copy on file with the author). (Emphasis in original.) The document notes the expenditures were directed to 'urbanisation', 'basic infrastructure' (964 km of roads, three airports, three sea ports) and 'drinking water supply'.

reparations claim.[39] It is the entire result of exploiting Western Sahara's natural resources that must be considered. How international law applies, to which we turn next, is vital to understanding how Western Sahara's natural resources are allowed to be taken.

III. Western Sahara's resources and the law

The international law which applies to the development and export of Western Sahara's natural resources is now mature. It has evolved in the modern era, including by cases in the International Court of Justice, the International Criminal Court and international criminal tribunals.[40] What makes the law remarkable when it comes to Western Sahara is how widely and continually it has been disregarded. The problem is enforceability. The measures available in law are for states to act on, and not the Saharawi people or an incompletely recognized Saharawi Republic. Two bodies of international law prohibit the taking of Saharawi resources. The first is the permanent sovereignty of non-self-governing peoples over their natural resources.[41] The second is international humanitarian law, and it is the more restrictive, prohibiting commercial exploitation of Western Sahara's resources except to meet the immediate needs of the original Saharawi population.[42]

During the 40 years of Western Sahara's occupation, there has been little declared interest in applying international humanitarian law in the territory, and less so in protecting the civil population by safeguarding public and private property including natural resources. The UN and the organized international community have been unwilling to declare that this body of law, IHL, applies. To insist on its application would be to acknowledge that the territory is occupied as defined in the Geneva and Hague Conventions and related customary international law, thereby raising the question of whether international criminal law applies. A declaration confirm-

---

39   The SADR government has presented a reparations claim to a phosphate purchasing company, Potash Corporation, stating: ' Our purpose in writing is to deliver to Potash Corporation notice of a pending or eventual claim for compensation resulting from your company's purchase of phosphate mineral rock from occupied Western Sahara ... The historical record and precedent bear out a claim for reparations, recalling the examples of the United Nations (Iraq–Kuwait) Compensation Commission and the mechanisms in the 1998 *Rome Statute* of the International Criminal Court ... We calculate the claim conservatively to be at least $400 million (in 2014 dollars).' SADR Petroleum and Mines Authority letter of January 10, 2014 (unpublished, copy on file with the author).

40   The leading ICJ decision on the right of non-self-governing peoples to self-determination is the *Kosovo Advisory Opinion (Accordance with International Law of the Unilateral Declaration of Independence in Respect of Kosovo*, Advisory Opinion), ICJ Reports 2010, 403. 'During the second half of the twentieth century, the international law of self-determination developed in such a way as to create a right to independence for the peoples of non-self-governing territories and peoples subject to alien subjugation, domination and exploitation.' Ibid., at para. 79 (citations omitted). The ICJ has not pronounced on the legality of resource development in non-self-governing territories or those considered occupied within international humanitarian law.
It is the right of permanent sovereignty to resources, coupled with the right to self-determination, that requires Morocco as an administering state in Western Sahara to ensure the consent of the original inhabitants of the territory is obtained to resource development, and that the benefits of such development accrue to them. This was the basis for the governance of Namibia's resources under occupation, by decree of the UN Council for Namibia, created in the 1960s and discussed below.
The leading international criminal law decisions for the taking of public resources under occupation remain those of the International Military Tribunal after the Second World War, for which see the discussion in James G. Stewart, *Corporate War Crimes: Prosecuting the Pillage of Natural Resources* (New York: Open Society Initiative, 2010).

41   This body of law traces back to the UN's decolonization mission with the UN General Assembly issuing its 1962 declaration, *Permanent Sovereignty over Natural Resources*, GA Res 1803 (XVII) (December 14, 1962), discussed below. Arguably, because Spain could not assign or transfer responsibility for self-determination of the Saharawi people to other states, Spain remains responsible for resource development in Western Sahara, that is, ensuring the consent of and benefit to the Saharawi people from such activity.

42   International humanitarian law and international criminal law is discussed below. As noted above, Spain's courts have accepted the application of international criminal law in recent months. Pillage may result in the setting of an international or a non-international armed conflict, from the taking of public and private resources. The Fourth Geneva Convention, 1949 and the Rome Statute 1998 of the International Criminal Court, discussed below, govern. Because of the stricter obligation to protect an occupied population, Morocco is arguably first bound to comply with international humanitarian and criminal law in its administration of Western Sahara.

ing the occupation was made early on by the General Assembly, but it has not been acted on.[43] Recognizing the annexation of Western Sahara as a continuing occupation would make inescapable the obligation on states to deny support to Morocco in its project. That is something the organized international community has not been prepared to accept. As with East Timor (Timor-Leste) until 1999, the occupation of Western Sahara remains disregarded under this branch of international law. Even as IHL rapidly developed in the first decade of the new millennium, including a creation of the International Criminal Court with a war crimes jurisdiction that includes pillage, there has been no interest in applying its criminal law adjunct to Western Sahara. That changed in the second half of 2014, and there are now two criminal appeals decisions in Spain which have directed investigations to proceed against alleged serious crimes in the occupation of Western Sahara on the basis of international criminal law.[44]

The reluctance of the organized international community to contemplate the application of international law in general to Western Sahara and within that its resources is the result of several factors. To begin with, few states have any interest in the legal protection of the territory's natural resources. This position is understandable when it is recalled that they defer to the United Nations in its oversight role for self-determination. The problem in having states recognize and apply international legal obligations is something that comes from treating the 'question' of Western Sahara exclusively as an incomplete self-determination project. In any event, and apart from Palestine's particular status, the case of Western Sahara is one now largely singular, almost unique. The treatment of Western Sahara therefore remains one of self-determination (that is, of completing decolonization) and not the reality of territorial acquisition through *re-colonization*. Considered this way, and consistent with the history of colonizing nations having particular and apparently non-transferable obligations to complete self-determination for peoples who were once a part of their imperiums, the UN's decolonization project arguably no longer has much useful application. Portugal, it seems, was the last colonizing state to realize its obligations, acting in 1999 to assure for the Timorese people their right to self-determination. (France in New Caledonia must be noted as a contemporary example.) When it is recalled that the Saharawi people have been consistent in expressing their desire for independence should self-determination eventuate (as well as their relatively uncontroversial declaration of independence in 1976), the UN decolonization project is revealed as fading in importance. A better approach might now be to categorize cases as either secessionary (including those of state dissolution) or the occupation of non-self-governing territories by (usually) neighboring states.

Another factor that has restricted the application of international law to Western Sahara (across several subjects, notably that of human rights) is found in the locus of international responsibility for the Saharawi people and their territory. Spain renounced its continuing colonial ('administering power') role despite half-hearted later statements that it did not intend to abandon the territory under the Madrid Accords.[45] Without Spain the Saharawi people have no colonial interlocutor to pursue diplomatic or legal redress for self-determination. But that does not

---

43 Resolution 34/37 'deeply [deplored] the aggravation of the situation resulting from the continued occupation of Western Sahara by Morocco and the extension of that occupation to the territory recently occupied [until August 1979] by Mauritania'. *Question of Western Sahara*, GA Res 34/37 (November 21, 1979).

44 The first was a decision of the *Audencia Nacional* directing an investigating magistrate to proceed on a criminal complaint about the death of a dual Saharawi/Spanish citizen at Gdeim Izek in November 2010. The court concluded that international criminal law applied in the territory as a result of Spain's adoption of such law into its national legal system. The same court concluded the following April that an investigation for genocide could proceed against 11 Moroccan citizens in the early years of Western Sahara's occupation. See the Decisions of the *Audiencia Nacional*, Auto no. 40/2014 (July 4, 2014), and Sumario 1/2015 (April 9, 2015). The latter decision effectively set aside Spain's November 1975 statute that purported to abrogate the country's colonial responsibility for Western Sahara, Ley 40/1975. See Fernando J. Pérez, 'Ruz procesa 11 mandos militares marroquies por genocidio en el Sáhara', *El País*, April 9, 2015.

45 Spain formally legislated an end to its responsibility. See *Ley* [Law] *40/1975, de 19 de noviembre, sobre descolonización del Sahara*. 'The Government is authorized to perform such acts and adopt measures as may be necessary for

mean the responsibility has become Morocco's. The obligation to ensure decolonization after 1991 has remained with the United Nations. By resolution and precedent, this responsibility in the UN system should fall first to the General Assembly, something that had its apogee in the case of Namibia.[46] The discussion of Western Sahara in the General Assembly and in a Security Council content to annually renew the mandate of the UN self-determination mission in the territory, MINURSO, has not been one in which annexation of territory or an occupation has featured.[47]

The two areas of law concerning natural resources, permanent sovereignty and IHL, are usefully returned to. The first prohibits states and individuals from taking the territory's natural resources without the consent of the Saharawi people and a benefit to them. The obligation to respect a people's sovereignty to resources originates from the United Nations Charter. Articles 73 and 74 of the Charter were intended to ensure the well-being of peoples of non-self-governing territories until they are no longer colonized. The duty for colonizing, administering and occupying states has several aspects. There must be consultation with the people of the colonized territory. They must give free consent, arrived at on an informed basis, to the exploitation of their natural resources. It is they who are to have the benefit of the exploitation. Settlers introduced by a colonizing state or an occupying power do not qualify.

> Members of the United Nations which have or assume responsibilities for the administration of territories whose peoples have not yet attained a full measure of self-government recognize the principle that the interests of the inhabitants of these territories are paramount, and accept as a sacred trust the obligation to promote to the utmost, within the system of international peace and security established by the present Charter, the well-being of the inhabitants of these territories.[48]

The obligation for consent has resulted from the two General Assembly Resolutions on which the UN self-determination process is founded, Resolutions 1514 (XV) and 1541 (XV) of 14 December 1960.[49] Resolution 1514 declares that 'peoples may, for their own ends, freely dispose of their natural wealth and resources … based on the principle of mutual benefit and international law' in order to realize the right to 'freely pursue their economic, social and cultural development'. In the five decades since, the two have uncontroversially entered into international law and are the core of Saharawi sovereignty over the resources of occupied Western Sahara.

In 1962 the General Assembly addressed permanent sovereignty over natural resources, declaring in Resolution 1803 that 'economic and financial agreements between the developed and the developing countries must be based on the principles of equality and of the right of peoples and nations to self-determination'.[50] That sovereignty to natural resources is vested in the

---

the decolonization of the non-autonomous territory of the Sahara, safeguarding Spanish interests.' (Translation by the author.)

46 The UN General Assembly-created Council for Namibia had legislative and executive jurisdiction for the territory after the termination of South Africa's mandate, exercising it including by legal action in the protection of natural resources. See *The Question of Namibia*, GA Res 2248 (S-V) (May 19, 1967). In November 2011, the Frente Polisario first called for UN oversight and possibly a form of trusteeship of natural resources in Western Sahara.

47 UN Security Council Resolution S/2218 (April 28, 2015) is the most recent annual extension of MINURSO's mandate. The UN assumed the obligation to ensure Saharawi self-determination in its referendum agreement with Morocco and the Frente Polisario which took effect in September 1991. The agreement is detailed in two reports of the UN Secretary-General, S/21360 (June 18, 1990) and S/22464 (April 19, 1991). 'The two parties, namely the Kingdom of Morocco and the Frente POLISARIO, recognize in the settlement proposals that the sole and exclusive responsibility for the organization and conduct of the referendum is vested in the United Nations.' S/22464, para. 9.

48 Article 73, *Charter of the United Nations* (June 26, 1945) 1 UNTS 16 (in force October 24, 1945). The UN Secretary-General noted the application of Article 73 in his annual report to the UN Security Council of April 10, 2015, above.

49 *Declaration of the Granting of Independence to Colonial countries and Peoples*, GA Res 1514 (XV) (December 14, 1960) and *Principles which should Guide Members in Determining whether or not an Obligation Exists to Transmit the Information called for under Article 73e of the Charter*, GA Res 1541 (XV) (December 14, 1960). See also *Permanent Sovereignty over Natural Resources*, GA Res 1803 (XVII) (December 14, 1962).

50 Ibid., *Sovereignty over Natural Resources* resolution.

people of a non-self-governing territory – and not an occupying or administering state – is clear by the resolution: 'The right of peoples and nations to permanent sovereignty over their wealth and natural resources must be exercised in the interest of their natural development and of the well-being of the people of the State concerned.' The General Assembly has observed that a '[v]iolation of the rights of peoples and nations to sovereignty over their natural wealth and resources is contrary to the spirit and principles of the Charter of the United Nations'.[51]

The Saharawi people's sovereignty over natural resources could theoretically be enforced by any state. That is because there exists a universal (*erga omnes*) requirement on all states to uphold the law in this respect.[52] The organized international community accepts the protection of non-self-governing peoples' sovereignty to natural resources, as the work of the UN Council for Namibia, and the Nauru and Palestine Wall decisions of the International Court of Justice have shown.[53] Although by 1990 there were only a few remaining self-determination cases, the obligation of administering-occupying states to safeguard the resources of such territories had become a peremptory norm of international law. The most recent UN General Assembly Resolution on the subject emphasizes

> the right of the peoples of the Non-Self-Governing Territories to self-determination in conformity with the Charter of the United Nations and with General Assembly resolution 1514(XV) ... as well as their right to the enjoyment of their natural resources and their right to dispose of those resources in their best interest.[54]

The development of this area of the law was discussed by Judge Christopher Weeramantry in his dissent to the ICJ's 1995 *East Timor (Portugal/Australia)* decision. He concluded that the 1989 Timor Gap Treaty was illegal, noting the obligation *erga omnes* on states to oppose the operation of the treaty:

> At such time as the East Timorese people exercise their right to self-determination, they would become entitled as a component of their sovereign right, to determine how their wealth and natural resources should be disposed of. Any action prior to that date which may in effect deprive them of this right must thus fall clearly within the category of acts which infringe on their right to self-determination, and their future sovereignty, if indeed full and independent sovereignty be their choice. This right is described by the General Assembly, in its resolution [1803] ...
> The exploration, development and disposition of the resources of the Timor Gap, for which the Timor Gap Treaty provides a detailed specification, has most certainly not been worked out in accordance with the principle that the people of East Timor should 'freely consider' these matters, in regard to their 'authorization, restriction or prohibition'.

---

51   Ibid., Articles 1 and 7, respectively.
52   *Legal Consequences of the Construction of a Wall in the Occupied Palestinian Territory,* Advisory Opinion, 2004 ICJ Reports 136 [*Palestine Wall,* Advisory Opinion]. Paragraph 159 of the Opinion is worth recalling: 'Given the character and the importance of the rights and obligations involved, the Court is of the view that all States are under an obligation not to recognize the illegal situation resulting from the construction of the wall in the Occupied Palestinian Territory, including in and around East Jerusalem. They are also under an obligation not to render aid or assistance in maintaining the situation created by such construction. It is also for all States, while respecting the United Nations Charter and international law, to see to it that any impediment, resulting from the construction of the wall, to the exercise by the Palestinian people of its right to self-determination is brought to an end. In addition, all the States parties to the Geneva Convention relative to the Protection of Civilian Persons in Time of War of 12 August 1949 are under an obligation, while respecting the United Nations Charter and international law, to ensure compliance by Israel with international humanitarian law as embodied in that Convention.' The Court noted that the taking of resources for construction of the wall was to be remedied, including payment of compensation. Ibid., para. 153.
53   Respectively, *Case concerning Phosphate Lands in Nauru (Nauru v Australia),* Preliminary Objection, 1992 ICJ Reports 240, *East Timor (Portugal v Australia),* 1995 ICJ Reports 139 [*East Timor*], and *Palestine Wall,* Advisory Opinion, ibid.
54   *Economic and Other Activities which Affect the Interests of the Peoples of Non-Self-Governing Territories,* GA Res 69/98 (December 16, 2014), paragraph 1.

The Timor Gap Treaty, to the extent that it deals with East Timorese resources prior to the achievement of self-determination by the East Timorese people, is thus in clear violation of this principle.[55]

In 2002, the law of non-self-governing peoples' sovereignty to natural resources was considered by Hans Corell, then the UN Under-Secretary-General for Legal Affairs. The Security Council had requested his opinion on the legality of seabed petroleum exploration on the coast of Western Sahara. Corell was not asked to consider the territory's fishery and phosphate resources.

> The conclusion is, therefore, that, while the specific [petroleum exploration] contracts which are the subject of the Security Council's request are not in themselves illegal, if further exploration and exploitation activities were to proceed in disregard of the interests and wishes of the people of Western Sahara, they would be in violation of the international law principles applicable to mineral resource activities in Non-Self-Governing Territories.[56]

There is an additional source of international law to be recalled when it comes to the Saharan fishery. All EU states, the EU itself and Russia are signatories to the UN Convention on the Law of the Sea; Morocco acceded in 2007.[57] UNCLOS states have an obligation to comply with Resolution III of the Final Act of the Law of the Sea Conference to ensure that for a 'people [who] have not attained full independence ... or a territory under colonial domination, provisions concerning rights and interests under the Convention [are] implemented for the benefit of the people of the territory with a view to promoting their well-being and development'.[58] The phrasing is consistent with General Assembly Resolution 1803. Resolution III has been overlooked in the case of Western Sahara.

The UN and the organized international community could be motivated to apply international law to Western Sahara if the principles of territorial integrity were recalled.[59] It is, after all, in the interest of the international community to promote the norm, as the response to Iraq's attempt to annex Kuwait in 1990 and by Western states to the incorporation of Crimea into Russia in 2014 have demonstrated. Dealing with the territorial integrity of Western Sahara would mean having to accept that international humanitarian law applies. Even if the facts on the ground are compelling – and they include the international nature of the conflict, the parties' 1991 cease-fire referendum arrangement, the presence of a substantial occupying force, the building of the berm and, not least, Morocco's admission that Western Sahara remains 'technically, a war zone' – what has been a deference to the UN to ensure self-determination displaces the suggestion that international humanitarian law can apply, even given the stark circumstances of a separated and refugee Saharawi people.[60]

When it comes to IHL, although 1991 brought an end to active hostilities between the Frente Polisario and Morocco, the occupation of Western Sahara continues. As such, there continues the

---

55 Dissenting Opinion in *East Timor*, 198.

56 'Report of the UN Office of Legal Affairs on the Legality of the Oil-Contracts Signed by Morocco over the Natural Resources of the Western Sahara' (letter dated January 29, 2002), UN doc. S/2002/161 (February 12, 2002), http://www.arso.org/UNlegaladv.htm (accessed December 1, 2014).

57 United Nations *Convention on the Law of the Sea*, 1982, December 10, 1982, 21 ILM 1261 (in force November 16, 1994) [UNCLOS].

58 UNCLOS Resolution III, para. 1. There has been virtually no mention of Resolution III in the context of the 'question' of Western Sahara by any state, the UN, or any commentator.

59 Territorial integrity finds its starting place in the UN Charter, at Article 2. The basis to assert the territorial integrity of Western Sahara has several dimensions, including the necessity of such a circumstances in order to ensure the exercise of the Saharawi people's right to self-determination, the commitments of the parties in the 1990–91 ceasefire and referendum arrangements, the principle of *uti posseditis* in the maintenance of the inviolability of Western Sahara's territory and, notably, the conclusion of the ICJ that Morocco has not basis in law for a territorial claim to the Sahara. The UN General Assembly's declaration of Western Sahara to be occupied and the African Union's position on the nature of Morocco's presence in the territory, discussed above, are a part of this imperative.

60 US diplomatic cable, 'Seven Saharawi activists charged with intelligence cooperation with a foreigner' (US embassy Rabat) (October 16, 2009), http://www.wikileaks.ch (accessed December 1, 2014).

obligation to protect the territory's original population. The Fourth Geneva Convention prohibits pillage after cessation of hostilities for the entire period a state or territory is occupied:

> In the case of occupied territory … the Occupying Power shall be bound, for the duration of the occupation, to the extent that such Power exercises the functions of government in such territory, by the provisions of [the articles against pillage and introducing settlers into occupied lands, among other provisions] of the present Convention.[61]

No state recognizes Morocco's claim to Western Sahara. As with Namibia, East Timor and Palestine, Morocco's annexation of the territory continues to be universally rejected.[62] That is a useful start to making out the norm of territorial integrity as it applies to Western Sahara and accepting the legal circumstances of the existence of an occupation. The discussion recalls the ICJ's task 'to assist the General Assembly to determine its future decolonization policy and in particular to pronounce on the claims of Morocco and Mauritania to have had legal ties with Western Sahara involving the territorial integrity of their respective countries' by its 1975 *Western Sahara* advisory opinion.[63] The court concluded:

> [T]he materials and information presented to it do not establish any tie of territorial sovereignty between the territory of Western Sahara and the Kingdom of Morocco or the Mauritanian entity. Thus the Court has not found legal ties of such a nature as might affect the application of resolution 1514 (XV) in the decolonization of Western Sahara and, in particular, of the principle of self-determination through the free and genuine expression of the will of the peoples of the Territory.[64]

If the rules of international law are clear enough in the case of Western Sahara's natural resources, we are left with the question of why they have not been applied. The answer should not be complicated, but it has become so. It includes the lack of any single state interested in upholding international law coupled with a leaving of the matter to a United Nations unwilling to act outside of a self-determination referendum approach. The consequence for international law is just as much the inability of any state or the Saharawi people being able to apply it to their circumstances as it is the creation of another precedent for the violation of territorial integrity, denial of self-determination and pillage of occupied lands. The taking of Saharawi resources damages the law in more ways than one. The organized international community has been slow to appreciate that.

IV.   Pillage made good

If the value of Western Sahara's natural resources can be approximated, the consequences of their taking have not been wholly understood. The exploitation of resources is only a part of Morocco's efforts to annex the territory. The historical record strongly suggests that Western Sahara would have been invaded by Mauritania and Morocco whatever resource potential the territory had.[65] However, as we have seen, the two states were quick to divide resources between them, although Mauritania does not seem to have benefited from the fishery. And several years were needed for Morocco to reestablish production at Bu Craa. Resource exploitation certainly acquired greater

---

61   *Fourth Geneva Convention*, Article 6.
62   Consider the statements of United States, Norway and Switzerland that their free trade agreements with Morocco do not apply to Western Sahara.
63   *Western Sahara*, Advisory Opinion, para. 161
64   Ibid., para. 162.A useful fact in applying international humanitarian law is Mauritania's admission of its wrongful occupation of Western Sahara, made in its 1979 treaty with the Frente Polisario. If a court has yet to pronounce definitively on the legal situation resulting from Morocco's occupation, the statement of an occupier asserting a similar historic claim as Morocco (and which agreed with Morocco to partition the territory in 1976) is compelling.
65   The best historical record is that presented in voluminous records to the ICJ by Spain, Mauritania and Morocco in the 1975 advisory opinion proceedings. Mauritania could never hope to share in the phosphate reserves at Bu Craa. The most in-depth discussion of the 'siren call' of resources and the idea sometimes suggested that Morocco hoped to acquire a monopoly of global phosphate production by its annexation is that of Tony Hodges, *Western Sahara: The Roots of a Desert War* (Westport, CT: Lawrence Hill, 1983).

importance because an economy was needed for settlers after 1975 (who entered in increased numbers after the 1991 ceasefire). While revenue from the trade in resources is important, the real benefit to Morocco has been to create the appearance of a viable annexation. Work available for settlers in the resource sector serves as the basis for a labor market, with employment for Moroccan nationals justifying the success of settlement. The purported return of resource revenues back into the local economy as something that benefits the 'local' population – now a majority of Moroccan citizens – helps satisfy international concerns that resource revenues are being properly applied in the territory.

The consequences of taking natural resources from occupied Western Sahara can be categorized as: (i) Morocco's unrealized financial enrichment; (ii) a present and perhaps future denial of natural resources to the Saharawi people; (iii) the consolidation of Morocco's occupation including the settlement of its nationals in the territory (together with the related problem of the delay of a self-determination referendum); and (iv) the promotion of the appearance of legitimacy for the occupation through the 'credibility mechanism' of trade in resources. An additional problem beyond these four, and noted above, is the diminished application and availability to the Saharawi people of international law along with a further incident of state practice which erodes the two basic norms of international law: territorial sovereignty and the protection of peoples under occupation. These consequences are not isolated from each other, being connected in their causes and having a common point of a delayed self-determination.

The consequences are now considered in turn. Over four decades the annexation of Western Sahara has resulted in a financial loss to Morocco. Its hold on the territory is one secured by large expenditures. Just as it is difficult to determine the extent to which the benefits of Western Sahara's resources have been applied in the territory, so it is equally difficult to gauge the cost of an occupation that allows for the taking of resources. It may be reasonable to conclude that recent revenues from resources – annually averaging $300 to $400 million from 2010 through 2014 – if directed back into the occupied territory, would substantially provide for the civil economy, meeting at least the basic cost of sustaining settler and Saharawi populations within existing Moroccan state expenditures (including taxation benefits and commodities subsidies) but not the cost of the military presence in the territory.[66]

The ongoing result for the Saharawi people from the taking of their resources is not something that is easily quantified. The Saharawi have a subordinate (or marginalized) role in the economy of Western Sahara. However, it is not accurate to say that the Saharawi population inside the occupied territory is deprived of all benefits from development of natural resources. Small numbers of Saharawi are employed by Phosboucraa, in the fishery and in related services. Labor figures are not reliable; however, the number of Saharawi employed in the formal sector appears to be between 25,000 and 40,000, less than a majority of the adult population in the occupied territory.[67] But few of these are involved directly or secondarily in resource industries, no more than several thousand. What is known is that preferred employment, housing and amenities overwhelmingly favor Moroccan settlers.[68]

---

66 There are few available figures about the cost of Morocco's military presence in Western Sahara. The CIA's 2014 *World Factbook* notes that the Kingdom's annual military spending in 2012 was 3.55% of a $105 billion GDP (2013 estimated), https://www.cia.gov/library/publications/the-world-factbook/geos/mo.html (accessed March 1, 2015). Morocco's reported state (government) budget for 2013 was estimated at $34.5 billion. (Transparency International states GDP in 2010 at $90.8 billion.) On the basis that one-third of Morocco's armed forces and military support infrastructure, including as many as 100,000 FAR members, is located in Western Sahara, the annual *military cost* of the occupation is approximately $1.2 billion.

67 Personal interviews, Saharawi government officials at the Boujdour and Rabouni refugee camps, October 2010 and December 2012.

68 In late 2010 the Saharawi protest camp at Gdeim Izek near el Aauin and others in the occupied territory were expressions of Saharawi discontent over marginalized economic circumstances. See Association Sahraouie des Victimes des Violations Graves des Droits de l'Homme Commises par l'Etat du Maroc, *Rapport de l'ASVDH sur le campement de Gdeim Izik et les événements qui ont suivi son démantèlement* (Tindouf, Algeria: January 2011).

That half the Saharawi population – those who live in the camps at Tindouf – is denied any benefit of their natural resources is a significant problem, a matter also overlooked during the early conflict. In recent years, the annual direct and indirect donor support including food aid and essential commodities to this population of perhaps 140,000 has been between €40 and 60 million.[69] The amount is small in comparison to the revenue in the same period from phosphate and the fishery. As far as the occupied territory is concerned, there is no reason why resource revenues could not be allocated to both Saharawi and Moroccans, including indirectly through employment schemes. However, Morocco has not been prepared to acknowledge any right of the Saharawi people to their resources and, in any event, the large settler population in the occupied territory, outnumbering the Saharawi population by at least two to one, depends on continued financial support from Rabat.[70]

The long-term value of Western Sahara's natural resources and so their potential loss to the Saharawi people in the future turns on three factors. The first is the uncertainty of the remaining time until the Saharawi people achieve self-determination. Changes in market prices for the two leading resources is another. (East Timor's experience with increases and the late 2014/15 decline in petroleum prices after independence is recalled.) A third factor is petroleum development in a time of unstable world prices for the commodity, which has now tentatively started in the territory.

An optimistic prediction might be made that fish stocks will continue undiminished. A 2011–12 fisheries research program, the Northwest Africa Ecosystem Survey (a joint undertaking of the UN Food and Agriculture Organization and Norway's Institute of Marine Research), will provide data about long-term sustainability in the area including the Saharan fishery.[71] The history of fishing in Saharan waters since 1975 should be recalled, for there have frequently been too many vessels involved. The allowance for more than 100 European vessels under the Fisheries Partnership Agreement has continued the tradition. Concerns persist that some stocks are overexploited.[72]

The extent of phosphate reserves at Bu Craa is uncertain, with present estimates ranging from a low of 100 million tonnes to 1.3 billion tonnes.[73] The latter figure seems too high and may come from outdated survey data. In its 2014 debt financing prospectus issued through the Irish Stock Exchange, OCP claims present reserves at Bu Craa (known also as Oued Eddahab) to be 500 million tonnes.[74] Phosphate extraction will continue to be limited by the capacities of the conveyor belt to el Aauin and facilities at the coast.

Overall, an annual revenue of about $300 million can be forecast to come from Western Sahara's resources over the next few years, until petroleum and mineral resources come to be

---

69   See UN Office for the Coordination of Humanitarian Affairs (Financial Tracking Services), 'Aid to Saharawi Refugee Camps in 2013' (December 12, 2014), http://fts.unocha.org (accessed April 1, 2015). In 2013, a total of $24 million was given by various governments (e.g. Spain) and agencies (WFP, UNHCR, UNICEF) as aid into the Tindouf camps. The SADR government has few sources of revenue, but obtains modest operating funds of perhaps $10 million annually from AU member states. Algeria offers considerable in-kind and material support to the Tindouf camps, including electricity and, through the Algerian Red Crescent, cooking gas. In the author's visits to the camps, discussion with aid agency managers, and interviews of SADR officials, the figure of €40–60 million for 2014 is arrived at.

70   Petrol is taxed less in occupied Western Sahara than in Morocco and is supplied by chartered vessels to El Aauin and Dakhla. See Western Sahara Resource Watch, 'Fuelling the Occupation: The Swedish Transport of Oil to Occupied Western Sahara' (WSRW: Brussels, July 2014).

71   The work is part of the UN Food & Agriculture Organization's Canary Current Large Marine Ecosystem (CCLME) Project. See the UNFAO project website: http://www.canarycurrent.org (visited April 1, 2015).

72   See the 2010 report prepared by the consultancy Oceanic Développement, 'Framework Contract Fish/2006/20 Convention Specifique N°26: Evaluation ex-post du protocole actuel d'accord de partenariat dans la domaine de peche entre l'union europeenne et le royaume du maroc, etude d'impact d'un possible future protocole d'accord – Rapport – Décembre 2010', http://www.fishelsewhere.eu/files/dated/2012-03-05/evaluation-app-maroc-2010.pdf (accessed December 1, 2014).

73   WSRW, P for Plunder, 9. Toby Shelley put the 'known exploitable reserves' in 2004 at 132 million tonnes, Shelley, Endgame in the Western Sahara, 70.

74   OCP 2014 Prospectus, 79. The figure is stated as 1% of 50 billion tonnes under control by OCP SA, i.e. Morocco, from the January 2013 United States Geological Survey published 'Mineral Commodities Summaries'.

exploited in commercial quantities.[75] Of course, the future value of resources should account for how much will remain for the Saharawi people at independence. As with East Timor, the international community has an interest in preserving such resources, the better to make a viable economy for an independent Saharawi Republic after self-determination is resolved. Along the way, the question of Western Sahara's two primary resources should not detract from the preservation of other resources including groundwater, the territory's limited arable land, and environmental protection generally.[76]

Another consequence of the development and export of resources from Western Sahara has been what seems to be a useful domestic political and international gaining of support (or at least a tacit acceptance) of the annexation. In general, development and trade in the resources has created a useful internal legitimacy for the Moroccan monarchy, its armed forces and civil society. The 'national project' to acquire Western Sahara, in other words assuring the success of returning to the Kingdom its lost southern provinces, is made more acceptable by apparent financial gain and economic activity in the territory. Moreover, the presence of a standing army in Western Sahara has been partly justified by the necessity to protect resources. (That there was no phosphate production at Bu Craa for several years before the berm was built bears this out.) The taking of resources also offers a greater stake for Moroccan government agencies, state corporations and individuals in the continued occupation of the territory. Perhaps most importantly, resource development serves as a pretext for economic activity to support Morocco's settlers. This is especially true given the absence of industry and manufacturing in Western Sahara. In other words, the acceptance by Moroccan society of repossessing the Sahara has been more readily perpetuated because of apparent productive activity and financial return.

On the international stage, states have for the most part avoided commenting about the trade in Western Sahara's phosphate. Norway is a rare exception; in late 2011 its government directed the state pension fund to sell off interests in the FMC Corporation and Canada's Potash Corporation.[77] To their credit, Norway, Switzerland and the United States declared that their post-2000 free trade agreements with Morocco do not extend to products from Western Sahara. (However, Saharawi phosphate enters the United States free of import taxes.)

It is the fishery which most secures for Morocco international support for its exploitation of the territory's resources. The European Commission has been satisfied to have the benefit of the FPA be realized by the entire population of Western Sahara, side-stepping the question of Saharawi resource rights.[78] Although not as well known, the same has been true for the recent Russia–Morocco fisheries treaties. The absence of measures to ensure compliance with the law of sovereignty to natural resources has reinforced the willingness of states to tolerate Morocco's presence in Western Sahara. An example is the statement in an internal document from the

---

75 Metalex Resources Ltd. of Canada has conducted aerial surveys in a joint venture with Morocco's state oil and mineral development agency, ONHYM. See the company website at: http://www.metalexventures.com (accessed April 1, 2015) and the 2013 ONHYM annual report at page 32: http://www.onhym.com (accessed April 4, 2015). Exploration for petroleum on land continues, for which see again the ONHYM 2013 annual report. Hanno Resources of Australia has extensively surveyed the liberated zone and found extensive deposits of iron ore and other minerals, under technical cooperation agreements with the SADR government.

76 Groundwater resources and water use in urban areas of occupied Western Sahara is not well understood.

77 See the website of Norway's state pension fund, http://www.regjeringen.no/en/dep/fin/pressesenter/pressemeldinger/2011/statens-pensjonsfond-utland-nye-beslutni/statens-pensjonsfond-utland-to-selskaper.html?id=665637 (accessed December 15, 2014). The Swedish state pension fund has also more recently divested itself of share ownership in Western Sahara resource-receiving companies.

78 See Smith, 'Fishing for Self-determination' and the observations of the EU Parliament Fisheries Rapporteur Carl Haglund, 'Report to the EU Parliament Fisheries Committee, 2011', http://www.europarl.europa.eu/sides/getDoc.do?type=REPORT&reference=A7-2011-0394&language=EN (accessed December 1, 2014).

Moroccan government published by a whistle-blower on 21 November 2014.[79] Titled 'La Fédération de Russie et la Question du Sahara Marocain', it explains that:

> To this objective, Morocco has to … implicate Russia in activities in the Sahara, as is already the case in the field of fisheries. Oil exploration, phosphates, energy and touristic development are, among others, the sectors that could be involved in this respect … In return, Russia could guarantee a freeze on the Sahara file within the UN, the time for the Kingdom to take strong action with irreversible facts with regard to the *marocanité* of the Sahara.[80]

For its part, the United Nations would do well to consider how the two areas of law described above can be used to help achieve Saharawi self-determination. Eliminate a substantial reason for the annexation of Western Sahara – the taking of its resources – and Morocco's capacity and justification to maintain its annexation should be diminished. The reasoning of the International Court of Justice in its *Palestine Wall* advisory opinion is relevant:

> The Court would observe that the obligations violated by Israel include certain obligations erga omnes. As the Court indicated in the Barcelona Traction case, such obligations are by their very nature 'the concern of all States' and, 'In view of the importance of the rights involved, all States can be held to have a legal interest in their protection' … The obligations erga omnes violated by Israel are the obligation to respect the right of the Palestinian people to self-determination, and certain of its obligations under international humanitarian law. […]
>
> In addition, all the States parties to the Geneva Convention relative to the Protection of Civilian Persons in Time of War of 12 August 1949 are under an obligation, while respecting the United Nations Charter and international law, to ensure compliance by Israel with international humanitarian law as embodied in that Convention.[81]

It is unfortunate that the well-established rules of international law have been made marginal in the case of Western Sahara. If the law is considered properly, Morocco's annexation of Western Sahara will be again revealed as illegal. For the present, there continues a tacit acceptance of the occupation and so the approval of the taking of resources from the Saharawi people's territory.

V. Will the taking of the Sahara continue?

The organized international community meets the 'question' of Western Sahara most directly through trade in the territory's natural resources. The other aspects of Morocco's occupation and the stalled right of self-determination for the Saharawi people are not so much the concern of states, deferring as they have to the United Nations to ensure decolonization. None of the concern for a large Saharawi refugee population at Tindouf, the problem of human rights abuses inside occupied Western Sahara or the partition of the territory by the berm have sufficed to overcome a status quo that has prevailed since 1991. If international law in its various forms can be applied to the question of Western Sahara, it will be over natural resources, as the EU Parliament's rejection in 2011 of the Fisheries Partnership Agreement – if only partly out of concern for the Saharawi people – demonstrated.

A few predictions can be ventured. It is unlikely that the United Nations, whether the General Assembly or the Security Council, will act to apply international law to the taking of Western Sahara's natural resources. Enforcing obligations to ensure for the Saharawi people their right of sover-

---

79   Government of Morocco, 'La Fédération de Russie et la Question du Sahara Marocain' (undated), http://www.arso. org/Coleman/Note_Russie_Saharacorrige.pdf (accessed January 5, 2015). The Moroccan government has not contested the validity of much of the leaked documents. See e.g. TelQuel, 'Chris Coleman: le government dénonce finalement une campagne <enragée>' (December 12, 2014); *Le Monde*, 'L'étrange marocain' (January 4, 2015); *Le Monde*, 'Un hacker ne peut déstabiliser à lui tout seul la monarchie marocaine' (January 6, 2015).

80   The document was made available through a Twitter account: @chris_coleman24 on November 21, 2014. It is undated, but contains information suggesting it was created after 2010. The Twitter account has sometimes been taken offline. See e.g. TelQuel, 'Twitter a supprimé le compte de Chris Colement, sans s'expliquer' (December 17, 2014).

81   *Palestine Wall* Advisory Opinion, paras. 155 and 159 [citation omitted]. *Legal Consequences of the Construction of a Wall in the Occupied Palestinian Territory, Advisory Opinion, I. C. J. Reports 2004, p. 136*

eignty over natural resources, even where the UN has an interest in the future availability of those resources to an independent Saharawi Republic restored to its territory, would mean confronting Morocco. The UN's declared aim of resolving the question of Western Sahara on a 'just, lasting and mutually acceptable basis' suggests that it will not prefer the application of the law to the detriment of one of the parties, no matter how serious the violation. That proved to be the case in the aftermath of self-determination in Timor, and is arguably what prevails in Palestine.[82] And so it appears to be the same over the short term when it comes to the natural resources of Western Sahara. In the short term, the best that might be hoped for from the UN is that it supports initiatives of the Personal Envoy of the Secretary-General to have the Frente Polisario and Morocco engage over natural resources.[83]

Another prediction is that international law will inevitably, if slowly, come to be applied to the case of Western Sahara, including international humanitarian law. Morocco, of course, remains immune to legal action for the occupation and plunder of Western Sahara. The kingdom is not a member of the International Criminal Court; nor can it be expected to join while the occupation of Western Sahara continues. And it will not consent to proceedings against it in any international forum, not when its defeat in the *Western Sahara* advisory case is recalled. If there are to be legal remedies against the taking of Saharawi resources, noting there is no similar recourse to challenge the fact of the occupation or human rights violations in Western Sahara, they will necessarily be against third states trading with Morocco for the resources, and individuals and corporations involved with purchasing those resources. The current docket of the International Criminal Court, together with the precedent of the UN Council for Namibia seeking civil remedies to protect natural resources, suggest the law can be applied in the defence of Saharawi resources.[84]

Ultimately, international law can only work at the margins of the Western Sahara case. The problem of Western Sahara is one of a stalled right of self-determination, impeded by an occupation and displacement of the Saharawi people. No body of law yet exists that is sufficient to force the resolution of such matters. We are left with an ordering norm of clear but unenforceable rules for those involved in the taking of Western Sahara's resources. Recent successes reveal the promise of reminding those involved about such norms, noting the successes in Norway and Sweden to withdraw government pension funds from phosphate trading companies and the EU Parliament in 2011 rejecting the FPA's extended first protocol.

There are good reasons for the organized international community to reject Morocco's annexation of Western Sahara. Self-interest in the preservation of the principle of territorial integrity is one. The general acceptance of the desirability of self-determination of non-self-governing peoples is another. The tragic circumstances of the Saharawi people in occupied Western Sahara and at the Tindouf camps is a third. A fourth is to ensure for a future Saharawi Republic sufficient resources for a functioning national economy. Where the international community concerns itself with Western Sahara's natural resources it will be to end the international trade in them, or least ensure Saharawi consent and benefit to their use, thereby reducing a pretext for an illegal occupation that has been allowed to continue too long.

Disclosure statement

No potential conflict of interest was reported by the author.

---

82   The United Nations Secretariat had called on the government of an independent Timor-Leste after 2002 to consider pursuing criminal investigations into serious human rights violations during Indonesia's occupation from 1975 until 1999 and notably arising in the months prior to the August 1999 self-determination referendum, without result. See Mohamed C. Othman, *Accountability for International Humanitarian Law Violations: The Case of Rwanda and East Timor* (New York: Springer, 2005).

83   See the 2014 'Report of the Secretary-General on the situation concerning Western Sahara' which noted continuing protests over resources (April 10, 2014), UN doc. S/2014/258.

84   As noted above, Spanish criminal law and therefore Spain's complementary jurisdiction under the Rome Statute of the International Criminal Court now appear to apply in Western Sahara.

Western Sahara, resources, and international accountability

Stephen Zunes

University of San Francisco, San Francisco, California, USA

The illegality of facilitating the exploitation of natural resources by an occupying power in non-self-governing territories is well-established in international law, yet – as in such cases as Namibia and East Timor – the legal principles are often overlooked by foreign corporations and their governments. The resource-rich territory of Western Sahara, under Moroccan occupation since 1975, is no exception, as European, North American, and Australian companies have sought to take advantage of lucrative fishing grounds or mineral deposits. While some have tried to claim that such resource extraction is legal since Morocco reinvests the money it receives into the territory through ambitious development programs, the benefits of such 'development' have largely gone to Moroccan settlers and occupation authorities, not the indigenous population. As with Namibia and East Timor, it may fall to global civil society to pressure such companies, through boycotts and divestment campaigns, to end their illegal exploitation of Western Sahara's natural resources.

Introduction

The significance of the debate over natural resources in Moroccan-occupied territory in Western Sahara goes beyond the relatively small number of people in that country who are most directly affected, but to broader questions involving decolonization, self-determination, and international law. Ongoing Moroccan control of what is often referred to as 'Africa's last colony' in violation of a series of United Nations Security Council resolutions and a landmark ruling of the International Court of Justice is a direct challenge to the UN Charter and other longstanding international legal principles and has placed the kingdom's continued extraction of non-renewable resources in the territory as a major issue of international contention. The failure of the United Nations to enforce Moroccan compliance with international norms, due large part to the pro-Western monarchy's close economic and strategic ties to veto-wielding members of the Security Council, has given special impetus to global civil society to step in to push for a just resolution to the conflict.

Background

Western Sahara is a sparsely populated territory about the size of Italy, located on the Atlantic coast in northwestern Africa, just south of Morocco. Traditionally inhabited by nomadic Arab tribes, collectively known as Sahrawis and famous for their long history of resistance to outside domination, the territory was occupied by Spain from the late 1800s through the mid-1970s. With Spain holding onto the territory well over a decade after most African countries had achieved their freedom from European colonialism, the nationalist Polisario Front launched an armed independence struggle against Spain in 1973. This – along with pressure from the United Nations – eventually forced Madrid to promise the people of what was then known as the Spanish Sahara, a referendum on the fate of the territory by the end of 1975. The International Court of Justice (ICJ) heard irredentist claims by Morocco and Mauritania and ruled in October of 1975 that – despite pledges of fealty to the Moroccan sultan back in the nineteenth century by some tribal leaders bordering the territory and close ethnic ties between some Sahrawi and Mauritanian tribes – the right of self-determination was paramount.[1] A special visiting mission from the United Nations engaged in an investigation of the situation in the territory that same year and reported that the vast majority of Sahrawis supported independence under the leadership of the Polisario, not integration with Morocco or Mauritania.[2]

During this same period, Morocco was threatening war with Spain over the territory and assembled over 300,000 Moroccans to march into Western Sahara to claim it as theirs regardless of the wishes of the indigenous population whose dialect, dress, and culture was very different to that of the Moroccan Arabs to their north. Though the Spaniards had a much stronger military, they were preoccupied with the terminal illness of their longtime dictator, General Francisco Franco. At the same time, Spain was facing increasing pressure from the United States, which wanted to back its Moroccan ally, King Hassan II, and did not want to see the leftist Polisario come to power.[3] As a result, Spain reneged on its promise of self-determination and instead agreed in November 1975 to allow for Moroccan administration of the northern two-thirds of the Western Sahara and for Mauritanian administration of the southern third.[4]

Only hours after the ICJ released its opinion affirming Western Sahara's right to self-determination, King Hassan announced a planned march of 350,000 unarmed Moroccans into the Spanish colony to reclaim the territory. The 'Green March' only penetrated a few kilometers into Western Sahara, but armored columns of invading Moroccan forces moved into the territory en masse supported by large-scale aerial bombardment, resulting in nearly half of the population fleeing into neighboring Algeria, where they and their descendants remain in refugee camps to this day. Morocco and Mauritania rejected a series of unanimous United Nations Security Council resolutions calling for the withdrawal of foreign forces and recognition of the Sahrawis' right of self-determination. The United States and France, meanwhile, despite voting in favor of these resolutions, blocked the United Nations from enforcing them. At the same time, the Polisario – which had been driven from the more heavily populated northern and western parts of the country – 'declared' independence as the Sahrawi Arab Democratic Republic (SADR).

Thanks in part to the Algerians providing significant amounts of military equipment and economic support, Polisario guerrillas fought well against both occupying armies and defeated Mauritania by 1979, making them agree to turn their third of Western Sahara over to the Polisario. However, the Moroccans then annexed the remaining southern part of the country.

The Polisario then focused their armed struggle against Morocco and by 1982 had liberated nearly 85% of their country. Over the next four years, however, the tide of the war turned in Morocco's favor thanks to the United States and France dramatically increasing their support for the Moroccan war effort, with US forces providing important training for the Moroccan army in counterinsurgency tactics. In addition, the Americans and French helped Morocco construct a 1200-kilometer 'wall', primarily consisting of two heavily fortified parallel sand berms,

---

1 International Court of Justice, *Advisory Opinion on Western Sahara* (The Hague: International Court of Justice, 1975).
2 United Nations General Assembly, 'Report of the United Nations Visiting Mission to Spanish Sahara', *Official Records: Thirtieth Session*, Supplement no. 23, vol. 3, chap. XIII, A/10023/Add.5 (New York: United Nations, 1977).
3 Jacob Andrew Mundy, 'Neutrality or Complicity? The United States and the 1975 Moroccan Takeover of the Spanish Sahara', *Journal of North African Studies* 11, no. 3 (2006): 275–306.
4 'Declaration of Principles on Western Sahara by Spain, Morocco, and Mauritania', *United Nations Treaty Series, 1975*, November 19, 1975, 988, 1-14450, 259.

which eventually shut off more than three-quarters of Western Sahara – including virtually all of the territory's major towns and natural resources – from the Polisario.

Meanwhile, the Moroccan government, through generous housing subsidies and other benefits, successfully encouraged tens of thousands of Moroccan settlers – some of whom were from southern Morocco and of ethnic Sahrawi background – to immigrate to Western Sahara. By the early 1990s, these Moroccan settlers outnumbered the remaining indigenous Sahrawis by a ratio of more than two to one.

While rarely able to penetrate into Moroccan-controlled territory, the Polisario continued regular assaults against Moroccan occupation forces stationed along the wall until 1991, when the United Nations ordered a ceasefire to be monitored by a United Nations peacekeeping force known as MINURSO (the French acronym for United Nations Mission for the Referendum in Western Sahara).[5] The agreement included provisions for the return of Sahrawi refugees to Western Sahara followed by a United Nations-supervised referendum on the fate of the territory, which would allow Sahrawis native to Western Sahara to vote either for independence or for integration with Morocco.[6] Neither the repatriation nor the referendum took place, however, due to the Moroccan insistence on stacking the voter rolls with Moroccan settlers and other Moroccan citizens whom it claimed had tribal links to the Western Sahara. Secretary General Kofi Annan enlisted former US Secretary of State James Baker as his special representative to help resolve the impasse. Morocco, however, continued to ignore repeated demands from the United Nations that it cooperate with the referendum process, and French and American threats of a veto prevented the Security Council from enforcing its mandate.

Legal Status

In 1963, the United Nations placed Spanish Sahara on its list of known colonies. In 1965, following deliberations in the Fourth Committee, the General Assembly passed, in a nearly unanimous vote, Resolution 2072, which 'Urgently' requested that 'the Government of Spain … take immediately all necessary measures for the liberation of the Territory of Ifni and Spanish Sahara from colonial domination'.[7] Morocco, Mauritania and Algeria voted for the resolution; Spain and Portugal were the only two nations to vote against it; the abstainers were the governments of France, South Africa, the United Kingdom and the United States. (Ifni was returned to Morocco in 1968.)

In 1966, the General Assembly passed Resolution 2229,[8] which contained the basic formula for a referendum in Western Sahara that the United Nations would use in the 1990s, although the questionable status of some of the 'exiles' complicated efforts to ensure that only 'indigenous' Western Saharans voted. Morocco, Mauritania and Algeria voted in support of the resolutions; Portugal and Spain continued their lonely dissent.

In 1971 the Fourth Committee and the General Assembly decided to wait a year before addressing Spain's Saharan colony. When it returned to the issue in 1972, the General Assembly's Resolution 2983[9] not only reaffirmed 'the inalienable right of the people of the Sahara to self-determination', but also 'to independence'. The Spanish government convinced several Latin American dictatorships, along with fascist Portugal and apartheid South Africa, to join it in

---

5 United Nations Security Council Resolution 690, *The Situation Concerning Western Sahara* (April 29, 1991), http://www.un.org/en/sc/repertoire/89-92/Chapter%208/AFRICA/item%2008_Western%20Sahara_.pdf.

6 *Official Records of the Security Council*, Forty-fifth Year, Supplement for April, May, June 1990, S/21360.

7 United Nations General Assembly Resolution 2072, 'Ifni and Spanish Sahara', *United Nations Yearbook 1965* (New York: United Nations Office of Public information, 1967), 585.

8 United Nations General Assembly Resolution 2229, *Question of Ifni and Spanish Sahara* (December 20, 1966), http://daccess-dds-ny.un.org/doc/RESOLUTION/GEN/NR0/005/32/IMG/NR000532.pdf?OpenElement.

9 United Nations General Assembly Resolution 2983, *The Question of Spanish Sahara* (December 14, 1972), http://daccess-ods.un.org/TMP/7801474.33280945.html.

voting against the resolution. The United States government abstained with a number of countries, including Morocco.[10]

The Spanish government announced in July 1974 that it intended to hold a self-determination referendum in early 1975. In response to a Moroccan request, supported by Algeria, the General Assembly passed Resolution 3292 (XXIX) on 14 December 1974, asking the International Court of Justice for an advisory opinion regarding Moroccan and Mauritanian claims to Spain's colony, and whether or not those claims trumped the Western Saharans' right to self-determination. It also called for a special visiting mission to assess the realities on the ground.[11] Spain agreed to postpone the referendum.

The ICJ held hearings on the question of Western Sahara from late June to late July 1975. This came almost a month after the UN visiting mission went to the region in May. The latter's findings, which confirmed broad indigenous support for both independence and Polisario in Western Sahara, were released on 15 October.[12] The ICJ's ruling, which recognized the Saharawis' right to self-determination, was issued the following day.[13]

When it became clear that, rather than abide by the ICJ's ruling, the Moroccans would attempt to seize the territory through the Green March, the Spanish government immediately brought the issue to the attention of the United Nations Security Council while simultaneously beginning urgent discussions with King Hassan. The Security Council opened debate on a draft resolution calling on the Moroccan government to 'desist from the proposed march on Western Sahara'. Instead, on 22 October 1975, the Security Council, under pressure from the United States and France, adopted Resolution 377[14] that appealed for 'restraint' on all sides and requested the Secretary-General to enter into consultations with the parties.[15] With this weak response from the United Nations, Spain was forced to pursue direct negotiations with Morocco simultaneously, which resulted in a postponement of the march until November. As ordered by the Security Council, the Secretary-General toured the region between 25 and 28 October but obtained little cooperation from King Hassan, who favored keeping up the pressure until Spain relented.

The following week, on 2 November, the Security Council answered another Spanish request for a further emergency meeting 'to oblige the Government of Morocco to desist from the march it has announced'[16] by adopting Resolution 379, urging all parties to avoid any actions that might escalate tensions and requesting the Secretary-General to intensify his mediation efforts.[17] As the Moroccan government began ferrying marchers to the border on the evening of 5 November, the Spanish representative to the United Nations again pressed the Security Council for action. The President of the Council quickly sent an 'urgent request to put an end forthwith to the declared march into Western Sahara' to King Hassan, who replied that until the Spanish government agreed to 'undertake urgent bilateral negotiations' the march would continue.[18] The Security

---

10 United Nations Office of Public Information, 'Spanish Sahara', *United Nations Yearbook 1972* (New York: United Nations Office of Public Information, 1975), 569–70, 579–80.

11 United Nations General Assembly Resolution 3292, 'Spanish Sahara', *United Nations Yearbook 1974* (New York: United Nations Office of Public information, 1977), 794, 805–6.

12 United Nations General Assembly, 'Report of the United Nations Visiting Mission to Spanish Sahara, *Official Records: Thirtieth Session*, Supplement no. 23, vol. 3, chap. XIII, A/10023/Add.5 (New York: United Nations, 1977).

13 For analysis, see Thomas M. Franck, 'The Stealing of the Sahara', *American Journal of International Law* 70, no. 4 (1976): 694–721; Thomas M. Franck, ''Theory and Practice of Decolonization', in *War and Refugees: The Western Sahara Conflict*, ed. Richard Lawless and Laila Monahan (New York: Pinter, 1987).

14 United Nations Security Council Resolution 377, *The Situation Concerning Western Sahara* (October 22, 1975), http://daccess-ods.un.org/TMP/7421183.58612061.html.

15 Karel Wellens, ed., *Resolutions and Statements of the United Nations, 1945–1989* (Leiden: Martinus Nijhoff Publishers, 1990), 49.

16 United Nations Security Council, *Documents Officiels* 30 (1975): 29.

17 Wellens, *Resolutions and Statements of the United Nations, 1945–1989*, 49.

18 United Nations Security Council, *Presidential Appeal*, November 6, 1975.

Council finally passed a more strongly worded resolution (380) late on 6 November, which 'deplored' the Green March, called on the Moroccans to withdraw immediately, to respect the Western Saharans' right to self-determination, and to cooperate with the Secretary-General's mediation efforts.[19]

However, France and the United States made sure that this resolution was not enforced. According to the United States' ambassador to the United Nations, Daniel Patrick Moynihan,

> The United States wished things to turn out as they did, and I worked to bring this about. The Department of State desired that the United Nations prove utterly ineffective in whatever measures it undertook. This task was given to me, and I carried it forward with no inconsiderable success.[20]

Not only was Resolution 380 not enforced, it was the last Security Council action on the Western Sahara issue for 10 years. Unable to obtain any meaningful response from the Security Council to stop Hassan's invasion, Spain decided to cut a secret trilateral deal with Morocco and Mauritania, finalized between 12 and 14 November 1975 in Madrid.[21]

Notwithstanding the trilateral agreement in Madrid, the United Nations Fourth Committee held hearings between 14 November and 4 December, where the Western Sahara was a major focus of the agenda. The Committee forwarded two draft resolutions to the General Assembly. One resolution (3458A), adopted by a vote of 88 to zero on 10 December, with 41 abstentions (including the United States), called on Spain, with the help of the Secretary-General, to hold a popular referendum on self-determination in the Western Sahara.[22] The other resolution (3458B), passed by a vote of 56 to 42, with 34 abstentions, took note of the Madrid Agreement and requested that the parties to the agreement 'ensure' that all persons originating from the territory 'exercise their inalienable right to self-determination'.[23]

Throughout 1976, the United Nations, with attention focused on the guerrilla war and the massive refugee exodus triggered by the Moroccan invasion, failed to address the underlying issue of self-determination. That December, the General Assembly passed resolution 31/45, in which the body decided to hold off further deliberations on the matter until the United Nations could learn the results of a scheduled extraordinary session of the Organization of African Unity on the Western Sahara.[24] Resolutions adopted over the next three years revealed that the United Nations had deferred the matter totally to the Organization of African Unity.[25]

The Security Council again became involved in the conflict in 1990 with a series of resolutions which put in place a ceasefire between Moroccan and Polisario forces, the stationing of United Nations' peacekeeping forces in the country, and an internationally supervised referendum in which the remaining Saharawi population in Western Sahara, combined with repatriated refugees, would take part in a referendum. A series of United Nations Security Council resolutions urged the referendum process to move forward (Resolutions 690, 725, 809, 973, 995, 1002, 1017, 1033 and 1056),[26] but Morocco remained intransigent.

---

19 Wellens, *Resolutions and Statements of the United Nations, 1945–1989*, 49–50.
20 Daniel Patrick Moynihan, *A Dangerous Place* (Boston: Little, Brown, 1980), 247.
21 'Declaration of Principles on Western Sahara by Spain, Morocco, and Mauritania', *United Nations Treaty Series, 1975*, November 19, 1975, 988, 1-14450, 259.
22 United Nations General Assembly Resolution 3248A, *Question of Western Sahara* (December 10, 1975), http://daccess-dds-ny.un.org/doc/RESOLUTION/GEN/NR0/001/71/IMG/NR000171.pdf?OpenElement.
23 United Nations General Assembly Resolution 3248B, *Question of Western Sahara* (December 10, 1975), http://daccess-dds-ny.un.org/doc/RESOLUTION/GEN/NR0/001/71/IMG/NR000171.pdf?OpenElement.
24 United Nations General Assembly Resolution 31/45, *Question of Western Sahara* (December 1, 1976), http://daccess-dds-ny.un.org/doc/RESOLUTION/GEN/NR0/302/28/IMG/NR030228.pdf?OpenElement. The Organization of African Unity (OAU) was the precursor to the African Union (AU).
25 See, for example, United Nations General Assembly, *Question of Western Sahara* (November 21, 1979), http://www.un.org/documents/ga/res/34/a34res37.pdf.
26 See United Nations Security Council Resolutions, http://www.un.org/en/sc/documents/resolutions/.

In 1997, UN Special Envoy Baker oversaw the signing of the Houston Accords which codified the modalities of the referendum process, including identification of voters. However, despite a series of additional United Nations Security Council resolutions),[27] Morocco refused to allow the referendum to go forward and, as they had done since the beginning of United Nations Security Council involvement, French and American threats of a veto prevented the Security Council from enforcing its mandate.

Subsequent developments

For more than 40 years, the United Nations had been recognizing the question of Western Sahara as that of an incomplete decolonization, a non-self-governing territory which had the right of self-determination, including the option of independence. However, Morocco's major allies – France and the United States – pushed the idea that Western Sahara was not an occupied territory but instead a 'disputed' territory. Were the latter designation to be accepted, the transfer of Moroccan settlers into the territory and the exploitation of its natural resources would no longer be illegal.

In 2000, the Clinton administration successfully convinced Baker and Annan to give up on efforts to proceed with the referendum as originally agreed by the United Nations 10 years earlier and instead to accept Moroccan demands that Moroccan settlers be allowed to vote on the fate of the territory along with the indigenous Saharawi. This proposal was incorporated into the first Baker Plan presented to UN Secretary General in early 2001, which would have held the plebiscite under Moroccan rule after a four- to five-year period of very limited autonomy with no guarantee that independence would be one of the options on the ballot.[28]

Though this first Baker Plan received the enthusiastic backing of the French and US governments, most of the international community rejected the proposal, since it would have effectively abrogated previous United Nations resolutions granting the right of self-determination with the option of independence and would have led to the unprecedented action of the United Nations placing the fate of a non-self-governing territory in the hands of the occupying colonial power.

As a result, Baker then proposed a second plan where, as with his earlier proposal, both the Sahrawis and the Moroccan settlers would be able to vote in the referendum, but the plebiscite would take place only after Western Sahara had enjoyed far more significant autonomy for the four to five years prior to the vote, independence would be an option on the ballot, and the United Nations would oversee the vote and guarantee that advocates of both integration and independence would have the freedom to campaign openly. The United Nations Security Council approved the second Baker plan in the summer of 2003.

Under considerable pressure, Algeria, and eventually the Polisario, reluctantly accepted the new plan, but the Moroccans – unwilling to allow the territory to enjoy even a brief period of autonomy and risk the possibility they would lose the plebiscite – rejected it. Once again, the United States and France blocked the United Nations from enforcing its mandate by pressuring Morocco to comply with its international legal obligations.

In what has been widely interpreted as rewarding Morocco for its intransigence, the Bush administration subsequently designated Morocco as a 'major non-NATO ally' in June of 2004, a coveted status currently granted to only 15 key nations, such as Japan, Israel and Australia. The following month, the Senate ratified a free trade agreement with Morocco by an 85–13 margin, making the kingdom one of only a half dozen countries outside of the Western hemisphere to enjoy such a close economic relationship with the United States. US aid to Morocco grew five-fold under the Bush administration, ostensibly as a reward for the kingdom undertaking

---

27 See United Nations Security Council Resolutions 1182, 1215, and 1359, available at http://www.un.org/en/sc/documents/resolutions/.

28 United Nations Security Council, *Report of the Secretary-General on the Situation Concerning Western Sahara*, S/2001/613 (June 20, 2001).

a series of neoliberal economic reforms and to assist the Moroccan government in 'combating terrorism'. While there has been some political liberalization within most of Morocco in recent years under the young King Mohammed VI, who succeeded to the throne following the death of his father in 1999, gross and systematic human rights violations in the occupied Western Sahara and Saharawi-populated segments of southern Morocco continues unabated, with public expressions of nationalist aspirations and organized protests against the occupation and human rights abuses routinely met with severe repression.

The Obama administration pressed Morocco on its human rights record and briefly joined other nations calling on the Security Council to expand MINURSO's mandate to include monitoring the human rights situation in both the occupied territory and the refugee camps in Algeria.[29] France and Morocco successfully blocked the effort, however, and MINURSO remains the only UN peacekeeping force without such a mandate.

The illegality of the exploitation of natural resources

UN General Assembly Resolution 1514, passed as part of a series of resolutions addressing the rights of inhabitants of non-self-governing territories, declares that 'peoples may, for their own ends, freely dispose of their natural wealth and resources ... based on the principle of mutual benefit and international law' in order to realize the right to 'freely pursue their economic, social and cultural development'.[30] Resolution 1803, passed two years later, underscores that 'economic and financial agreements between the developed and the developing countries must be based on the principles of equality and of the right of peoples and nations to self-determination'. The resolution makes clear that sovereignty over natural resources belongs to the indigenous inhabitants of a non-self-governing territory rather than the occupying power in noting, 'The right of peoples and nations to permanent sovereignty over their wealth and natural resources must be exercised in the interest of their natural development and of the well-being of the people of the state concerned.' The resolution further put the General Assembly on record emphasizing that 'Violation of the rights of peoples and nations to sovereignty over their natural wealth and resources is contrary to the spirit and principles of the Charter of the United Nations'.[31]

A series of decisions by the International Court of Justice regarding Namibia, Nauru, East Timor and Palestine further codified protection of the peoples of non-self-governing territories to sovereignty over their natural resources.[32] As recently as 2011, the General Assembly reiterated 'the right of the peoples of the Non-Self-Governing Territories to self-determination in conformity with the Charter of the United Nations and with General Assembly resolution 1514(XV) ... as well as their right to the enjoyment of their natural resources and their right to dispose of those resources in their best interest'.[33]

---

29 Louise Charboneau and Aziz el Yaakoubi, 'U.S. Proposes U.N. Western Sahara Rights Monitor; Morocco Warns of "Missteps"', *Reuters*, April 17, 2013, http://uk.reuters.com/article/2013/04/17/uk-westernsahara-un-idUKBRE93G00Z20130417.

30 United Nations General Assembly Resolution 1514, *Declaration on the Granting of Independence to Colonial Countries and Peoples* (December 14, 1960), http://daccess-dds-ny.un.org/doc/RESOLUTION/GEN/NR0/152/88/IMG/NR015288.pdf?OpenElement.

31 United Nations General Assembly Resolution 1803, *Permanent Sovereignty over Natural Resources* (December 14, 1962), http://www.ohchr.org/Documents/ProfessionalInterest/resources.pdf.

32 See, for example, International Court of Justice, 'Certain Phosphate Lands in Nauru' (Nauru v. Australia), *Application Instituting Proceedings Filed in the Registry of the Court on 19 May 1989* (The Hague: International Court of Justice, 1989); International Court of Justice, 'East Timor' (Portugal v Australia), *Application Instituting Proceedings Filed in the Registry of the Court on 22 February 1991* (The Hague: International Court of Justice, 1991).

33 UN General Assembly Resolution 52/72, *Economic and Other Activities which Affect the Interests of the Peoples of the Non-Self-Governing Territories* (December 10, 1997), http://www.un.org/ga/documents/gares52/res5272.htm.

The application of these legal principles to Western Sahara was examined by UN Under-Secretary for Legal Affairs Hans Corell in regard to a request from the Security Council regarding oil exploration off the Western Sahara coast. He concluded:

> while the specific contracts which are the subject of the Security Council's request are not in themselves illegal, if further exploration and exploitation activities were to proceed in disregard of the interests and wishes of the people of Western Sahara, they would be in violation of the international law principles applicable to mineral resource activities in Non-Self-Governing Territories.[34]

As with other issues regarding the illegality of Morocco's occupation of Western Sahara, however, the United States and France blocked the Security Council from taking further action on this question.

In late 2001, Morocco announced hydrocarbon exploration in Western Sahara and offshore. That September, Morocco's National Office for Petroleum Exploration and Exploitation (Onarep) signed contracts with French-based 'supermajor' TotalFinaElf (now Total) and the United States-based firm Kerr-McGee. As president of the Security Council in November 2001, Jamaica requested an official opinion from the Under-Secretary-General for Legal Affairs, which resulted in Corell's report, released on 5 February 2002. The opinion not only highlighted Morocco's precarious legal position in the territory (i.e. illegally obtaining status as the de facto administering power), it also clearly reiterated that Western Sahara is a non-self-governing territory (i.e. a colony) requiring self-determination. Its conclusion, however, was that resource exploration in itself, what the Moroccan concessions offered, would not be illegal under international law. However, it would be illegal for the Moroccan government, as the de facto colonizing power in a non-self-governing territory, to extract Western Sahara's resources without adequate approval from the population.

The acquisition of Western Sahara adds significant sources of revenue to Moroccan state coffers. Foremost are the phosphate deposits at Boucraa, first developed by Spain in the 1960s and now exploited by Morocco. Even without Western Sahara, Morocco is the world's leading exporter of this fast dwindling resource, which is key to modern industrial agriculture. The reserves in Western Sahara are of an extremely high quality and are close to the surface, though they still only account for a small percentage of Moroccan phosphate exports. Perhaps of more value to Morocco has been the rich fishing grounds found off the coast of Western Sahara, which is of increasing importance in light of the decline of fishing stocks off Morocco itself. In addition to Moroccan fleets, the government has signed lucrative contracts with other countries and, more recently, the European Union. Furthermore, there are numerous other sources of revenue yet to be explored or exploited, whether minerals or hydrocarbons.

Though not explicit on Western Sahara's two main exports, fisheries and phosphates, the opinion clearly implied that profits gained from those industries by the Moroccan government were in contravention of international law. In the Security Council, the opinion provoked a debate on Morocco's ambiguous and illegal status in Western Sahara, though members of the Council and Secretariat dismissed such talk as unproductive.[35]

Petroleum resources remain a particularly significant question. Unlike fisheries, which in most cases can be regenerated, fossil fuels are a finite resource. The burgeoning interest by industrialized countries in offshore oil in West Africa has added a significant geostrategic component. On the one hand, petroleum prospects in the Western Sahara are not a phenomenon unique to the new century. In the late 1950s, the Spanish government made moves towards exploiting known

---

34 United Nations Security Council, *Letter dated 29 January 2002 from the Under-Secretary-General for Legal Affairs, the Legal Counsel, addressed to the President of the Security Council*, S/2002/161 (February 12, 2002).

35 Ibid. See also Carola Hoyos and Toby Shelley, 'UN Throws Doubt on Oil Deals in Western Sahara', *Financial Times*, February 6, 2002, 7; 'Security Council Disagrees Over Oil Prospecting in W Sahara', *Agence France Presse*, February 20, 2002.

and assumed reserves. By the mid-1960s, different contractors had found over 27 different potential inland sites, although none were considered worth the effort. North of the Spanish Sahara, the Moroccan government commissioned an offshore study by the firm Esso, which apparently discovered a 60-mile-long field stretching off the coast of Tarfaya into the Spanish-administered waters. Following the Moroccan–Mauritanian takeover of the Western Sahara, different companies accepted various exploration contracts for the Tarfaya region yet the collapse of global oil prices inhibited interest.[36]

A number of countries, particularly the United States, have shown serious interest in tapping into potential West African sources. Despite the numerous conflicts that plague West Africa, the move towards offshore sources translated into a 'stable' source of oil for the United States, unlike Middle Eastern and Central Asian providers. Vice President Dick Cheney's National Energy Policy report noted that West Africa had become 'one of the fastest-growing sources of oil and gas for the American market'.[37] Some estimates have predicted that West African oil could soon provide up to 25% of US petroleum imports. The Institute for Advanced Strategic and Political Studies, a Jerusalem-based think tank, convened a working group comprised of US business and policy leaders called the African Oil Policy Initiative Group. Among its list of recommendations, it advised the US government to declare the Gulf of Guinea an area of 'Vital Interest'.[38] Just south of Western Sahara, Mauritania signed agreements to begin oil and gas production at 75,000 barrels a day from its offshore wells by the year 2005.[39] However, when production finally began in 2006, output was revised significantly downward several times, eventually below 50% of the original assessment, which had been based on a single test well. Still, the increasing importance of West African oil may make it even more difficult for influential foreign governments to discourage their companies from taking advantage of Western Saharan oil resources.

Parsing the 2002 opinion, Morocco and its supporters seized on the fact that simple exploration was deemed legal. As an oil-importing country, the Moroccan regime had good reason to secure any potential Western Saharan oil reserves. Off the coast of Western Sahara the US 2000 Geological Survey of World Energy thought that reserves could be 'substantial', whereas sources in Morocco proper were 'low and insecure'.[40] The Moroccan regime's moves in late 2001 towards exploration and exploitation specifically targeted the waters off the coast of the Western Sahara. The firm conducting the exploration for Kerr-McGee and Total, TGS-Nopec, however, came under intense grassroots pressure from Norwegian activists, citing the company's activities as complicit with the Moroccan occupation.[41] These efforts led TGS-Nopec to hastily withdraw from the affair, but only after it had completed most of its survey.

With all of this talk of oil in Western Sahara, Baker's own oil interests began to be called into question, especially his connections with Kerr-McGee as well as the Bush–Cheney administration, known for its close ties with Big Oil. Indeed, one US journalist claimed that the Bush administration's first ambassador to Morocco, Margaret Tutwiler, a very close and personal friend of Baker and who had served as State Department spokesperson when he was Secretary

---

36 Tony Hodges and Anthony G. Pazzanita, *Historical Dictionary of Western Sahara*. 3rd ed. (Lanham, MD: Scarecrow Press, 2006), 347–50.
37 Quoted in Simon Robinson, 'Black Gold', *Time*, October 28, 2002, A10.
38 Institute for Advanced Strategic and Political Studies, 'African Oil: A Priority for US National Security and African Development' (Jerusalem: IASPS, 2002).
39 Toby Shelley, 'Premier Oil Acquires Stakes in West Africa', *Financial Times,* May 29, 2003: 25; Toby Shelley, 'Oil Groups Target NW Africa: The Little-Explored Region is Attracting Much International Interest', *Financial Times*, July 12, 2002, 28.
40 Stefan Armbruster, 'Western Sahara's Future Hinges on Oil', *BBC News Online*, March 4, 2003, http://news.bbc.co.uk/1/hi/business/2758829.stm (accessed October 8, 2004).
41 Janos Besenyo, *Western Sahara* (Pecs: Publikon Publishers, 2000), 18.

of State, was specifically placed in Rabat to, among other things, expedite oil deals.[42] With the Total–Kerr-McGee deal unfolding in the context of Baker's pro-Moroccan Framework Agreement, it was difficult for observers not to think that Western Sahara was being sold out to US energy interests. Baker, however, would prove a more honest broker, and supporters of international law in the US Congress made sure that Western Sahara was specifically exempt from provisions of a free trade agreement with Morocco. As US trade representative (and future World Bank president) Robert Zoellick noted, 'The United States and many other countries do not recognize Moroccan sovereignty over Western Sahara'.[43] By then, 2004, Total had dropped out of Western Sahara ostensibly for business reasons. Isolated, Kerr-McGee came under increasing pressure, even from conservative Christian activists in its home state of Oklahoma. In 2005, Norway's Government Pension Fund, the world's largest sovereign-wealth fund, began divesting its $52 million investment in Kerr-McGee stock because their Western Sahara operations constituted an 'unacceptable risk for contributing to other *particularly serious violations of fundamental ethical norms*'.[44] Kerr-McGee finally withdrew in 2006.

The Moroccan government, however, has continued to seek companies interested in exploring and exploiting potential Western Saharan oil and gas. In a counter-move, the SADR signed an exploration contract in 2003 with the Anglo-Australian oil company Fusion to access the entire acreage off the coast of the Western Sahara.[45] Then, in 2005, SADR signed contracts with seven different companies covering areas onshore and offshore, mostly British and Australian companies. Knowing their favorable position under international law, SADR officials hoped these concessions could force some kind of international legal battle regarding sovereignty over Western Sahara, which would be to the advantage of those seeking self-determination. Yet the prospects that there might be significant deposits on- or offshore Western Sahara continue to be treated with significant skepticism, even when global oil prices were at all-time highs in 2006.

Subsequently, the Moroccan state oil company Office National des Hydrocarbures et des Mines (ONHYM) has granted five licenses for oil exploration and production in Western Sahara without the consent of the population. Kosmos Energy Offshore Morocco HC, a subsidiary of the US-based but Bermuda-registered firm Kosmos Energy Ltd, holds the license once held by Kerr-McGee off the shore from Boujdour. Total SA has signed new licenses for an offshore block to the south in 2011, 2012 and 2013. Both companies have signed agreements with ONHYM for future production. The British companies San Leon Morocco Ltd and the PetroMaroc (formerly known as Longreach Oil and Gas Ventures) hold two onshore exploration licenses in conjunction with ONHYM, primarily consisting of oil shale, in the northwestern corner of the territory.

Efforts for self-determination were set back when the European Union, in an apparently illegal move, signed a fisheries agreement with Morocco in early 2006 which included areas off Western Sahara. Organizing efforts by human rights groups in various European countries, particularly the Norwegian-based Western Sahara Resource Watch, led to it not being extended in 2011. However, in December 2013 it was surprisingly renewed, with vague references about benefits to the 'local population', but with no specific mention of the Sahrawis.[46] Former United

---

42 Wayne Madsen, 'Big Oil and James Baker Target the Western Sahara', *Counter Punch*, January 8, 2003, http://www. counterpunch.org/madsen01082003.html (accessed October 8, 2004). See also Frank Bruni, 'A Loyal Lieutenant [i.e. Tutwiler] Re-enlists to Serve the Bush Brigade', *New York Times*, March 26, 2001, A12.

43 Quoted in Jacob Mundy, 'Mixing Occupation and Oil in Western Sahara', *CorpWatch*, July 21, 2005, http://www. corpwatch.org/article.php?id=12506 (accessed September 2006).

44 Ministry of Finance, Norway, 'Recommendation on Exclusion from the Government Petroleum Fund's Investment Universe of the Company Kerr-McGee Corporation', June 6, 2005, http://www.regjeringen.no/nb/dep/fin/tema/ statens_pensjonsfond/ansvarlige-investeringer/tilradninger-og-brev-fra-etikkradet/Recommendation-on-Exclusion- from-the-Government-Petroleum-Funds-Investment-Universe-of-the-Company-Kerr-McGee-Corporation.html? id=419582.

45 Petroleum Exploration Society of Australia (PESA), *PESA News*, April–May 2003, 53–8.

46 European Commission, *Proposal for Council Decision on the Conclusion of the Protocol between the European Union and the Kingdom of Morocco Setting out the Fishing Opportunities and Financial Contribution Provided*

Nations legal counsel Corell declared that 'The E.U.'s interpretation of the legal opinion is preposterous. It is utterly embarrassing that the international community has been unable to solve this conflict. Since Morocco is able to capitalize in Western Sahara, there will be no incentive at all to change the situation'.[47]

The Moroccan government and its supporters point to its ambitious large-scale development projects in Western Sahara, particularly in the urban areas. Morocco claims it has invested more than US$2 billion in infrastructure development in the territory, significantly more than Morocco has procured from Western Sahara's natural resources and more than they would be likely to obtain in the foreseeable future.[48] For this reason, the Moroccan government and its supporters argue that they have fulfilled the requirements regarding interests, well-being, and development needs of the indigenous population.[49] However, most of the infrastructure development has involved the elaborate internal security system of military bases, police facilities, prisons, surveillance, and related repressive apparatuses; housing construction, subsidies, and other support for Moroccan settlers; and airport, seaport, and other transportation development designed to accelerate resource extraction, not build up the standard of living for the territory's people. More fundamentally, the decisions on how to use the proceeds from resource extraction are being made by the Moroccan government in the capital of Rabat, not by the indigenous people of Western Sahara.

As a result, international pressure has been increasing. In March of 2015, the Peace and Security Council of the African Union called on the UN Security Council to intervene to stop the illegal exploitation of Western Sahara's natural resources and called for a 'global boycott of products of companies involved in the illegal exploitation of the natural resources of Western Sahara'.[50] International outcry placed former US Senator and Secretary of State Hillary Clinton – a leading contender in the 2016 US presidential race – on the defensive when it was revealed that the Office Cherifien des Phosphates (OCP), a Moroccan government-owned mining company that controls one of the world's largest phosphate mines in the occupied Western Sahara, was the primary donor to the May 2015 Clinton Global Initiative conference in Marrakech.[51]

The future

Since the 1991 ceasefire, the Sahrawis have fought for their national rights primarily by legal and diplomatic means, not through armed struggle. Unlike a number of other peoples engaged in national liberation struggles, the Saharawi have never committed acts of terrorism. Even during their armed struggle against the occupation, which ended 15 years ago, Polisario forces restricted their attacks exclusively to the Moroccan armed forces, never targeting civilians. The failure of the international community to defend the legal rights of the Sahrawis despite this moderation effectively sends a signal that such moderation will not be rewarded.

---

for in the Fisheries Partnership Agreement in Force between the two Parties (Brussels: European Commission, 2013), http://eur-lex.europa.eu/legal-content/EN/TXT/PDF/?uri=CELEX:52013PC0648&from=EN.

47 Per Liljas, 'There's a New Terrorist Threat Emerging in Western Sahara, and the World Isn't Paying Attention', *Time*, August 8, 2014.

48 Sarah A. Topol, 'Amid Moroccan Investment in Western Sahara, Tensions Simmer', *Bloomberg Business*, May 30, 2013, http://www.bloomberg.com/bw/articles/2013-05-30/amid-moroccan-investment-in-western-sahara-tensions-simmer.

49 Aidan Lewis, 'Morocco's Fish fight: High Stakes over Western Sahara', *BBC News*, December 15, 2011, http://www.bbc.com/news/world-africa-16101666.

50 African Union, *Communiqué of the Peace and Security Council of the African Union (AU), at its 496th meeting held on 27 March 2015, on the situation in Western Sahara*, http://www.peaceau.org/en/article/communique-of-the-peace-and-security-council-of-the-african-union-au-at-its-496th-meeting-held-on-27-march-2015-on-the-situation-in-western-sahara#sthash.TYOHI9YB.dpuf.

51 Stephen Zunes, 'Hillary Clinton, Phosphates, and the Western Sahara', *National Catholic Reporter*, May 12, 2015.

The nonresolution of the Western Sahara conflict has important regional implications. It has encouraged an arms race between Morocco and Algeria and, on several occasions over the past four decades, has brought the two countries close to war. Perhaps even more significantly, it has been the single biggest obstacle to a fuller implementation of the goals of the Arab Maghreb Union – consisting of Morocco, Algeria, Libya, Tunisia, and Mauritania – to pursue economic integration and other initiatives which would increase the standard of living and political stability in the region. The lack of unity and greater coordination among these nations and their struggling economies has contributed to the dramatic upsurge in illegal immigration to Europe and the rise of radical Islamist movements.

Over the past three decades, the Sahrawi Arab Democratic Republic has been recognized as an independent country by more than 80 governments, with Kenya and South Africa becoming the latest to extend full diplomatic relations. The SADR has been a full member state of the African Union (formerly Organization for African Unity) since 1984 and most of the international community recognizes Western Sahara as Africa's last colony. (By contrast, with only a few exceptions, the Arab states – despite their outspoken opposition to the Israeli occupation of Palestinian and Syrian land – have supported Morocco's occupation of Western Sahara.)

With Morocco's rejection of the second Baker Plan and the threat of a French and American veto of any Security Council resolution that would push Morocco to compromise, a diplomatic settlement of the conflict looks highly unlikely. With Morocco's powerful armed forces protected behind the separation wall, and Algeria unwilling to support a resumption of guerrilla war, the Polisario appears to lack a military option as well.

As happened during the 1980s in both South Africa and the Israeli-occupied Palestinian territories, the locus of the Western Sahara freedom struggle has recently shifted from the military and diplomatic initiatives of an exiled armed movement to a largely unarmed popular resistance from within. In recent years, young activists in the occupied territory and even in Saharawi-populated parts of southern Morocco have confronted Moroccan troops in street demonstrations and other forms of non-violent action, despite the risk of shootings, mass arrests, and torture. The construction of a tent city of up to 12,000 Sahrawi human rights activists on the outskirts of Al Aioun in the fall of 2010 was met by severe repression from Moroccan authorities.[52]

The failure of the Kingdom of Morocco and the Polisario Front to agree on the modalities of the long-planned United Nations-sponsored referendum on the fate of Western Sahara, combined with a growing non-violent resistance campaign in the occupied territory against Morocco's 40-year occupation, has led Morocco to propose granting the former Spanish colony special autonomous status within the kingdom. The plan has received the enthusiastic support of the American and French governments as a reasonable compromise to the abiding conflict. As illustrated below, there are serious problems with this proposal. However, the very fact that Morocco has felt obliged to propose a special status for the territory constitutes an admission that its previous insistence that Western Sahara was simply another part of Morocco was false. As visitors to Western Sahara in recent years have noticed, not only has Morocco's 40-year campaign of assimilation failed, but the younger generation of Saharawis are at least as nationalistic as their parents.

It is unfortunate, therefore, that the Moroccan plan for autonomy falls so well short of what is required to bring about a peaceful resolution to the conflict. Moreover, it seeks to set a dangerous precedent which threatens the very foundation of the post-World War II international legal system.

To begin with, the proposal is based on the assumption that Western Sahara is part of Morocco, a contention that has long been rejected by the United Nations, the ICJ, the African Union, and a broad consensus of international legal opinion. To accept Morocco's autonomy

---

52 Stephen Zunes, 'Upsurge in Repression Challenges Nonviolent Resistance in Western Sahara', *Open Democracy*, November 17, 2010.

plan would mean that, for the first time since the founding of the United Nations and the ratification of its Charter more than 60 years ago, the international community would be endorsing the expansion of a country's territory by military force, thereby establishing a very dangerous and destabilizing precedent.

If the people of Western Sahara accepted an autonomy agreement over independence as a result of a free and fair referendum, it would constitute a legitimate act of self-determination. However, Morocco has explicitly stated that its autonomy proposal 'rules out, by definition, the possibility for the independence option to be submitted' to the people of Western Sahara, the vast majority of whom – according to knowledgeable international observers – favor outright independence.

Even if one takes a dismissive attitude toward international law, there are a number of practical concerns regarding the Moroccan proposal as well.

One is that the history of respect for regional autonomy on the part of centralized authoritarian states is quite poor, and has often led to violent conflict. For example, in 1952, the United Nations granted the British protectorate (and former Italian colony) of Eritrea autonomous, federated status within Ethiopia. In 1961, however, the Ethiopian emperor unilaterally revoked Eritrea's autonomous status, annexing it as his empire's fourteenth province, resulting in a bloody 30-year struggle for independence and subsequent border wars between the two countries, which have claimed hundreds of thousands of lives.

Based upon Morocco's habit of breaking its promises to the international community regarding the United Nations-mandated referendum for Western Sahara and related obligations based on the ceasefire agreement 18 years ago, there is little to inspire confidence that Morocco would live up to its promises to provide genuine autonomy for Western Sahara. Indeed, a close reading of the proposal raises questions as to how much autonomy is even being offered. Important matters such as control of Western Sahara's natural resources and law enforcement (beyond local jurisdictions) remain ambiguous.

In addition, the proposal appears to indicate that all powers not specifically vested in the autonomous region would remain with the Kingdom. Indeed, since the king of Morocco is ultimately invested with absolute authority under article 19 of the Moroccan Constitution, the autonomy proposal's insistence that the Moroccan state 'will keep its powers in the royal domains, especially with respect to defence, external relations, and the constitutional and religious prerogatives of His Majesty the King' appears to afford the monarch considerable latitude in interpretation.

While encouraging such compromise, or 'third way' between independence and integration, as a possible win/win situation can often be a successful formula for conflict resolution in some ethnic conflicts and many international disputes, Western Sahara is a clear-cut case of self-determination for a people struggling against foreign military occupation. This is not a matter of 'splitting the difference', given that one party is under an illegal foreign military occupation and the other party is the occupier. This is why the international community rejected Iraq's proposals in 1990–91 for some kind of compromise regarding its occupation of Kuwait. The Polisario Front has already offered guarantees to protect Moroccan strategic and economic interests if allowed full independence.[53] To insist that the people of Western Sahara must give up their moral and legal right to genuine self-determination is therefore not a recipe for conflict resolution, but for far more serious conflict in the future.

Morocco has succeeded in resisting its international legal obligations for more than four decades through support from permanent members of the United Nations Security Council. As a result of the French and US veto threats, the Security Council has failed to place the Western Sahara issue under Chapter VII of the United Nations Charter, which would give the international

---

53 United Nations Security Council, *Letter dated 16 April 2007 from the Permanent Representative of South Africa to the United Nations addressed to the President of the Security Council*, S/2007/210 (April 16, 2007).

community the power to impose sanctions or other appropriate leverage to force the Moroccan regime to abide by the United Nations mandates it has to date disregarded. Polisario's unwillingness to compromise further should not be seen as the major obstacle impeding the resolution of the conflict.

Similar support from Western industrialized nations for Indonesia for many years prevented resolution to the occupation of East Timor. It was only after human rights organizations, church groups and other activists in the United States, Great Britain, and Australia successfully pressured their governments to end their support for Indonesia's occupation that the Jakarta regime was finally willing to offer a referendum which gave the East Timorese their right to self-determination. It may take similar grassroots campaigns in Europe and North America to ensure that Western powers live up to their international legal obligations and pressure Morocco to allow the people of Western Sahara to determine their own destiny.

The growth of the non-violent resistance struggle in the occupied territories offers a unique opportunity to build international awareness of the conflict among civil society organizations that could offer much-needed solidarity with the freedom struggle inside Western Sahara. Such massive non-violent action and other forms of non-cooperation provides an important signal to the Moroccan occupiers and the international community that the people of Western Sahara still demand their freedom and will not accept any less than genuine self-determination. The use of nonviolent methods of resistance also makes it easier to highlight gross and systematic violations of international humanitarian law by Moroccan occupation forces, gain sympathy and support from the international human rights community, and provide greater pressure on the French, American, and other governments which continue to provide security assistance to Morocco and otherwise support the Moroccan occupation.

Human rights groups have increasingly been highlighting the poor human rights situation in Western Sahara, which has contributed to recent diplomatic rows between Morocco and the United States, Spain, and France. Freedom House has ranked Western Sahara as having one of very worst human rights situations in the world.[54] In April 2015, a Spanish court indicted 11 Moroccan former officials for genocide in connection with killings and torture in Western Sahara.[55] The following month, Amnesty International issued another scathing report on the human rights situation, targeting the widespread torture of political prisoners.[56]

There is a small but growing movement in Europe supporting the Saharawi's right to national self-determination, as well as similar civil society efforts in South Africa, other African countries, Australia, Japan, and the United States. More focus on the issue of the illegal exploitation of natural resources in Western Sahara could provide proponents of international law and human rights an issue through which to challenge governments and companies which take advantage of the occupation is such a way through campaigns advocating boycotts, divestment, and sanctions. At this point, however, such movements are too small to have much impact on government policies, particular those of France and the United States, which are the two governments most responsible for the failure of the United Nations to enforce its resolutions dealing with the conflict. This can change, however. Just over 20 years ago, there was relatively little civil society activism regarding East Timor, but a dramatic growth in such activism in the late 1990s contributed to East Timor's eventual independence.

A similar campaign may be the best hope for the people of Western Sahara and the best hope we have to save the vitally important post-World War II principles enshrined in the United Nations Charter.

---

54 Human Rights Watch, *Freedom in the World 2013* (Washington, DC: Human Rights Watch, 2013).
55 Carolotta Gall, 'Spanish Judge Accuses Moroccan Former Officials of Genocide in Western Sahara', *New York Times*, April 10, 2015.
56 Amnesty International, 'Morocco: Endemic Torture Used to Incriminate Suspects, Gag Dissent', *Amnesty International*, May 19, 2015, https://www.amnesty.org/en/latest/news/2015/05/morocco-endemic-torture/.

If the international community cannot fulfill its responsibilities on this issue – where the legal and moral imperatives are so clear – how can it deal with more complex issues? If the international community cannot uphold the fundamental right of self-determination, how can it successfully defend other human rights? If the international community cannot enforce a series of United Nations Security Council resolutions regarding such a blatant violation of the UN Charter as a member state invading, occupying, annexing, and colonizing a neighboring country, how can it enforce other provisions of international law?

The stakes are not simply about the future of one small country, but the question as to which principle will prevail in the twenty-first century: the right of self-determination, or the right of conquest? The answer could determine the fate not just of the Western Sahara, but that of the entire international legal order for many decades to come.

Disclosure statement

No potential conflict of interest was reported by the author.

The status of Western Sahara as occupied territory under international humanitarian law and the exploitation of natural resources

Ben Saul

Professor of International Law and Australian Research Council Future Fellow, University of Sydney, Australia

Much of the international legal analysis of dealings in natural resources in Western Sahara has focused on its status as a Non-Self-Governing Territory, as well as the right of self-determination of the Sahrawi people. Surprisingly overlooked in the legal debates is a close examination of the application of the international law of occupation under international humanitarian law (IHL). This article considers whether and why Western Sahara is 'occupied territory' under IHL, discussing some of the unique peculiarities that complicate the legal answer. It then considers issues of state responsibility and individual criminal liability under international law for unlawful dealings with natural resources in Western Sahara by Moroccan and foreign companies.

Introduction

Both the international community and scholars have paid surprisingly little attention to whether Western Sahara is occupied territory under international humanitarian law (IHL), as well to the legal implications of Moroccan occupation for dealings with natural resources there. This article explores these questions and argues that Western Sahara has met the legal criteria for occupation under IHL from early 1976 to the present (2015). It further argues that certain commercial dealings with Western Saharan resources, from phosphates to fisheries, are prohibited by the international law of occupation and may attract individual criminal responsibility as war crimes.

In its resolutions since the Moroccan invasion of Western Sahara in November 1975, the UN Security Council has not characterized Western Sahara as 'occupied' under IHL,[1] including in its extensive documentation on the UN Mission for the Referendum in Western Sahara since 1991.[2] While the General Assembly twice deplored Morocco's 'occupation' of Western Sahara (in resolutions in 1979 and 1980),[3] it has refrained from repeating that characterization in the 35 years since.[4] In its *Western Sahara Advisory Opinion* of 16 October 1975, the International Court of Justice (ICJ) did not consider question of occupation because at that time Morocco had not yet

---

1 Christine Chinkin, 'Laws of Occupation', paper presented at the Conference on Multilateralism and International Law with Western Sahara as a Case Study, South African Department of Foreign Affairs and the University of Pretoria, December 4–5, 2008 (Pretoria Conference), 198, 199–200.
2 MINURSO was created by UNSC resolution 690 (April 29, 1991). See UN Documents on MINURSO, Resolutions of the Security Council, http://www.un.org/en/peacekeeping/missions/minurso/resolutions.shtml.
3 UNGA resolutions 34/37 (November 21, 1979) and 35/19 (November 11, 1980).
4 Chinkin, 'Laws of Occupation', 200. See also Marcel Brus, 'The Legality of Exploring and Exploiting Mineral Resources in Western Sahara', in *International Law and the Question of Western Sahara*, ed. Karin Arts and Pedro Pinto Leite (Leiden: International Platform of Jurists for East Timor, 2007), 201, 206.

invaded Western Sahara. As one author observes, Morocco is 'rarely described as an occupying power',[5] although this may reflect political considerations as much as definitive legal positions or uncertainties. In the scholarly literature too, while it has occasionally been suggested that Western Sahara is occupied under IHL,[6] most sources do not provide detailed legal analyses.

One reason for the relative inattention to IHL in debates over the exploitation of natural resources in Western Sahara is that most of the focus has been on other legal paradigms. It is widely accepted that Western Sahara remains a Non-Self-Governing Territory under Chapter XI of the United Nations Charter.[7] As such, according to the then UN Legal Counsel, resource exploitation 'in disregard of the interests and wishes of the people of Western Sahara would be in violation of the international law principles applicable to mineral resource activities in Non-Self-Governing Territories'.[8] Such law encompasses the principles of self-determination and permanent sovereignty over natural resources.[9] Further, as recognized by the International Court of Justice (ICJ) in the *Western Sahara Advisory Opinion* (1975), Morocco does not possess sovereignty over Western Sahara, whose people enjoy a right of self-determination.[10] Such right encompasses a right of the Sahrawi people to freely pursue their 'economic ... development' and to, 'for their own ends, freely dispose of their natural wealth and resources' and to not 'be deprived of ... [their] own means of subsistence'.[11]

Such legal considerations apply to Morocco's exploitation, or licensing of foreign corporate exploitation, of resources such as oil, minerals and fisheries in Western Sahara. Much scholarly commentary has considered self-determination in Western Sahara,[12] including its political[13] and economic[14] dimensions. Further, as noted by the ICJ in the *Israeli Wall Advisory Opinion* (2004), other states owe an obligation *erga omnes* (that is, to all other states) not to recognize the illegal situation created by the denial of self-determination, not to render aid or assistance in maintaining such illegality, and to remove impediments to the realization of

---

5   Jacob Mundy, 'The Legal Status of Western Sahara and the Laws of War and Occupation', *Collaborations* no. 1790, Strategic Studies Group, June 22, 2007.

6   Chinkin, 'Laws of Occupation', 199–200; Stuart Casey-Maslen, ed., *The War Report 2012* (Oxford: Oxford University Press, 2013), 63–5; Vincent Chapaux, 'The Question of the European Community-Morocco Fisheries Agreement', in *International Law and the Question of Western Sahara* (see note 4), 217, 224–6; Hans-Peter Gasser, 'The Conflict in Western Sahara – An Unresolved Issued from the Decolonization Period', *Yearbook of International Humanitarian Law* (2002): 375, 379; Rule of Law in Armed Conflicts Project (RULAC), 'Morocco: Applicable International Law' (Geneva Academy of International Humanitarian Law and Human Rights), http://www.geneva-academy.ch/rulac-project/profile/pages/140/morocco/8/applicable-international-law.html; Stephanie Koury, 'The European Community and Member States' Duty of Non-Recognition under the EC-Morocco Association Agreement: State Responsibility and Customary International Law', in *International Law and the Question of Western Sahara* (see note 4), 172.

7   On which see Carlos Ruiz Miguel, 'Spain's Legal Obligations as Administering Power of Western Sahara', in Pretoria Conference (see note 1), 222.

8   Letter dated January 29, 2002 from the Under Secretary-General for Legal Affairs, the Legal Counsel, addressed to the President of the Security Council, UN Doc S/2002/161, February 12, 2002 (Corell Opinion), para. 25.

9   Ibid., paras. 9–14. See in particular UNGA resolutions: 1514 (XV) (December 14, 1960): Declaration of the Granting of Independence to Colonial Countries and Peoples; 1541 (XV) (December 14, 1960): Principles which should guide members in determining whether or not an obligation exists to transmit the information called for under Article 73e of the Charter; 1542 (XV) (December 15, 1960): Transmission of information under Article 73(e) of the Charter; 1803 (XVII): Permanent Sovereignty over Natural Resources (December 14, 1962).

10 *Western Sahara (Advisory Opinion)*, ICJ Rep 12, October 16, 1975, para. 70.

11 International Covenant on Economic, Social and Cultural Rights (adopted December 16, 1966, entered into force January 3, 1976, 993 UNTS 3), Article 1(1) and (2). See Ben Saul, David Kinley, and Jacqueline Mowbray, *The International Covenant on Economic, Social and Cultural Rights: Commentary, Cases and Materials* (Oxford: Oxford University Press, 2014), chapter 2.

12 See, e.g., Thomas Franck, 'The Stealing of the Sahara', *American Journal of International Law* 70 (1976): 694; Roger Clark, 'Western Sahara and the Right to Self-Determination', in *International Law and the Question of Western Sahara* (see note 4), 45; Catriona Drew, 'The Meaning of Self-Determination: "The Stealing of the Sahara" Redux?', in ibid., 87; Stephen Zunes, 'East Timor and Western Sahara: A Comparative Analysis of Prospects for Self-Determination', in ibid., 109.

13 See, e.g., Carlos Ruiz Miguel, 'The Self-Determination Referendum and the Role of Spain', in *International Law and the Question of Western Sahara* (see note 4), 305.

14 See, e.g., Koury, 'The European Community', 170–2, 176–8.

self-determination.[15] This has implications, for instance, for foreign states' dealings with Western Saharan resources,[16] including in relation to the licensing of foreign fishing in waters under Moroccan sovereignty or jurisdiction;[17] permitting national corporations to exploit resources; and allowing the import or export of goods related to such exploitation.

In principle, the abovementioned legal frameworks provide considerable normative constraints on Morocco's utilization of Western Saharan resources and substantial protections for the proprietary interests of the Sahrawi people. However, these paradigms – the law on Non-Self-Governing Territories, permanent sovereignty over natural resources, and self-determination – principally operate only on the legal plane of (inter-)state responsibility. That is, the states concerned owe obligations to one another and the breach of an international obligation attracts state responsibility and triggers obligations to make reparation (typically in the form of cessation, restitution and compensation, apology and guarantees of non-repetition). While self-determination is also a human right, the UN human rights treaty bodies have refused to admit individual petitions alleging violations of this collective right.[18]

The application of IHL to Western Sahara, and the classification of the conflict, deserve more detailed consideration, which this article undertakes. Under international law, the existence of an armed conflict or occupation is an objective matter which does not depend on the subjective determination of the political organs of the United Nations or individual states, though such assessments are relevant facts. This chapter explores whether Western Sahara is 'occupied' under IHL, then discusses the provisions of IHL governing natural resources in occupied territory. It finally considers the criminal law consequences of characterizing Western Sahara as occupied territory in the context of natural resource exploitation.

IHL makes a distinctive contribution to regulation of the Western Sahara dispute. Like the other legal frameworks already mentioned, the law of occupation establishes state responsibility for breaches of IHL obligations governing natural resources. Under common article 1 of the Geneva Conventions of 1949, states parties also have a duty to ensure respect for IHL[19] and to take measures to suppress breaches of IHL.[20] In addition, however, there exists individual criminal responsibility for war crimes under international law, whether as 'grave breaches' of certain IHL treaties, other violations of the laws and customs of war, or pursuant to specific international criminal law regimes such as the 1998 Rome Statute of the International Criminal Court (ICC).[21] Specifically, under the Geneva Conventions, states must establish criminal jurisdiction over war crimes (including extraterritorially), search for suspects, and prosecute or extradite them.[22] Further, because of such treaty-based quasi-universal jurisdiction under the Geneva Conventions and the 1998 Rome Statute of the ICC, many states have enacted domestic legislation which enables them to prosecute war criminals in domestic courts. In addition, some national laws

---

15 *Legal Consequences of the Construction of a Wall in the Occupied Palestinian Territory* (2004) ICJ Rep 136 (*Israel Wall Advisory Opinion* (2004)), paras. 154–9 and 163. Cf. *Portugal v Australia* (1995) ICJ Rep 90, paras. 31–2.

16 See generally New York City Bar (Committee on United Nations), Report on Legal Issues Involved in the Western Sahara Dispute: Use of Natural Resources, April 2011; Erik Hagen, 'The Role of Natural Resources in the Western Saharan Conflict, and the Interests Involved', Pretoria Conference (see note 1), 292.

17 See, e.g., Koury, 'The European Community', 180–97.

18 *Chief Bernard Ominayak and Lubicon Lake Band v Canada*, UN Human Rights Committee Communication No. 167/1984, UN Doc. CCPR/C/38/D/167/1984 (March 26, 1990), para. 13.3.

19 See also *Israel Wall Advisory Opinion* (2004), para. 163(D).

20 See, e.g., Geneva Convention IV Relative to the Protection of Civilian Persons in Time of War (adopted August 12, 1949, entered into force October 21, 1950) (Fourth Geneva Convention 1949), Article 146(3).

21 Respectively: see, e.g., Fourth Geneva Convention 1949, ibid., Article 147; ICRC, *Customary International Humanitarian Law* (Cambridge: Cambridge University Press, 2005) (ICRC Customary IHL Study), Rules 151 (individual criminal responsibility) and 156 (war crimes); and Rome Statute of the International Criminal Court (adopted July 17, 1998, entered into force July 1, 2002), 2187 UNTS 3, Article 8 (war crimes). On the technical distinction between 'grave breaches' and war crimes (which is not the subject of the present article), see Marko Öberg, 'The Absorption of Grave Breaches into War Crimes Law', *International Review of the Red Cross* 91 (2009): 163.

22 See, e.g., Fourth Geneva Convention 1949, Article 146(1)–(2).

provide for corporate criminal liability for war crimes. Accordingly, if certain dealings with Western Saharan natural resources are contrary to the international law of occupation under IHL, the individuals and companies involved not only bear direct criminal responsibility under international law, but may be liable to prosecution in national courts. Further, pursuant to international obligations of cooperation, other states may be required to assist in the investigation and extradition of suspects.

Classification of armed conflict: is Western Sahara 'occupied territory'?

Under common article 2 of the 1949 Geneva Conventions, an international armed conflict can arise in two relevant situations – first, where there are armed hostilities between two or more states, including through the use of irregular forces 'belonging' to a state;[23] and secondly, where one state partially or totally occupies the territory of another state, 'even if the said occupation meets with no armed resistance'.[24] A territory is considered 'occupied' under IHL where the local authority is displaced and 'when it is actually placed under the authority of the hostile army',[25] and regardless of whether underlying sovereign title to the territory is contested.[26]

An international conflict can also arise between national liberation or self-determination movement and a state party under Additional Protocol I of 1977, which alters the pre-existing characterization of such conflicts as non-international.[27] Morocco ratified Protocol I in 2011, long after signing it 1977. In June 2015 Polisario deposited a unilateral declaration of adherence to the Geneva Conventions and Protocol I under the procedure provided for in article 96(3) of Protocol I. The depository state, Switzerland, duly notified the declaration to states parties, formally accepting the first ever article 96(3) declaration. A non-international armed conflict exists under common article 3 of the 1949 Geneva Conventions where there is sufficiently intense armed violence between a state and an organized non-state armed group, or between two or more organized groups.[28]

The violence that engulfed Western Sahara in 1975 was complex because it involved an array of state and non-state armed actors at varying levels of intensity, in a rapidly changing security environment, and affected by legally significant intervening events. This article focuses only on whether Western Sahara is occupied territory as a result of Morocco gaining control of the territory, commencing in late November 1975. It should be mentioned, however, that it is likely that there were a series of parallel armed conflicts of different kinds during this period – a non-international armed conflict between Spain and Polisario in 1974–75; a brief international armed conflict between Spain and Morocco in 1975, constituted by a number of armed engagements between regular forces;[29] a non-international conflict between Polisario and Mauritania from 1975 to 1979, in both Western Saharan and Mauritanian territory;[30] and a brief and low-intensity international conflict between

---

23 Geneva Conventions I–IV 1949, common Article 2(1).
24 Ibid., common Article 2(2).
25 Hague Regulations Respecting the Laws and Customs of War on Land (adopted October 18, 1907, entered into force January 26, 1910) (Hague Regulations 1907), Article 42.
26 *Israel Wall Advisory Opinion* (2004), para. 95.
27 Protocol I Additional to the Geneva Conventions of August 12, 1949 and Relating to the Protection of Victims of International Armed Conflicts (adopted June 8, 1977, entered into force December 7, 1978), 1125 UNTS 3 (Additional Protocol I 1977), Article 1(4).
28 *Prosecutor v Tadic (Interlocutory Appeal on Jurisdiction)*, ICTY, IT-94-1, October 2, 1995, para. 70; *Prosecutor v Limaj et al.*, ICTY, IT-03-66-T, November 30, 2005, para. 83; *Prosecutor v Boskoski*, ICTY, IT-04-82-T, July 10, 2008.
29 *Keesings Contemporary Archives* (1975), vol. XXI, November 3–9, 1975, 27416; ibid., 27418; see also Stephen Zunes and Jacob Mundy, *Western Sahara: War, Nationalism and Conflict Irresolution* (Syracuse, NY: Syracuse University Press, 2010), 4.
30 See Tony Hodges, *Western Sahara: Roots of A Desert War* (Westport, CT: Lawrence Hill, 1983), 230–1; *Keesings Contemporary Archives* (1976), vol. XXII, February 13, 1976, 27579; ibid., May 28, 1976, 27746; Zunes and Mundy, *Western Sahara*, 11–12; John Mercer, *The Sahrawis of Western Sahara*, Minority Rights Group Report

Morocco and Algeria in 1976.[31] The principal active hostilities, between Polisario and Morocco from 1975 to the present, have probably constituted a non-international conflict between a state and a non-state actor, taking place in occupied territory but legally distinct from international conflict.[32] After Morocco's ratification of Protocol I in 2011, those hostilities were transformed from a non-international conflict into an international conflict, alongside the continuing international conflict constituted by the persisting occupation of Spanish Sahara since 1975.

International armed conflict by occupation: Morocco in Spanish Sahara 1975–present – timeline of legally significant events

After the ICJ delivered its Western Sahara *Advisory Opinion* on 16 October 1975, Morocco announced a peaceful 'Green March' of 350,000 Moroccans into Spanish Sahara to claim the territory for Morocco. Spain told the Security Council on 20 October 1975 that such an 'invasion' would threaten international peace and security, and on 2 November 1975 warned in the Council that Spain would 'repel it with all means at her disposal, including use of armed force'.[33] Algeria also protested. The UN intensified its diplomatic efforts. Spain commenced negotiations with Morocco, Mauritania, Algeria and Polisario.[34]

On 25 October, Spain and Morocco reached a 'tacit agreement' to permit the marchers to enter Spanish Sahara up to a limited distance and for a brief period,[35] seemingly to avert a military confrontation with Moroccan civilians (and their military backers). On 28 October 1975, Spain imposed a curfew on the territory, and then dismissed its Sahrawi soldiers, evacuated European civilians, withdrew its troops to a fortified 'dissuasion line' some miles from the Moroccan border, and mobilized nearby warships, aircraft and reserve troops.[36] Moroccan and Algerian forces also mobilized on their borders.

Spanish concessions to Moroccan demands had, however, gone further than was evident from Spain's public position. By 4 November, the essence of a trilateral agreement between Spain, Morocco and Mauritania had been agreed, to transfer sovereignty and administration to the latter states.[37] On 5 November, Morocco gave an ultimatum to Spain to immediately negotiate to cede Spanish Sahara to Morocco and Mauritania or Morocco's marchers would be ordered to proceed to the dissuasion line, and if Spain attempted to stop them, Morocco would militarily intervene.[38] The marchers entered Spanish Sahara on 6 November 1975 and the Security Council deplored the march that day and called for its withdrawal.[39] The marchers' numbers swelled until 9 November, when Morocco called off the march.[40] Spain's Cabinet had decided on 8 November to cede the territory without a referendum.[41] All of the marchers were consequently withdrawn from Western Sahara by 13 November.[42]

---

no. 40 (1979), 13; Letter dated August 18, 1976 from the Permanent Representative of Mauritania to the United Nations addressed to the Secretary General, UN Doc S/2002/161 (February 12, 2002).

31 *Keesings Contemporary Archives* (1976), vol. XXII, 28 May 1976, 27746; ibid., 27748.
32 See, e.g. *Hamdan v Rumsfeld*, US Supreme Court, 548 US (2006), 126 S Ct 2749 (on the interpretation of common Article 3 of the Geneva Conventions). Cf. the approach taken in *Public Committee against Torture in Israel v Government of Israel*, Supreme Court of Israel, HCJ 769/02, December 11, 2005, paras. 18, 21 (all hostilities in occupied territory are part of the international conflict, even if involving non-state actors).
33 *Keesings Contemporary Archives* (1976), vol. XXII, February 13, 1976, 27575.
34 *Keesings Contemporary Archives* (1975), vol. XXI, November 3–9, 1975, 27413.
35 Hodges, *Western Sahara*, 216–17.
36 *Keesings Contemporary Archives* (1976), vol. XXII, February 13, 1976, 27576.
37 Hodges, *Western Sahara*, 220.
38 Ibid., 222.
39 UNSC resolution 380 (November 6, 1975).
40 *Keesings Contemporary Archives* (1976), vol. XXII, February 13, 1976, 27576.
41 Hodges, *Western Sahara*, 222.
42 Ibid., 223.

WESTERN SAHARA

Talks in Madrid from 11 November 1975 led to the conclusion, on 14 November 1975, of the tripartite Madrid Agreement between Spain, Morocco and Mauritania. Spain agreed to decolonize Western Sahara and end its responsibilities and powers as administering power; establish a provisional administration involving Morocco and Mauritania, in cooperation with the Spanish Sahara General Assembly of Sahrawi representatives (the *Yemaá*); appoint two assistant governors from Morocco and Mauritania; and end its presence by 28 February 1976. While the Agreement provided that '[t]he views of the inhabitants of the Sahara as expressed through the *Yemaá* shall be respected', and for 'respect for the principles of the UN Charter', there was no provision for a referendum. Side agreements preserved certain Spanish economic interests, including fishing rights, a 35% share in the Bou Craa phosphate mine, and compensation for its citizens.[43] The November talks had involved the Director General of the Office chérifien des phosphates (OCP), the Moroccan state phosphate company.[44] The Madrid Agreement reflected a secret arrangement between Morocco and Mauritania in October 1974 to partition Spanish Sahara and share its economic exploitation.[45] Morocco and Mauritania agreed on the actual partition of the territory on 14 April 1976.

Morocco ordered the marchers to return home from the border on 18 November 1975, after the Spanish Parliament approved a decolonization law giving effect to the Madrid Agreement.[46] On 18 November Spain informed the UN Secretary General of its intention to terminate its presence in Western Sahara by 28 February 1976.[47] On the same day, Polisario described these events to the UN decolonization committee as a 'Moroccan aggression' and 'military invasion'.[48] The Moroccan and Mauritanian assistant governors were appointed on 22–23 November and by 1 December 'military and civilian officials from both countries had taken over most public services and government posts in the territory'.[49] From 1 January 1976, residents ceased to be Spanish citizens and Morocco was already issuing passports and identity cards, and appointing regional administrators.

As Spanish administrative and military personnel withdrew, Moroccan military forces rapidly entered to secure the territory. In fact, Spanish forces had begun withdrawing from outer regions by 30 October 1975, with Polisario taking over many posts.[50] On 31 October, Moroccan forces secretly entered Spanish Sahara to take over three of the outposts (Jdiriya, Haousa and Farsia) evacuated by Spanish troops.[51] By 13 November – the day before the Madrid Agreement – Moroccan forces had reached Tifariti, near the Mauritanian border.[52]

After the Madrid Agreement purported to legalize Morocco's presence, hundreds of advance Moroccan troops entered the administrative capital El Aaiún on 25 November with Moroccan officials.[53] Around 5000 more troops entered El Aaiún on 11 December, with Spanish forces leaving on 20 December, and Moroccan forces assuming control over airfields and military bases by 28 December. Moroccan forces also took over the second largest town, Smara, on 27 November. The Bou Craa phosphate mine was under Moroccan control by late December. Moroccan forces spread throughout the territory and reached Villa Cisneros (now Dakhla) in the south by 11 January 1976, joined by Mauritanian troops; and, in the north-east, reached Tifariti,

---

43 Ibid., 224. By February 7, 1976 Spain had sold 65% of Fosbucraa to Morocco, retaining 35%; the remaining 35% was divested in 2003.
44 *Keesings Contemporary Archives* (1976), vol. XXII, February 13, 1976, 27577.
45 *Keesings Contemporary Archives* (1975), vol. XXI, November 3–9, 1975, 27417.
46 *Keesings Contemporary Archives* (1976), vol. XXII, February 13, 1976, 27577.
47 UN Doc. S/11880 (November 19, 1975).
48 *Keesings Contemporary Archives* (1976), vol. XXII, February 13, 1976, 27577.
49 Ibid., 27577.
50 Hodges, *Western Sahara*, 219.
51 Ibid., 220.
52 Ibid., 223.
53 Ibid., 229.

Bir Lehlou and Mahabes in the first weeks of February.[54] Polisario held on to some smaller settlements for some months, with heavy fighting,[55] but by 19 April 1976 Morocco had taken all of the major former Spanish settlements and outposts.[56] The International Committee of the Red Cross (ICRC) reported 40,000 Sahrawis displaced by early January 1976 and most Sahrawis had fled by mid-1976.[57] Today Morocco controls (with over 100,000 troops)[58] around 80% of Spanish Sahara, but for the so-called 'liberated territories' east of the fortified military sand wall (the 'berm') constructed by Morocco from 1980. It has extended its control through development plans, the sedentarization and 'modernization' of the nomadic population, the exploitation of resources,[59] and mass Moroccan migration.

The last Spanish troops departed around 8–12 January 1976[60] and the remnants of the Spanish administration by 26 February. Spain announced to the UN on 26 February that its participation in the temporary administration established under the Madrid Agreement had immediately ceased and that it 'considers itself henceforth exempt from any responsibility of an international nature in connection with the administration of the said Territory'.[61] It added, however, that '[t]he decolonization of Western Sahara will reach its climax when the views of the Saharan population have been validly expressed'. That caveat was a response to the unanimous vote by the Sahrawi *Yemaá*, originally appointed by the Spanish authorities and identified as expressing the 'views' of Sahrawis under the Madrid Agreement, to ratify the Agreement on 26 February 1976. Only 57 of 102 members of the *Yemaá* attended,[62] the rest having joined Polisario or fled to Algeria.[63] Polisario claimed that the *Yemaá* had dissolved itself on 28 November 1975, at a meeting attended by 67 members,[64] and had regarded the *Yemaá* as elderly, conservative colonial collaborators not representative of all Sahrawis.[65]

The UN similarly did not regard the above process as an exercise of self-determination. UN General Assembly resolution 3458A of 10 December 1975, adopted by 88 votes to none, with 41 abstentions, provided that Spain as administering power was to organize the exercise of self-determination in Spanish Sahara. On the same day, resolution 3458B, supported by Morocco, and with much less support – 56 votes in favour to 42 against, with 34 abstentions – noted the Madrid Agreement and provided that the interim administration was to ensure self-determination through free consultations assisted by a UN representative, including by consulting 'all the Saharan population originating in the territory'. The UN representative who visited Western Sahara in early February 1976 concluded that genuine consultation was impossible because of the military presence, political oppression, displacement and conflict.[66] On 25–26 September 1976, both Spain and UN Secretary General Waldheim stated that self-determination had not been exercised in the required manner.[67]

---

54 Ibid., 232.
55 Ibid., 229.
56 Ibid., 238.
57 Ibid., 229.
58 Eyal Benvenisti, *The International Law of Occupation* (Princeton: Princeton University Press, 2004), 152.
59 David Price, *The Western Sahara*, The Washington Papers, vol. VII (Sage Publications, 1979), 38–41.
60 *Keesings Contemporary Archives* (1976), vol. XXII, February 13, 1976, 27578; Hodges, *Western Sahara*, 230.
61 Letter dated February 26, 1976 from Spain's Permanent Representative to the United Nations addressed to the UN Secretary General, UN Doc. S/11997.
62 Hodges, *Western Sahara*, 237.
63 *Keesings Contemporary Archives* (1976), vol. XXII, May 28, 1976, 27747.
64 Mercer, *The Sahrawis of Western Sahara*, 10.
65 Hodges, *Western Sahara*, 224.
66 Ibid., 236.
67 Ibid., 237.

The legal test for belligerent occupation

In assessing whether Western Sahara is occupied territory under IHL, it is clear that Morocco has actual[68] or effective governmental and administrative control over most of Western Sahara, secured by the presence of its military forces. Having successfully substituted its authority for that of Spain by early 1976, the decisive legal question is whether Morocco *forcibly* displaced the Spanish authorities in the course of the events of 1975–76 described above. As mentioned earlier, IHL envisages that occupation can arise by a classic invasion involving inter-state hostilities, or by 'bloodless occupation' of foreign territory involving no actual hostilities. As noted earlier, there were a handful of minor skirmishes between Spanish and Moroccan forces in 1975, and large-scale civilian penetration of Spanish Saharan borders in the Green March of November 1975, but no active armed hostilities after the Madrid Agreement of November 1975. Western Sahara was accordingly not occupied in this orthodox sense under article 2(1) of the Geneva Conventions.

The situation is arguably more assimilable to a so-called 'bloodless invasion' under article 2(2) of the Geneva Conventions, by which Morocco occupied Spanish Saharan territory without active hostilities against Spain. Technically the lack of *consent* of the legitimate authority to the presence of foreign forces is not an explicit precondition for the existence of an occupation under IHL treaties. It is, however, widely accepted that the absence of consent is 'a central element and a precondition for establishing occupation'.[69] In doctrine and practice, a state that validly consents to the presence of foreign troops is not considered 'occupied'. Consent must be 'genuine, valid and explicit', not 'engineered' (as in the cases of the United States invasion of Panama in 1989 or the Soviet Union's occupation of Czechoslovakia in 1968) or coerced (as in the cases of Haiti in 1994 and the Indonesian invasion of East Timor in 1975).[70] Coercion may be usefully articulated in the IHL context by reference to broader international law,[71] particularly the law on treaties. Article 52 of the Vienna Convention on the Law of Treaties 1969 (VCLT) provides that a treaty is void for 'coercion' 'if its conclusion has been procured by the threat or use of force in violation of' the UN Charter.[72] Article 52 reflects customary international law.[73] In addition, a treaty is void under article 53 of the VCLT 'if, at the time of its conclusion, it conflicts with a peremptory norm [*jus cogens*] of general international law'.[74] The prohibition on the use of force, the related prohibition on the acquisition of title to territory by force, and self-determination are three potentially relevant *jus cogens* principles.[75]

In the light of the factual situation leading up to and including the Madrid Agreement, the critical question is whether Spain validly consented to Morocco and Mauritania's entry, so as to preclude the existence of an occupation under IHL, or whether Spain's consent was invalidated by coercive threats of, or the use of, force, thus resulting in a 'bloodless' occupation. There is a closely related question of whether Spain's apparent consent to the entry of Morocco and

---

68 *Armed Activities on the Territory of the Congo* (*Democratic Republic of the Congo v Uganda*), ICJ Judgment, December 19, 2005 (*Congo v Uganda* (2005)), para. 173.

69 ICRC, 'Occupation and Other Forms of Administration of Foreign Territory', Expert Meeting, March 2012, 21.

70 Ibid. On Portuguese Timor, see Ben Saul, 'Prosecuting War Crimes at Balibo under Australian Law: The Killing of Five Journalists in East Timor by Indonesia', *Sydney Law Review* 31 (2009): 3.

71 ICRC, 'Occupation and Other Forms of Administration of Foreign Territory'.

72 Vienna Convention on the Law of Treaties (adopted May 23, 1969, entered into force January 27, 1980) (VCLT 1969), Article 52.

73 *Dubai–Sharjah Border Arbitration*, Award, October 19, 1981, *International Law Reports* 91 (1981): 543, 569.

74 VCLT 1969, Article 53 defines a peremptory norm as 'a norm accepted and recognized by the international community of States as a whole as a norm from which no derogation is permitted and which can be modified only by a subsequent norm of general international law having the same character'.

75 The ICJ described self-determination as an obligation *erga omnes* (*Israeli Wall Advisory Opinion* (2004), para. 88; *East Timor v Portugal* (1995) ICJ Rep 102, para. 29) but did not characterize it as *jus cogens*.

Mauritania is alternatively or additionally invalid because it conflicts with the peremptory norms on the prohibition on the use of force, the non-acquisition of title to territory by force, and self-determination. The invalidation of Spain's consent on this basis would also mean that Moroccan and Mauritanian forces bloodlessly occupied Spanish territory under IHL, notwithstanding Spain's purported agreement.

Lack of valid consent: coercion

Spain's exit from Western Sahara in 1975–76 was motivated by a number of considerations. Spain had been on the way out since 1963, having committed to decolonization in principle by listing Western Sahara as a non-self-governing territory in that year.[76] Regularly from 1966 to 1973, the UN General Assembly had called on Spain to hold a referendum under UN auspices to enable the indigenous population to freely exercise self-determination.[77] Pressure from Sahrawi liberation movements grew from 1969, starting with demonstrations and progressing to violent resistance by Polisario and the Front de Libération et de l'Unité (FLU) from 1973.

Such pressures hastened Spain to announce, in August 1974,[78] a procedure for the exercise of Sahrawi self-determination: a referendum in the first half of 1975, postponed because of the request made of the ICJ in December 1974, resulting in the *Advisory Opinion* of 16 October 1975. As mentioned earlier, Moroccan military incursions and threats intensified throughout 1975, culminating in the civilian Green March of November 1975. In the midst of Morocco's provocations, a domestic political crisis threw Spanish policy into disarray, with General Franco becoming suddenly ill on 17 October and dying on 20 November. Spain also faced Basque separatism at home.[79] Spain abandoned its referendum proposal and agreed to the tripartite interim administration under the Madrid Agreement on 14 November 1975, leaving the territory entirely by 26 February 1976.

Under article 52 of the VCLT, a treaty is void due to coercion if it is 'procured' by the unlawful threat or use of force. The plain meaning of 'procure' is '[t]o obtain; to bring about'.[80] In the simplest case, coercion may be the *sole* reason a state consented to a treaty. However, in other cases, as in Spanish Sahara, consent may have been influenced by a combination of factors of varying weight in the decision-making process. The text of article 52, and the International Law Commission (ILC) Commentary on the draft on which it was based,[81] gives little guidance on when a treaty will be considered 'procured' by coercion where multiple motives drive a state's consent. At a minimum the term 'procured' suggests some 'causal link' is required, but the drafting record evidences little attention to this issue.[82] In principle, a spectrum can be envisaged: at one end, coercion might be the *sole* reason for consent; in the upper middle of the spectrum, it could be a dominant influence; at the lower middle, it could be a substantial or significant

---

76 By transmitting information under Article 73e of the UN Charter: see UN Doc. A/5446/Rev.1, annex 1. See also UNGA resolutions 2072 (December 17, 1965); 229 (December 20, 1966); 2354 (December 19, 1967); 2428 (December 27, 1968); 2591 (December 16, 1969); 2711 (December 14, 1970); 2983 (December 14, 1972); 3162 (December 14, 1973); and Miguel, 'Spain's Legal Obligations', 223, 237.

77 UNGA resolutions 2229 (XXI) (December 20, 1966); 2354 (XXII) (December 19, 1967); 2428 (XXIII) (December 18, 1968); 2591 (XXIV) (December 16, 1979); 2711 (XXV) (December 14, 1970); 2938 (XXVII) (December 14, 1972); 3162 (XXVIII) (December 14, 1973).

78 Letter dated August 20, 1974 from the Permanent Representative of Spain to the United Nations to the Secretary-General, UN Doc. A/9714.

79 Hodges, *Western Sahara*, 215.

80 Oxford English Dictionary, 'procure', online.

81 International Law Commission, Draft Articles on the Law of Treaties with Commentaries (1966) II Yearbook of the International Law Commission 187 (ILC Commentary), 247.

82 Olivier Corten, 'Article 52', in *The Vienna Conventions on the Law of Treaties: A Commentary*, vol. II, ed. Olivier Corten and Pierre Klein (Oxford: Oxford University Press, 2011), 1201, 1211.

factor, even if not dominant; and at the bottom end, coercion might simply be one of many factors, and not necessarily especially important. The first three approaches are consistent with the 'but for' test often deployed in various domestic legal contexts, namely, 'but for' the coercion, consent to a treaty, at the time of its conclusion, would not have been given.

Relevant international jurisprudence is sparse. In the *Fisheries Jurisdiction* case, the ICJ held briefly that a treaty 'concluded under' the threat or use of force is void, but on the facts of that case the Court found that the agreements 'were freely negotiated by the interested parties on the basis of perfect equality and freedom of decision on both sides'.[83] After the Second World War a Dutch national court took the view that coercion required that the victim state 'could not escape' the effects of coercion;[84] a similar approach is reflected in the *Aminoil Arbitration* ('the absence of any other possible course')[85] and was favoured by the jurist Hersch Lauterpacht ('unable to resist').[86] However, the manifest nature of coercion in some of these cases arguably accounts for the restrictive approaches adopted.[87] A more liberal view is that a treaty is procured by coercion where it would not have been entered into in the absence of the coercion.[88] On this view, coercion may be 'a decisive influence' but it need not entail a 'total absence of choice', or be the exclusive or essential reason.[89]

The latter approach is also consistent with developments in national laws. Domestic jurisprudence is of qualified utility in that treaties are not assimilable to contracts under domestic law and are governed by international not domestic law. Domestic contract law also varies between civil and common law states on basic matters, including the legal significance and effects of coercion or duress, such as whether a contract thus affected is void or voidable at the election of a party. Further, coercion in those contexts is typically unlike the threat or use of force in international relations, although it may involve threats to the person. It is also inapposite to simply transpose terminology from other legal contexts to interpret what it means to 'procure' a treaty by coercion, such as criminal law concepts of complicity in the procuring of offences (which can entail stricter notions of causation).[90]

Comparable domestic principles may nonetheless be of some assistance, and particularly if they are sufficiently widespread to reflect general principles of (international) law.[91] In the common law of contract, for instance, a contract is affected by duress (including threats to life) where the agreement to contract was induced by an illegitimate threat amounting to compulsion.[92] Duress may be crystallized by a series of threats.[93] Importantly, the case law establishes that the pressure need not be the sole or even principal cause of the decision to contract.[94] It is sufficient for the duress to be *an* inducement to contract,[95] in part because 'any degree' of duress taints the

---

83 *Fisheries Jurisdiction (Federal Republic of Germany v Iceland)*, Judgment of February 2, 1973, *ICJ Reports* (1973) 49, at 59, para. 24.

84 *Amato Narodni Podnik v Julius Keilwerth Musikinstrumentenfabrik*, District Court of The Hague, December 31, 1955–November 11, 1956, *International Law Reports* 24 (1957): 437 (concerning the 1938 Munich Agreements and the German–Czechoslovak Nationality Treaty).

85 *Kuwait v The American Independent Oil Company (Aminoil)*, Arbitral Award, March 24, 1982, para. 43.

86 Cited in Corten, 'Article 52', 1212.

87 Ibid., 1213.

88 Ibid.

89 Ibid.

90 See, e.g., *Attorney-General's Reference (No. 1 of 1975)* [1975] 2 All ER 684 at 686, at 687.

91 Pursuant to Article 38(1)(c) of the Statute of the International Court of Justice, annexed to the Charter of the United Nations 1945.

92 John Carter, 'Chapter 23: Duress', in *Carter on Contract* (LexisNexis, Service 40: February 2015), database.

93 *Ampol Ltd v Caltex Oil (Australia) Pty Ltd* (unreported, NSW SC, Foster J, 82/9033, December 22, 1982).

94 See e.g. *Barton v Armstrong* [1976] AC 104; [1973] 2 NSWLR 598, PC; *Crescendo Management Pty Ltd v Westpac Banking Corp* (1988) 19 NSWLR 40 at 45 per McHugh JA; *Vantage Navigation Corp v Suhail and Saud Bahwan Building Materials LLC (The Alev)* [1989] 1 Lloyd's Rep 138, Hobhouse J; *Hawker Pacific Pty Ltd v Helicopter Charter Pty Ltd* (1991) 22 NSWLR 298, CA.

95 Carter, 'Chapter 23: Duress', [23-030] (citing *Crescendo Management Pty Ltd v Westpac Banking Corp* (1988) 19 NSWLR 40, CA).

contract's foundation.[96] Further, the common law cases establish that the victim need not be so 'overborne' by duress as to deprive him or her of any free will and thereby vitiate consent.[97] Rather, it is recognized that the victim still exercises a choice, from amongst alternatives, to knowingly enter into the contract, even if the alternatives are constrained or costly (and even involve death).[98] Duress thus constitutes an improper pressure rather than one which vitiates consent.[99] The focus is therefore on the quality of consent[100] rather than if it was voluntary, wilful, compelled, coerced and the like.

The domestic principles provide useful analogies in the interpretation of article 52 of the VCLT. They support an interpretation to the effect that a treaty may be 'procured' by coercion where the threat or use of force induces a state to agree to the treaty, even if the coercion is not the sole or even the dominant cause of the state giving its consent. Such an approach is consistent with the language of article 52, which does not provide that coercion must be 'exclusively', 'solely', 'predominantly' or 'substantially' procured by force; rather, coercion is *a* reason the treaty was procured. This approach is also consistent with the object and purpose of the strict prohibition on the threat or use of force under the UN Charter to which article 52 is pegged. A breach of the prohibition on the threat or use of force is recognized as one of the most fundamental wrongs in the international legal order. As such, a treaty tainted by it to *any extent* deserves to be treated as void.

Applying this interpretive approach, it is strongly arguable that Spain would not have entered into the Madrid Agreement – at that time (14 November), and on those terms – but for the coercion arising from a series of Moroccan threats and use of force in the lead-up to it. Morocco had sponsored the FLU attacks on Spanish Sahara since 1973. There was a build-up of 25,000 Moroccan troops on the border by May 1975, with no apparent defensive purpose given Spain's lack of aggressive intent. This was followed by border skirmishes in May 1975. Regular Moroccan forces mounted a number of incursions and attacks inside Spanish Sahara in June, July and August 1975. On 16 October 1975, Morocco announced that it would take over Spanish Sahara through a civilian Green March and later warned Spain that attempts to stop it would provoke a military response. The march took place from 6 to 13 November 1975, rendering Spain's position untenable. Already by 31 October, Moroccan forces were secretly occupying evacuated Spanish outposts.

The subjective intention of the coercive state is an important consideration.[101] Throughout this period Morocco had made it clear to Spain that it regarded Spanish Sahara as its own, and that it was prepared to take it forcibly; and Spain protested such threats of aggression, including to the Security Council. Further, as is required under article 52, Morocco's threats and uses of force were internationally unlawful, being neither in self-defence nor authorized by the Security Council, and being inconsistent with Spanish sovereignty and territorial integrity, and the right of self-determination of the Sahrawi people.

That Spanish forces could have ably resisted a Moroccan invasion if ordered to do so – Spain had superior military forces[102] – is not relevant; Spain, faced with the more harmful alternative of full-scale hostilities against Morocco, chose to de-escalate and not defend its territory. There are other examples of such 'bloodless invasions' procured by coerced agreements,

---

96 *Barton v Armstrong*, citing *Reynell v Sprye* (1852) 1 De GM & G 660 at 708.
97 As suggested in earlier cases: Carter, 'Chapter 23: Duress', [23-020].
98 Ibid. [23-020] (citing, among others, *Crescendo Management Pty Ltd v Westpac Banking Corp* (1988) 19 NSWLR 40, 45 per McHugh JA, CA).
99 Carter, 'Chapter 23: Duress', [23-020].
100 Ibid., [23-001] (citing, among others, *Commercial Bank of Australia Ltd v Amadio* (1983) 151 CLR 447, 474 per Deane J (Wilson J agreeing)).
101 Corten, 'Article 52', 1213.
102 Hodges, *Western Sahara*, 215.

such as Latvia's consent to Soviet occupation in 1940,[103] Czechoslovakian consent to Soviet forces in 1968,[104] or France's consent to a peace treaty with Thailand in 1941 in the face of Japanese threats.[105]

That Spain also secured economic concessions in the Madrid Agreement does not obviate the coercion; Spain still lost most, just not all, of its prior economic possessions, and an imbalance of benefits under a treaty can objectively indicate coercion.[106] Further, whereas the Security Council had authorized force in relation to a treaty imposed on Haiti under the threat of US military force in 1994,[107] there was no Council authorization in relation to Spanish Sahara.[108]

In sum, Morocco's actual and threatened use of force is a critical factor explaining how 'Spanish policy had turned full circle'[109] within a single month in late 1975 – from staunchly supporting Sahrawi self-determination and a referendum, and resolutely opposing Moroccan ambitions (with the Spanish military especially keen to preserve its honour), to transferring its administration to Morocco and Mauritania and rapidly quitting the territory. Other factors were certainly influential, such as the Sahrawi insurgency, Franco's illness and Spain's political transition. The Madrid Agreement also provided Spain with a quick exit from its decolonization responsibilities and the residual economic concessions softened the blow. But the Agreement would not have been concluded on that date, on those terms, but for Moroccan aggression. Moroccan coercion was more than a mere influence on Spain's consent; it was a decisive factor, even if it was not the sole or essential reason, or Spain could have resisted at considerable cost.

Lack of valid consent: jus cogens

A treaty is also void if, at the time of its conclusion, it conflicts with a peremptory norm. In terms, the Madrid Agreement did not authorize the unlawful use of force by Morocco or Mauritania against Spain contrary to the UN Charter. As discussed above, Morocco used and threatened force against Spain to coerce it into concluding the Agreement, obviating the need for further force, and the Agreement does not make provision for the military enforcement of its terms against Spain in the event of a breach of its obligations. Nor did the Agreement expressly authorize the forcible acquisition of sovereign title to territory; rather, the Agreement created a temporary administration by Morocco and Mauritania, in collaboration with the *Yemaá*, respecting the views of the Saharan population (through the *Yemaá*), and 'with due respect for the principles of the Charter of the United Nations, and as the best possible contribution to the maintenance of international peace and security'. Morocco's annexation of the territory was subsequent to the Agreement, even if Spain must have known that annexation was Morocco's aim, and that Morocco was contracting in bad faith.

---

103   *Kariņš and Others v Parliament of Latvia and Cabinet of Ministers of Latvia,* Latvian Constitutional Court, Case No. 2007-10-0102, November 29, 2007.

104   Treaty on the Temporary Sojourn of Soviet Forces in the Territory of the Czechoslovak Socialist Republic (adopted 16 October 1968).

105   Peace Convention between France and Thailand (adopted May 9, 1941).

106   Corten, 'Article 52', 1213.

107   Meinhard Schröder, 'Treaties, Validity', *Max Planck Encyclopedia of Public International Law*, online, last updated December 2010 (on the Agreement concerning the restoration of the Government of President Aristide (adopted September 18, 1994)).

108   On whether the UNSC can lawfully ratify post facto an agreement procured by coercion, see Serena Forlati, 'Coercion as a Ground Affecting the Validity of Peace Treaties', in *The Law of Treaties Beyond the Vienna Convention*, ed. Enzo Cannizzaro (Oxford: Oxford University Press, 2011), 320; and Jochen Frowein and Nico Krisch, 'Introduction to Chapter VII', in *The Charter of the United Nations: A Commentary*, ed. Bruno Simma. 2nd ed. (Oxford: Oxford University Press, 2002), 701, 711.

109   Hodges, *Western Sahara*, 223.

The Madrid Agreement is void for the different reasons that it conflicts with the peremptory norm of self-determination. Critically, the Agreement makes no provision for a referendum. Regularly from 1966 to 1973, the UN General Assembly had called on Spain to hold a referendum under UN auspices as the proper procedure to enable the indigenous population to freely exercise self-determination.[110] Self-determination thus required a free expression of the will of all Sahrawis, not only the *Yemaá*; and, in any event, there were serious doubts about both the representativeness, and ongoing capacity to function with all members, of the *Yemaá* during the relevant period.

Further, in the decolonization process Spain had responsibilities as the administering power of a Non-Self-Governing Territory to enable the exercise of Sahrawi self-determination. In the opinion of then UN Legal Counsel Hans Corell, the Madrid Agreement did not affect the international status of Western Sahara as a Non-Self-Governing Territory, or 'confer upon any of the signatories the status of administering Power, a status which Spain alone could not have unilaterally transferred'.[111] As a result, the Agreement conflicts with Sahrawi self-determination because it neither provides for a referendum to enable its full exercise, nor lawfully transfers the powers and responsibilities of the administering power to Morocco so as to enable decolonization through that UN Charter-based mechanism. Subsequent debate about who is now the administering power is immaterial;[112] the issue is whether the treaty was void due to conflict with a peremptory norm at the time of its conclusion.

Legal consequences of coercion and conflict with jus cogens

Under the law of treaties, a treaty procured by coercion or in conflict with *jus cogens* is 'void' *ab initio* under articles 52 and 53 of the VCLT. An ILC commentary on the draft provisions indicated that this language indicates that such treaties 'must be characterized as void rather than as voidable at the instance of the injured party'.[113] This is because, for instance, the prohibitions on the threat and use of force 'are rules of international law the observance of which is legally a matter of concern to every State'.[114] As such, a treaty procured by coercion is void *ab initio* '[e]ven if it were conceivable that after being liberated from the influence of a threat or of a use of force a State might wish to allow a treaty procured ... by such means'.[115]

Despite the plain textual meaning and drafting intention that such treaties are indeed 'void', articles 52 and 53 are still expressly subject to the procedure for impeaching the validity of a treaty under articles 65–68 of the VCLT, so that such treaties are, curiously, not automatically invalid.[116] Article 69 of the VCLT makes clear that a treaty is void only once its invalidity has

---

110 UNGA resolutions 2229 (XXI) (December 20, 1966); 2354 (XXII) (December 19, 1967); 2428 (XXIII) (December 18, 1968); 2591 (XXIV) (December 16, 1979); 2711 (XXV) (December 14, 1970); 2938 (XXVII) (December 14, 1972); 3162 (XXVIII) (December 14, 1973).

111 Corell Opinion, para. 6.

112 Morocco is not listed as administering power in the UN list of Non-Self-Governing Territories: http://www.un.org/en/decolonization/nonselfgovterritories.shtml. See also Corell Opinion, para. 7. Neither, however, is Spain, although it is listed as such in some UN Secretary General reports: Miguel, 'Spain's Legal Obligations', 243 (citing UN Docs. A61/70 (2006) and A/62/67 (2007)). Spain could be the de jure administering power in absentia; or its role as administering power may have lapsed due to ineffectiveness, the elapse of time, or (more doubtfully) its unilateral renunciation of its responsibilities.

113 ILC Commentary, 247.

114 Ibid.

115 Ibid. Any subsequent agreement between the same parties not tainted by coercion and to the same effect must also comply with other rules of the law on treaties, including conflict with peremptory norms under Article 53.

116 Annalisa Ciampi, 'Invalidity and Termination of Treaties and Rules of Procedure', in *The Law of Treaties* (see note 108), 360; see also Schröder, 'Treaties, Validity', para. 23; Alessandra Gianelli, 'Absolute Invalidity of Treaties and Their Non-Recognition by Third States', in *The Law of Treaties* (see note 108), 333. The procedure requires notification to the other parties; proposed measures of settlement; and a waiting period before implementing said measures. If another state objects, the parties must pursue the peaceful settlement of disputes in accordance with Article 33 of the UN Charter. If there is no solution within 12 months of the objection, in the case of Article 53

been established. One qualification in respect of a treaty that is 'void' is that a state cannot subsequently acquiesce to it (under article 45 of the VCLT) and thereby waive its right to seek to invalidate it.[117]

In relation to Western Sahara, none of Spain, Morocco or Mauritania has sought to impeach the validity of the Madrid Agreement on the basis of coercion or conflict with *jus cogens*. As noted, the subsequent conduct of the parties cannot amount to acquiescence to a treaty tainted by such defects, so as to waive the right to challenge the treaty in future. The fact remains that none of the parties has initiated the VCLT procedure and, on an orthodox view, the Madrid Agreement remains effective between the parties. Notwithstanding the earlier drafting intention signalled by the ILC, the VCLT as adopted enables a state, such as Spain, that is later liberated from the threat or use of force, to allow a treaty procured by coercion, simply by refraining from challenging its validity. As noted earlier, Spain was keen to decolonize Spanish Sahara; coercion hastened its timing and the form it took, but Spain had no interest in resuming its burden as administering power even if the coercion dissipated.

As regards the position of third states, non-parties to such a treaty cannot consider it invalid independently of the parties,[118] because article 42 of the VCLT provides that the validity of a treaty may only be impeached through the application of the VCLT, and the VCLT procedure only recognizes a right of states parties to seek to impeach validity. There is, however, some state practice indicating that third states have sometimes treated as invalid agreements which infringe self-determination. Thus UN General Assembly resolution 34/65 B (1979) described the Camp David Accords of 1978 as having 'no validity in so far as they purport to determine the future of the Palestinian people and of the Palestinian territories occupied by Israel since 1967'.[119] The resolution objected to the exclusion of the Palestinian Liberation Organization, 'the representative of the Palestinian people', from the negotiations, and provisions of the accords which 'ignore, infringe, violate or deny the inalienable rights of the Palestinian people'.

The resolution may indicate subsequent practice or agreement amongst the parties to the VCLT that third states (and international organizations) may claim that a treaty in conflict with a peremptory norm (or, equally, procured by coercion) is void, without depending on the parties to the treaty to impeach its validity pursuant to the VCLT procedures.[120] Alternatively, such an approach by third states could be based on qualifying the conclusion of such treaties as a wrongful act towards the international community as a whole,[121] given the interests at stake. The VCLT procedure for impeaching the validity of treaties has never been invoked in practice and it is unlikely that it reflects general international law rules.

Another example is the ICJ's *Case Concerning East Timor*, where Portugal alleged that Australia had violated the obligation to respect Portugal's powers as administrator of that Non-Self-Governing Territory by concluding the Timor Gap Treaty with Indonesia, to explore continental shelf resources.[122] While the case was found to be inadmissible because of Indonesia's non-participation, it focused the international community's disquiet about dealings in natural resources that conflicted with the right of self-determination.

---

     of the VCLT (*jus cogens*), a state may unilaterally initiate proceedings in the ICJ (or pursue arbitration by consent). As regards Article 52 (coercion), a state may invoke the Conciliation Commission under the VCLT.

117 Ciampi, 'Invalidity and Termination of Treaties'.
118 Gianelli, 'Absolute Invalidity of Treaties'.
119 UNGA resolution 34/65 B (November 29, 1979). See also UNGA resolution 33/28 A (1979); Gianelli, 'Absolute Invalidity of Treaties'; Ciampi, 'Invalidity and Termination of Treaties'.
120 Gianelli, 'Absolute Invalidity of Treaties', 336; see also Ciampi, 'Invalidity and Termination of Treaties', 330 (suggesting further that national courts are obliged to impeach the validity of such treaties).
121 Gianelli, 'Absolute Invalidity of Treaties'.
122 Treaty between Australia and the Republic of Indonesia on the Zone of Cooperation in an Area between the Indonesian Province of East Timor and Northern Australia (adopted December 11, 1989, entered into force February 9, 1991, [1991] ATS No. 9); *East Timor (Portugal v Australia)* [1995] ICJ Rep 90.

Regardless of whether the Madrid Agreement is void between the parties, or is considered void by third states, the position under the law of treaties must be carefully distinguished from the situation under IHL. As argued at the outset, a lack of genuine consent to the presence of foreign forces is an indispensable requirement of the existence of an occupation. In the absence of explicit guidance in IHL, reference to the grounds of invalidity under the law of treaties is a useful source of guidance in determining when consent under IHL may be considered free and genuine, or coerced or otherwise contaminated for conflicting with a peremptory norm. Both situations impermissibly taint the consent given under the law of treaties and under IHL.

However, under the law of treaties, the VCLT procedure must then be pursued to technically invalidate a treaty and render it definitively void. Under IHL, however, no such procedure is required to establish whether there exists a lack of genuine consent to foreign forces on either of these substantive grounds. The VCLT establishes a partially subjective regime that depends on a party choosing to impeach validity. In contrast, IHL is an objectively applicable legal regime which does not formally depend on a party electing to plead a lack of consent, or even a third state identifying a lack of consent. Rather, the lack of consent under IHL is an objective fact. The invalidation of a treaty in consequence of the VCLT procedure will certainly provide good evidence of a lack of genuine consent under IHL, but it is not indispensable in cases where a victim of aggression chooses not to impeach the treaty. The way in which treaty law substantively (not procedurally) assesses coercion or conflict with *jus cogens* is instead drawn upon as a source or analogue for the separate IHL assessment; it is a borrowing or transplant of principles, not an application of treaty law as *lex specialis*.

Final issues concerning Morocco's occupation

To summarize the argument so far, there are strong indications that Morocco's threat and use of force was an important factor in coercively procuring Spain's purported consent to the entry and presence of Moroccan forces under the Madrid Agreement. In addition, the consent given was not otherwise valid in that it conflicted with the peremptory norm of self-determination. The absence of free and valid consent to an Agreement authorizing the entry of foreign forces, the termination of Spanish administrative authority, and the substitution of Moroccan and Mauritanian authority can only be characterized as an occupation of foreign territory by a 'bloodless' invasion. This is so notwithstanding the many peculiarities of the situation, including Spain's mixed motives, which set it apart from orthodox occupations.

An issue remains whether the dispute over legal title to Western Sahara affects the application of IHL and the existence of an occupation there. In the *Israeli Wall Advisory Opinion*, Israel argued that the West Bank was not occupied because it was not sovereign Jordanian territory.[123] As such, despite there having been an armed conflict between Jordan and Israel in 1967, there was not an 'occupation of territory of a High Contracting Party' as required by common article 2(2) of the Geneva Conventions. By analogy, Morocco had contested Spain's title to Spanish Sahara prior to its entry in 1975, so that it might argue there was no occupation of the sovereign territory of another state.

Such an argument must be rejected for the reasons given in the *Israeli Wall Advisory Opinion*. The ICJ found that as long as an armed conflict has arisen between two states, IHL applies under common article 2(1) of the Geneva Conventions, 'in particular, in any territory occupied in the course of the conflict by one of the contracting parties' – and specifically including 'territories not falling under the sovereignty of one of the contracting parties'.[124] It observed that article 2 (2) emphasizes that an occupation can exist even if it meets no armed resistance, and is not

---

123 *Israeli Wall Advisory Opinion* (2004), paras. 91, 93.
124 Ibid., para. 95.

intended to restrict the scope of application of IHL. On this analysis, any dispute over legal title to Spanish Sahara is immaterial; an occupation arose there because of taking of territory held by Spain, even if there was no armed Spanish resistance. Further, as Corell's legal opinion notes, '[t]he Madrid Agreement did not transfer sovereignty over the Territory',[125] and Morocco cannot acquire sovereign title to Western Sahara by force or prolonged occupation.[126]

Regulation of natural resources under the law of occupation

The law of occupation provides a high level of protection for the proprietary interests of the inhabitants of occupied territory, while recognizing the military and administrative needs of the occupying power. First, it is forbidden to destroy private or public property (real or personal) in occupied territory 'except where ... rendered absolutely necessary by military operations'.[127] Secondly, it is prohibited to pillage (or steal) private or public property in occupied territory,[128] including, for instance, state companies.[129]

Thirdly, it is prohibited to confiscate moveable private property,[130] except military material,[131] or requisitions in kind and services 'for the needs of the army of occupation' and in proportion to the resources of the country.[132] Fourthly, moveable public property (including natural resources which have already been extracted or produced)[133] may only be requisitioned if it comprises military material;[134] or if it is for the needs of the occupying army (proportionate to the country's resources);[135] or if it could be used for military operations.[136] Taxes may also be levied to fund the military and administrative costs of occupation.[137]

Fifthly, the immovable public property of occupied territory (including natural resources *in situ*)[138] must be treated in accordance with the principle of trusteeship, for the benefit of the local inhabitants, and its capital must be safeguarded.[139] The occupant cannot appropriate,

---

125 Corell Opinion, para. 6.

126 Declaration on Principles of International Law Concerning Friendly Relations and Co-operation among States in accordance with the Charter of the United Nations, in UNGA resolution 2625 (October 24, 1970) (reflecting customary law); see also Benvenisti, *The International Law of Occupation*, 151–3.

127 Fourth Geneva Convention 1949, Article 53 and ICRC Commentary 1958 thereto; see also Hague Regulations 1907, Articles 46 and 56.

128 Fourth Geneva Convention 1949, Article 33 and ICRC Commentary; Hague Regulations 1907, Article 47; ICRC Customary IHL Study, rule 52.

129 *The IG Farben Trial: The Trial of Carl Krauch and 22 Others*, US Military Tribunal, Nuremberg, August 14, 1947– July 29, 1948, in UN War Crimes Commission, *Law Reports of Trials of War Criminals*, vol. X (London: HMSO, 1949), 1.

130 Hague Regulations 1907, Article 46. Private owners may, however, lawfully transact with the occupying power where their consent is voluntarily and not obtained by threats, intimidation, pressure, or exploitation: *The IG Farben Trial*, 46–7.

131 Hague Regulations 1907, Articles 46 and 53(2).

132 Ibid., Article 52; ICRC Customary IHL Study, rule 50.

133 See Iain Scobbie, 'Natural Resources and Belligerent Occupation: Perspectives from International Humanitarian and Human Rights Law', in *International Law and the Israeli-Palestinian Conflict: A Rights-based Approach to Middle East Peace*, ed. Susan Akram, Michael Dumper, Michael Lynk and Iain Scobbie (Abingdon: Routledge, 2011), 229, 234.

134 Hague Regulations 1907, Article 53(2). 'Munitions de guerre' includes arms, ammunition, transport, communications equipment, and other things that have a sufficiently close connection with direct military use, and does not include, for instance, crude oil in the ground: *NV de Bataafsche Petroleum Maatschappij v The War Damage Commission*, Singapore Court of Appeal, April 13, 1956 (in violation of Article 53 of the Hague Regulations 1907), *American Journal of International Law* 51 (1957): 802.

135 Hague Regulations 1907, Article 52.

136 Ibid., Article 53.

137 Ibid., Articles 48–9.

138 Scobbie, 'Natural Resources and Belligerent Occupation', 234.

139 Article 55 of the Hague Regulations 1907 provides that: 'The occupying State shall be regarded only as administrator and usufructuary of public buildings, real estate, forests, and agricultural estates belonging to the hostile State, and situated in the occupied country. It must safeguard the capital of these properties, and administer them in accordance with the rules of usufruct'. See also ICRC Customary IHL Study, rule 51.

WESTERN SAHARA

acquire title to, or sell such public assets,[140] but has the right to utilize the proceeds thereof for the benefit of the inhabitants.[141] Immovable public property may, however, be destroyed or seized where required by imperative military necessity.[142]

It is unlawful to appropriate or utilize foreign public property to benefit the occupying state's own economy or companies,[143] or its own civilian settlers transferred to occupied territory contrary to IHL.[144] The payment of a price does not relieve an appropriation of its unlawful character,[145] nor does the apparently legal form or purported voluntary character of a transaction.[146] Any transfers or dealings with property, rights and interests not justified by IHL are invalid,[147] including where a person or legal entity plans to subsequently acquire the property from those who unlawfully confiscated it.[148]

The principle of usufruct applies more strictly in the case of non-renewable than renewable natural resources,[149] given that the former is prone to exhaustion, particularly in cases of protracted occupation. An administrator should not exercise rights over immovable property in such a wasteful and negligent manner so as to seriously impair its value.[150] As such, an occupying power may continue to extract non-renewable resources at the ordinary pre-occupation rate, but may not abusively increase production of existing assets or permit new resource developments.[151]

Finally, the occupying power must respect, 'unless absolutely prevented', the laws in force at the time of occupying the territory.[152] This includes local property laws, insofar as such laws are consistent with international human rights law[153] and other relevant international laws. In the case of occupation of Non-Self-Governing Territories, this entails respect for the property laws of the legitimate administering power – Spain at the time of Morocco's occupation of Spanish Sahara – insofar as Spanish property laws respected the right of economic self-determination, and permanent sovereignty over natural resources, of the Sahrawi people.[154]

In the case law, numerous decisions have found violations of IHL by the exploitation of the resources of occupied territories without regard for the local economy,[155] including by state officials,[156] corporate actors[157] and individuals. In the Nazi occupation of Europe this included the

---

140 *In re Flick (US Military Tribunal at Nuremberg)*, 14 Ann Dig 266, 271; UK Ministry of Defence, *The Manual of the Law of Armed Conflict* (Oxford: Oxford University Press, 2004), 303. See Scobbie, 'Natural Resources and Belligerent Occupation', 233.

141 Scobbie, 'Natural Resources and Belligerent Occupation', 235.

142 ICRC Customary IHL Study, rules 50–51.

143 Koury, 'The European Community', 174; *The IG Farben Trial*, 50.

144 The transfer of civilian populations into occupied territory itself is unlawful under IHL: Fourth Geneva Convention 1949, Article 49(6); Rome Statute of the International Criminal Court, Article 8; see also *Israeli Wall Advisory Opinion* (2004), para. 120 (Israeli settlements in the West Bank violate international law).

145 *The IG Farben Trial*, 44.

146 Ibid., 45.

147 Ibid.

148 Ibid., 44.

149 Scobbie, 'Natural Resources and Belligerent Occupation', 234–5.

150 US Army Field Manual 27-10: The Law of Land Warfare, July 18, 1956, para. 402.

151 Scobbie, 'Natural Resources and Belligerent Occupation', 234–5; see, e.g., UK Ministry of Defence, *The Manual of the Law of Armed Conflict*, 303; *In re Krupp (US Military Tribunal at Nuremberg*, 1948), 15 Ann Dig 620, 622–5.

152 Hague Regulations 1907, Article 43.

153 Human rights law applies concurrently with IHL in armed conflict, including extraterritorially in occupied territory: *Israeli Wall Advisory Opinion* (2004), paras. 105–7.

154 On which, see Corell Opinion.

155 See, e.g., International Military Tribunal at Nuremberg, Judgment, 22 IMT 481, September 30, 1946; *In re Flick* (1947) US Military Tribunal at Nuremberg; *In re Krupp* (1948) US Military Tribunal at Nuremberg, in UN War Crimes Commission, (1949) 10 *Law Reports of Trials of War Criminals* 69; *In re Krauch* (1948) US Military Tribunal at Nuremberg (illegal transfer of shareholdings in private companies to industrialists of the occupying power).

156 E.g., German Finance Minister Schwerin von Krosigk responsible for the taking of oil, coal, ores and raw materials from Poland: UN War Crimes Commission, (1949) 14 *Law Reports of Trials of War Criminals* 784.

157 See, e.g., *The IG Farben Trial*; *In re Krupp*.

systematic requisitioning and taking to Germany of agricultural products, food, raw materials, tools, transportation, finished products and financial securities resulting in famine, inflation and black marketeering.[158] In the Japanese occupation in Asia it included the exploitation of immoveable oil reserves in existing oil production facilities for civilian and military use at home and abroad by the occupying power.[159] Iraq eventually paid compensation for the pillage of Kuwaiti state resources after the 1991 Gulf War.[160]

In *Congo v Uganda* (2005), the ICJ found Uganda responsible for pillage by failing to prevent its armed forces from looting, plundering and commercially exploiting Congolese resources including diamonds, gold, coffee, wildlife and forest agricultural products.[161] Such exploitation was unlawful because it was not carried out for the benefit of the local population.[162] Its focus on breaches of IHL may be significant for Western Sahara because the ICJ also determined (without explanation) that such exploitation did *not* constitute a violation of permanent sovereignty over natural resources. As mentioned earlier, much of the debate about the illegality of Moroccan dealings with Sahrawi resources has been based on Corell's legal opinion on the law governing Non-Self-Governing Territories, which in turn rests heavily on the principle of permanent sovereignty (in addition to self-determination).

Certain breaches of the above IHL prohibitions attract not only state responsibility but individual criminal liability. Pillage of private or public property is a war crime in international and non-international conflicts.[163] There is also a related war crime (in international conflicts only) of the 'extensive destruction and appropriation of property, not justified by military necessity and carried out unlawfully and wantonly'.[164] Any deprivation of property, including pillage, plunder, theft or requisition, is a form of appropriation.[165] Pillage and unlawful appropriation of property cover individual acts of looting for private gain as well as organized seizure and systematic exploitation of occupied territory.[166] In the case law, pillage has extended to receiving property illegally taken by others[167] (echoing common domestic offences such as receiving stolen goods). There is a further war crime in international and non-international conflict of 'destroying or seizing the enemy's property', where such property is protected by IHL and the destruction or seizure is not justified by military necessity.[168]

The contemporary modes of criminal participation for war crimes generally are reflected in article 25(3) of the Rome Statute of the ICC, namely to (a) commit an offence, (b) order, solicit or induce, (c) facilitate by aiding, abetting or otherwise assisting (including providing the means to commit), and (d) contribute to a crime by a group acting with a common purpose, with the aim of furthering the criminal activity or purpose, and with knowledge of

---

158   International Military Tribunal at Nuremberg, Judgment, 22 IMT 481, September 30, 1946.

159   *NV de Bataafsche Petroleum Maatschappij v The War Damage Commission.*

160   See UN Claims Commission for Kuwait, Report and Recommendations of Commissioners, UN Doc. S/A.22/1999/10 (1999).

161   *Congo v Uganda* (2005), paras. 222–50 (under the Hague Regulations 1907, Article 47; Fourth Geneva Convention, Article 33; and the African Charter on Human and Peoples' Rights, Article 21 (which requires restitution or compensation in the case or spoliation)).

162   *Congo v Uganda* (2005), para. 249.

163   ICC Rome Statute, Article 8(2)(b)(xvi) and (e)(v) (as a serious violation of the laws and customs of war).

164   Fourth Geneva Convention 1949, Article 147. Also ICC Rome Statute, Article 8(2)(a)(iv) (as a grave breach of the Geneva Conventions).

165   *Prosecutor v Blaskic*, ICTY Trial Chamber, ICTY-95-14-T, March 3, 2000), para. 184, and *Prosecutor v Delalic*, ICTY Trial Chamber, IT-96-21-T (November 16, 1998), para. 591, plunder was found to embrace all unlawful appropriation of property, including pillage. See also *Prosecutor v Kunarac*, ICTY Trial Chamber, ICTY-96-23/1-T, February 22, 2001, para. 15 (plunder and pillage are synonymous). 'Spoliation' and 'plunder' are also synonymous: *The IG Farben Trial*, 44.

166   *Prosecutor v Delalic* (1998), para. 590.

167   *Trial of Christian Baus*, Permanent Military Tribunal at Metz, Judgment of August 21, 1947, (1949) IX *War Crimes Reports* 68 (where a German caretaker was convicted for taking property from French farms which had been given to him by another German custodian of the farms).

168   Rome Statute, Article 8(2)(b)(xiii) (international conflict) and 8(2)(e)(xii) (non-international conflict).

the group's intention. There is, however, no state or corporate criminal liability under IHL, although state officials and corporate personnel may be held individually liable, and some national laws implementing war crimes in domestic law provide for corporate criminal liability.[169] Some national laws also apply additional modes of liability to war crimes, such as 'accessory after the fact' (by receiving, or assisting another to dispose of, the proceeds of crime),[170] or receiving stolen goods.

The application of the law of occupation is significant because it provides much greater protection in relation to natural resources than IHL applicable to non-international conflicts. While pillage of private or public property is also prohibited in the latter conflicts, there is no requirement of trusteeship over natural resources for the benefit of the local inhabitants. In ordinary civil wars, this is because the state is sovereign over the territory and has the right to make property laws, appropriate or nationalize natural resources, and exploit natural resources in exercising permanent sovereignty over them. In transnational non-international conflicts where the belligerent state is not the sovereign, powers are more limited (and still structured by the principles of self-determination and permanent sovereignty); but only under the law of occupation applicable in international conflicts are the full and detailed protections of the trusteeship principle applicable.

Conclusion: legal implications for exploitation of Sahrawi resources

Having established that Western Sahara has been occupied territory since early 1976, a number of general conclusions can be drawn below about the application of the law of occupation to dealings with its natural resources (including phosphate, oil, gas, minerals and fisheries). In sum, certain commercial dealings with Western Saharan natural resources are both prohibited by the international law of occupation and attract individual criminal responsibility as war crimes.

First, under IHL Morocco does not gain proprietary legal title to such resources, or the right to pass title to others, but is required to administer them on trust for the people of Western Sahara. The law of occupation accordingly cannot cure any legal defects in the purported transfer of legal title to phosphate and fishing rights by Spain to Morocco in the side deals to the Madrid Agreement (including a 65% share in Bou Craa mine). As discussed above, those agreements were entered into before the occupation was established but in principle were void by coercion and conflict with self-determination. While neither Spain nor Morocco has invoked the treaty law procedure to render them void, as noted earlier, non-party states must regard such agreements as legally ineffective to transfer property rights.

Secondly, Morocco must administer the natural resources of Western Sahara on trust for the benefit of the Sahrawi people and otherwise only to fulfil imperative military needs. As regards finite phosphate resources, IHL supposes that Morocco is entitled to maintain the pre-existing Spanish levels of production in 1975, with some leeway to account for both the pre-existing intended expansion of production (since the mine was then in its early stages of development) and the sustainable development of the Sahrawi people over the protracted period of the Moroccan occupation (of almost 40 years). Morocco is also not supposed to exploit new finite resources, such as by developing or licensing new mines or other minerals. Insofar as Morocco exploits or permits exploitation of renewable resources such as fisheries, this must be sustainable and not abusive, consistent with the inter-generational dimension of the trusteeship principle and concurrently applicable principles of international environmental law.[171]

---

169   E.g., Australian Criminal Code, s. 12.1.
170   See, e.g., Crimes Act 1914 (Australia), s. 6.
171   Stockholm Declaration of the UN Conference on the Human Environment (1972), principle 13; Rio Declaration on Environment and Development (1992), principle 15.

The critical legal question is whether Morocco's exploitation of resources is reasonably done for the benefit of the local inhabitants or otherwise out of military necessity. This requires a detailed factual assessment of the evidence as to how, to whom and for what purposes the Moroccan exploitation of Sahrawi natural resources accrues. This could include, for instance, evidence as to the profits made from resource exploitation, and whether these are repatriated into Morocco's general state revenues or quarantined for expenditure in Western Sahara; the level of expenditure on public administration, infrastructure and services, and whether this is linked to resources profits; and the costs of military occupation. Accurate information about some of these matters is not readily available on the public record. While a full assessment is therefore outside the scope of this article, some general considerations may be offered which cast grave doubt on the lawfulness of Moroccan resource exploitation.

First, the demographic balance in Western Sahara has been fundamentally altered by both the mass exodus of Sahrawi refugees and Morocco's sponsorship and facilitation of large-scale inward Moroccan migration. On one estimate, 400,000 people live in Moroccan-occupied Western Sahara, of which 250–300,000 are Moroccan civilian settlers and 100–150,000 are Sahrawis; in addition, there are perhaps 160,000 Moroccan military and police personnel.[172] In 1999, MINURSO identified 86,425 eligible Sahrawi voters for the referendum; and estimates of the Algerian refugee camp population vary from 90,000 to 155,000.

The key legal point is that profits from the exploitation of natural resources may only be lawfully directed under IHL to benefiting the indigenous inhabitants of occupied territory. That means the local population at the time the occupation is established, adjusted for subsequent natural growth. As a result, the fruits of natural resources cannot be spent on public administration, services and infrastructure to benefit Moroccan settlers (who comprise the majority of the territory's current population), or the military protection of such settlers. Employment opportunities in resource developments must also exclusively benefit Sahrawis, not settlers. Further, profits must be held on trust to benefit all Sahrawi people, including those in the liberated zone (perhaps 20–30,000 people) and in the Algerian and Mauritanian refugee camps (up to 160,000 people), or, at a minimum, the 86,425 registered by MINURSO. Since most of these Sahrawis are outside Morocco's jurisdiction, their share of the profits from resource exploitation should be held on trust and not expended.

Secondly, while the trusteeship principle does not require the consent of the inhabitants to resource exploitation, consent or lack thereof may be a relevant factual indicator of whether the trustee is discharging its obligation. Polisario, as the internationally recognized representative of the Sahrawi people, has resolutely opposed Moroccan resource exploitation, and even issued resource exploration licences of its own to counter Morocco's; and there does not appear to be any legitimate mechanism within Western Sahara for local consultation.

Thirdly, Morocco denies that it is the occupying power of occupied territory. As such, it necessarily does not, and cannot in good faith, argue that its exploitation of resources is justified by imperative military necessity under IHL. The benefits of the law of occupation run with the burdens, and a state cannot take advantage of the law if it denies that it applies. Further, even if Morocco seeks to rely upon its IHL powers as occupant, any utilization of resources to support its military needs cannot be out of proportion to the capacity of the local economy to bear such imposition. In other words, even if Morocco's military costs exceeded the profits from resource exploitation, Morocco may only utilize an amount in proportion to the capacity of the local economy, precisely so as not to deprive the inhabitants of their means of sustenance and their proprietary rights as beneficiaries. The occupant cannot fund its war effort by decimating

---

172   Norwegian Refugee Council, *Western Sahara: Occupied Countries, Displaced People*, NRC Reports, Issue 2, 2008, 4. The statistics are, however, uncertain. According to the UN, the total population of Western Sahara was 549,000 people in 2012: https://data.un.org/CountryProfile.aspx?crName=Western%20Sahara.

the local economy. Morocco's military needs must also be assessed in light of the existence of a ceasefire since 1991 and the cessation of active hostilities.

Fourthly, there is some historical evidence that Morocco's occupation of Western Sahara was partly motivated by its concerns in the 1970s about the adverse effects of Spanish phosphate mining on the domestic Moroccan phosphate industry. This was at a time when the Moroccan economy relied significantly on phosphate exports and the global commodity price had decreased markedly, undermining the Moroccan economy. The exploitation of resources in occupied territory is not permitted to improve the position of the occupant's economy.

As regards individual criminal liability, there are implications for a range of actors, depending on the nature of particular dealings with Western Saharan resources. Moroccan state and corporate personnel are most likely liable for the ordering and commission of war crimes. The crime of pillage is constituted by the appropriation of property; the intent to deprive the owner of it, and to take it for private or personal use (not out of military necessity); the absence of consent by the owner; and the existence of an armed conflict of which the perpetrator knew.[173] The crime of 'extensive destruction and appropriation of property' requires an appropriation of property that the perpetrator was aware is protected by IHL, that is extensive and deliberate, not justified by military necessity, and where the perpetrator was aware an international conflict existed.[174] The crime of 'destroying or seizing the enemy's property' requires that the property belongs to the enemy and is protected by IHL, the perpetrator was aware of the facts as to the property's status and the existence of a conflict, and the destruction or seizure is not justified by military necessity.[175]

The directors and employees of foreign companies that deal with Morocco and Moroccan companies in relation to the natural resources of Western Sahara may also bear individual criminal liability for war crimes. Contracting with Moroccan companies to buy and import phosphate, for instance, could variously amount to soliciting or inducing the commission of a war crime;[176] facilitating by aiding, abetting or otherwise assisting in a war crime (including providing the means, such as finance or orders to purchase, to commit it);[177] or contributing to a crime by a group acting with a common purpose, with the aim of furthering the criminal purpose, and with knowledge of the group's intention.[178] In general, perpetrators must intend their conduct to assist in the commission of the crime by another and be aware of the elements of the war crime. It is unnecessary, however, to show that such conduct caused another to commit the crime, or that the other person has been convicted of an offence.

The characterization of resource exploitation in Western Sahara as war crimes also has implications for all states. Under the Geneva Conventions of 1949, states parties have a duty to respect IHL and to ensure respect by others.[179] Specifically, states must establish universal criminal jurisdiction over war crimes, search for suspects and prosecute or extradite them.[180] No such obligations exist in relation to the legal principles governing Non-Self-Governing Territories, self-determination, or permanent sovereignty over natural resources. This is why the application of IHL and the law of occupation to Western Sahara matters most: it enables the punishment of those who unlawfully exploit others' natural resources, and in so doing may deter future wrongful conduct by states and corporations alike.

---

173 ICC, Elements of Crimes: Rome Statute, Article 8(2)(b)(xvi) and (e)(v), UN Doc. PCNICC/2000/1/Add.2 (2000).
174 Ibid., Article 8(2)(a)(iv).
175 Ibid., Article 8(2)(b)(xiii) and 8(2)(e)(xii).
176 Rome Statute, Article 25(3)(b).
177 Ibid., Article 25(3)(c).
178 Ibid., Article 25(3)(d).
179 See also *Israel Wall Advisory Opinion* (2004), para. 163(D).
180 See, e.g., Fourth Geneva Convention 1949, Article 146(1)–(2).

The prosecution of war crimes in domestic courts is likely to be the only practical means of bringing to justice those responsible for the illegal exploitation of Western Saharan resources. While such crimes also fall within the substantive criminal jurisdiction of the ICC, as outlined above, the ICC is unlikely to be able to exercise jurisdiction to prosecute. ICC jurisdiction is primarily territorial and largely depends on the consent of state parties to the Rome Statute,[181] but Morocco is not a party to it, and only states can become parties, thus ruling out consent by Polisario. Technically the UN Security Council could still refer the situation to the ICC prosecutor[182] – but that is highly unlikely given the close ties with Morocco by two veto-wielding permanent members, the US and France. Political will is ultimately required to effectively bring to justice the corporate thieves and pillagers who plunder the natural resources belonging to others.

Disclosure statement

No potential conflict of interest was reported by the author.

---

181 Rome Statute, Articles 12–14.
182 Ibid., Article 13(b).

The hidden cost of phosphate fertilizers: mapping multi-stakeholder supply chain risks and impacts from mine to fork

Dana Cordell, Andrea Turner and Joanne Chong

Institute for Sustainable Futures, University of Technology Sydney, Sydney, NSW, Australia

Without phosphorus, we could not produce food. Farmers need access to phosphate fertilizers to achieve the high crop yields needed to feed the world. Yet growing global demand for phosphorus could surpass supply in the coming decades, and the world currently largely relies on non-renewable phosphate rock that is mined in only a few countries. Morocco alone controls 75% of the remaining reserves, including those in the conflict territory of Western Sahara. While some argue that the market will take care of any scarcity, the market price of phosphate fertilizers fails to account for far-ranging negative impacts. Drawing on multi-stakeholder supply chain risk frameworks, the article identifies a range of negative impacts, including the exploitation and displacement of the Saharawi people, the destruction of aquatic ecosystems by nutrient pollution, and jeopardizing future generations' ability to produce food. This paper fills a crucial gap in understanding phosphorus impacts by mapping and discussing the nature of phosphorus supply chain risks, and the transmission of such risks to different stakeholder groups. It also identifies a range of potential interventions to mitigate and manage those risks. In addition, the paper highlights that while risks are diverse, from geopolitical to ecological, those groups adversely affected are also diverse – including the Saharawi people, farmers, businesses, food consumers and the environment. Potential risk mitigation strategies range from resource sparing (using phosphorus more sparingly to extend the life of high quality rock for ourselves and future generations), to resource diversification (sourcing phosphorus from a range of ethical sources to reduce dependence on imported phosphate, as a buffer against supply disruptions, and preferencing those sources with lower societal costs), and sharing the responsibility for these costs and consequences.

1 Introduction

The importance of phosphorus is well established: phosphorus underpins our ability to produce food anywhere in the world.[1] Like water, oxygen and carbon, phosphorus is a fundamental building block of life and there is no substitute for phosphorus in food production. The positive impact of applying phosphate fertilizers is evidenced by high crop yields compared to their unfertilized counterparts (Figure 1).[2] Higher crop yields in general mean greater agricultural productivity, higher returns for the farmer, increased food available to feed populations, and increased food security. Indeed, the use of phosphate fertilizers has contributed to feeding billions of people over the past century.[3]

---

1 A.E. Johnston, *Soil and Plant Phosphate* (Paris: International Fertilizer Industry Association, 2000).
2 K. Syers, A.E. Johnston, and D. Curtin, 'Efficiency of Soil and Fertilizer Phosphorus Use: Reconciling Changing Concepts of Soils Phosphorus Behaviour with Agronomic Information', *FAO Fertilizer and Plant Nutrition Bulletin* 18 (Rome: Food and Agriculture Organization of the United Nations, 2008).
3 IFPRI, *Green Revolution: Curse or Blessing?* (Washington, DC: International Food Policy Research Institute, 2002).

Figure 1. Agricultural test field indicating the results of phosphate fertilizer use on crop cover. Source: Tennessee Valley Authority, Franklin D. Roosevelt Presidential Library and Museum.

While the importance of phosphorus is well known within the agricultural sector, the negative impacts of the whole phosphorus fertilizer supply chain from production to end use are not fully accounted for, or well understood.[4] The world's agriculture today relies on phosphorus sourced from finite phosphate rock reserves mined in only a few countries. Much of this is inefficiently used and is lost or wasted along the supply chain, largely ending up in rivers and oceans where it causes pollution.[5]

The phosphorus supply chain spans the system of phosphorus use in the global food system, from mine to field to fork. It is highly globalized and includes sectors and processes related to mining, processing and trade of phosphate rock; production and trade of phosphate fertilizers; application of fertilizers in agriculture to crops and pastures; harvesting of phosphorus-containing crops; production, processing and distribution of food; consumption of food; and, finally, the management of phosphorus-containing wastewater, food waste and eutrophied waters (Figure 2).[6]

From a single-stakeholder perspective, each actor in the phosphorus supply chain has a specific objective, such as commercial farmers efficiently converting natural capital (phosphorus)

---

4 M. Bekunda et al., 'Phosphorus and food production', UN*EP Yearbook: Emerging Issues in Our Global Environment* (Paris: United Nations Environment Programme, 2011); D. Cordell and S. White, 'Life's Bottleneck: Sustaining the World's Phosphorus for a Food Secure Future', *Annual Review of Environment and Resources* 39, no. 1 (2014): 161–88, http://www.annualreviews.org/doi/full/10.1146/annurev-environ-010213-113300.
5 Cordell & White. Life's Bottleneck.
6 D. Cordell, J.-O. Drangert, and S. White, 'The Story of Phosphorus: Global Food Security and Food for Thought', *Global Environmental Change* 19, no. 2 (2009): 292–305, http://linkinghub.elsevier.com/retrieve/pii/S095937800800099X; J.J. Schroder et al., 'Sustainable Use of Phosphorus', Rep.357, European Union Tender ENV.B.1/ETU/2009/0025 (Wageningen, Netherlands: Plant Research International, 2010).

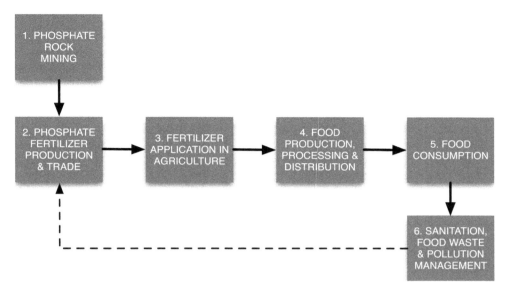

Figure 2. Key sectors directly involved in the phosphorus supply chain, from mining to application in agriculture through to environmental management. Arrows indicate material flows. A minimal amount of phosphorus reuse from organic waste sources is also indicated by the dotted line.

into financial capital (agricultural commodities) through productive farming. However, in this paper we take a multi-stakeholder, sustainable systems and food security perspective, where the fundamental objective of the phosphorus supply chain is to ensure that farmers have sufficient access to phosphorus to efficiently produce food for the global population while ensuring ecosystem integrity and supporting farmer livelihoods.[7] By taking this approach, we reveal a vast and diverse array of negative impacts, the 'sustainability costs', associated with mining and using phosphate rock for food production. Together, these impacts compromise humanity's ability to meet this fundamental objective.

This paper identifies the nature of the associated risks to different stakeholder groups, laying the conceptual foundations for why the sustainability costs associated with phosphate rock, from mine to fertilizer application, through to the dinner table need to be considered. However, it does not attempt to quantify these costs or impacts in monetary terms for reasons explained below.[8] Examples of interventions to mitigate and manage such risks are provided, ranging from market-based to social in nature.

2 Valuing the invaluable and the uncertain

In this section we briefly introduce two approaches to valuing impacts – monetizing approaches and risk-based approaches and explain why the latter is more appropriate in the case of the phosphorus supply chain.

2.1 *Monetizing approaches*

The need for assessing and quantifying impacts is not unique to phosphorus. Quantifying impacts in monetary terms is a long-established convention for weighing up costs and benefits to inform

---

7 D. Cordell, 'The Story of Phosphorus: Sustainability Implications of Global Phosphorus Scarcity for Food Security' Doctoral thesis, no. 509 (Linköping: Linköping University Press, 2010), http://liu.diva-portal.org/smash/record.jsf?pid=diva2:291760.
8 See section 2.

decision-making. With theoretical foundations in welfare economics,[9] the use of cost–benefit analysis and the net-present-value metric is the standard and in many cases regulated practice[10] for public policy-makers to test whether a policy, law or program should proceed. This approach considers whether the 'monetary sum' of positive impacts outweigh that of the negative impacts.

There are well-established taxonomies of methods for quantifying impacts in monetary terms, particularly those adapted from ecosystem services frameworks which link ecology and economics but are applicable to a wide range of other impacts.[11] These methods include 'revealed preference' approaches, which use price in associated or proxy markets; cost-based approaches, which consider the cost of measures to replace, mitigate or avoid damage; and stated preference approaches, which are based on survey and other methods that aim to elicit responses from a representative group to determine how much they would be willing to pay to avoid damage, or how much payment they would be willing to receive to bear the impact.

Such methods could be used to quantify the monetary impacts of some of the costs and risks associated with global phosphorus production and use. For example, the costs and risks associated with an algal bloom, based on the values frameworks established in the ecosystem services theory and practice,[12] include loss of a source of irrigation water; damage to a fish spawning ground; reductions in tourism; as well as lost 'intrinsic' value of ecosystems and nature. Methods to monetize these impacts include lost production value from agriculture and commercial fisheries; travel cost method for reductions in tourism; and a stated preference method to survey recreational fishers and the community more generally about existence value.

Many of these methods enable quantification of impacts that are 'negative externalities' – that is, those not taken into account in the direct market transactions in the supply chain of the global phosphorus industry. It is well accepted, at least in theory, that inclusion of externalities in decision-making is critical to ensure welfare is maximized. Valuation techniques enable environmental, social and cultural values and impacts to be considered 'on a par' with the more conventional production and consumption values, and have been successfully used to make the case for conservation and wise management of natural resources.[13] However, a drawback of focusing only on the monetization of impacts is the array of complexities and uncertainties in monetizing impacts, particularly those that are not associated with direct production or consumption. Methodological criticisms, particularly of non-market approaches, the cost of conducting robust stated-preference studies, and ethical debates about commodification,[14] can sideline the intent of highlighting these very impacts.

Furthermore, monetizing approaches, in practice, often draw attention to the quantification of a specific level (or range) of cost or impact when, in reality, the amounts and likelihoods are uncertain. Hence despite the wide-ranging application of monetary decision-making frameworks, this paper does not deal with valuation, but rather draws on more appropriate frameworks to identify impacts and risks.

---

9   N. Kaldor, 'Welfare Proposition of Economics and Interpersonal Comparisons of Utility', *Economic Journal* 49 (1939): 549–52.

10 Australian Government, *The Australian Government Guide to Regulation* (Canberra: Department of the Prime Minister and Cabinet, Commonwealth of Australia, 2014); OECD, *Cost–Benefit Analysis and the Environment: Recent Developments* (Paris: Organisation for Economic Co-operation and Development, 2006).

11 TEEB, 'The Economics of Ecosystems and Biodiversity: Mainstreaming the Economics of Nature: A Synthesis of the Approach, Conclusions and Recommendations of TEEB' (2010).

12 Ibid.

13 Millennium Ecosystem Assessment, 'Ecosystems and Human Well-being: Wetlands and Water Synthesis' (Washington D.C: World Resources Institute, 2005). Available: http://www.millenniumassessment.org/documents/document.358.aspx.pdf

14 C. Spash, S. Stagl, and M. Getzner, 'Exploring Alternatives for Environmental Valuation', in *Alternatives for Environmental Valuation*, ed. M. Getzner, C. Spash, and S. Stagl (Abingdon: Routledge, 2005).

2.2 *Assessing and managing risks*

Risk management approaches are diverse and are applied in a myriad of scales and fields, including assessing and managing organizational risks; epidemiological studies on public health risks; disaster risk management; negotiating risk-sharing in contracts; and management of corporate financial and reputational risks. However, all approaches aim to identify and manage risks to better meet objectives, and many of the underlying principles are the same, including that risk management should be systematic, based on the best available information, inform decision-making, and create and protect value.[15]

Supply chain risk literature typically draws attention to the identification and management of external or internal business risks that can adversely affect a firm's operational, market or financial performance.[16] Internal business risks can include process and control risks, while risks internal to the whole supply chain can include demand and supply-side risks.[17] Environmental risks external to both a firm and a supply chain can also adversely affect a firm's performance. Increasingly long and global supply chains, coupled with growing scarcity of critical resources, means effective management of supply chain risks is becoming increasingly important.[18]

Healthy supply chains are agile and proactive, and can both respond to and pre-empt potential disruptions. Because phosphorus is critical and non-substitutable in food production, it will be essential for supply chain managers to minimize supply disruptions to ensure customers (farmers) have access to fertilizers. However, in their typology of natural resource scarcity, Bell et al. warn that there is little research on mitigation strategies for supply chain managers to deal with the potential impacts of resource scarcity.[19] They also conclude that 'as resources become increasingly scarce … the value of interorganisational connections may play a significant role in a firm's ability to secure and use scarce resources in a cost- and time-efficient manner'.[20]

While there are numerous supply chain risk management frameworks related to natural resources and/or the agri-food system, few take a multi-stakeholder and systems approach. Matopoulos et al. comprehensively reviewed 96 papers related to resource-efficient supply chains (RESC) in the agri-food sector.[21] The authors identify four key characteristics of effective RESCs: resource awareness, resource sensitivity, resource sparing and resource responsiveness. Further, their framework captures current gaps and future needs, identifying a lack of comprehensive assessment linking all stages of an agri-food supply chain, and a need to better link different actors in the chain and consequently collaboratively identify and manage risks.

In this paper we draw from the World Bank's RapAgRisk Assessment conceptual framework to highlight phosphorus supply chain risks.[22] We choose this framework by way of example because, importantly, it takes a multi-stakeholder and systems approach to supply chain risk management. Taking an inherently systems approach to risk management involves multiple sectors and actors and implies the need for collective action to mitigate and manage risks. Causal links and influences

---

15 International Organization for Standardization, 'ISO 310000:2009 Risk Management – Principles and Guidelines' (2009).

16 R. Narasimhan and S. Talluri, 'Perspectives on Risk Management in Supply Chains', *Journal of Operations Management* 27, no. 2 (2009): 114–18.

17 M. Christopher et al., 'Approaches to Managing Global Sourcing Risk', *Supply Chain Management: An International Journal* 16, no. 2 (2001): 67–81.

18 J.E. Bell et al., 'A Natural Resource Scarcity Typology: Theoretical Foundations and Strategic Implications for Supply Chain Management', *Journal of Business Logistics* 33, no. 2 (2012): 158–66; Christopher et al., 'Approaches to Managing Global Sourcing Risk'.

19 Bell et al., 'A Natural Resource Scarcity Typology.

20 Ibid., 163.

21 A. Matopoulos, A. Barros, and J.G.A.J. Van der Vorst, 'Resource-Efficient Supply Chains: A Research Framework', *Literature Review and Research Agenda, Supply Chain Management: An International Journal* 20, no. 2 (2015): 218–36.

22 S. Jaffee, P. Siegel, and C. Andrews, 'Rapid Agricultural Supply Chain Risk Assessment, A Conceptual Framework', *Agriculture and Rural Development Discussion Paper* 47 (Washington D.C: The World Bank, 2010).

between sectors through the supply chain, such as the transfer of risks between stakeholder groups, are also important. Jaffee et al.'s framework provides a systematic approach to identify risks, the severity of impact, and risk management strategies that can be actions by individual or collective stakeholders within the supply chain, or by external stakeholders such as policy-makers. The framework enables the identification and assessment of risks from different stakeholder perspectives. Rather than solely a conceptual academic framework, RapAgRisk aims to provide practical guidance on how to systematically identify key vulnerabilities and priority actions to reduce risks and loss in a given agricultural commodity system.

3 Approach

In the remainder of this paper, while taking an interdisciplinary perspective, we use the RapAgRisk framework to identify and typologize a range of phosphorus supply chain risks from different stakeholder perspectives, and different stages in the supply chain. To do this, we draw on a synthesis of our own and others' extensive body of sustainable phosphorus research.[23] This research identifies multiple dimensions of phosphorus scarcity – physical, geopolitical, economic, institutional, managerial[24] – and the context-specific interactions and consequences in a phosphorus vulnerability assessment framework,[25] in addition to integrated sustainable phosphorus measures and governance structures[26] and other work in this new and rapidly growing field related to geopolitics,[27] ecological impacts[28] and fertilizer market dynamics.[29]

We also draw from and adapt a 'sustainability cost framework' that we developed for the water service provision sector.[30] This framework has been developed and applied through extensive work conducted in the water industry to identify and assess the broader sustainability costs of supply- and demand-side options in water service provision decision-making.[31] In this paper we define 'sustainability costs' as negative impacts – that is, loss of social, financial, physical or psychological capital to any stakeholder internal or external to the phosphorus supply chain as a consequence of supply chain activities. 'Risk' is defined as the likelihood and consequence of those negative impacts.

23 E.g. Cordell and White, 'Life's Bottleneck'.
24 Cordell et al., 'The Story of Phosphorus'.
25 D. Cordell and T.S.S. Neset, 'Phosphorus Vulnerability: A Qualitative Framework for Assessing the Vulnerability of National and Regional Food Systems to the Multi-dimensional Stressors of Phosphorus Scarcity', *Global Environmental Change* 24 (January 2014): 108–22, http://linkinghub.elsevier.com/retrieve/pii/S0959378013001970; D. Cordell et al., 'Adapting to Future Phosphorus Scarcity: Investigating Potential Sustainable Phosphorus Measures and Strategies', Phase II of the Australian Sustainable Phosphorus Futures project, prepared by Institute for Sustainable Futures, University of Technology Sydney (Canberra: Rural Industries Research and Development Corporation, Australian Government, 2014); P-FUTURES website: Transforming the Way Cities Secure Food & Water through Innovative Phosphorus Governance; 'Transformations to Sustainability' Programme, Future Earth, International Social Science Council, http://www.p-futurescities.net/.
26 E.g. D. Cordell and S. White, 'Sustainable Phosphorus Measures: Strategies and Technologies for Achieving Phosphorus Security', *Agronomy* 3, no. 1 (2013): 86–116; D. Cordell and S. White, 'Phosphorus Security: Global Non-governance of a Critical Resource for Food Security', in *Edward Elgar Encyclopedia of Global Environmental Politics and Governance*, ed. P. Pattberg and F. Fariborz Zelli (Cheltenham, UK & Northampton, MA, USA: Edward Elgar, 2015).
27 E.g. HCSS, *Risks and Opportunities in the Global Phosphate Rock Market: Robust Strategies in Times of Uncertainty* (The Hague: Hague Centre for Strategic Studies, 2012).
28 E.g. W. Dodds et al., 'Eutrophication of U.S. Freshwaters: Analysis of Potential Economic Damages', *Environmental Science & Technology*. 43, no. 1 (2009): 12–19.
29 E.g. IFA, 'Food Prices and Fertilizer Markets: Factors influencing variations in fertilizer market conditions' (Paris: International Fertilizer Industry Association, June 2011); IFDC, 'Fertilizer Supply and Costs in Africa' (Chemonics International Inc. and the International Center for Soil Fertility and Agricultural Development, 2007).
30 S. Fane, A. Turner, and C. Mitchell, 'The Secret Life of Water Systems: Least Cost Planning beyond Demand Management', in *2nd IWA Leading-Edge on Sustainability in Water-Limited Environments*, ed. M.B. Beck and A. Speers (London: IWA Publishing, 2006), 35–41.
31 Ibid.; A. Turner et al., 'Guide to Demand Management and Integrated Resource Planning' (paper prepared for the National Water Commission and the Water Services Association of Australia, Inc., at Institute for Sustainable Futures, University of Technology Sydney, 2010).

Due to the diversity and complexity of risks and impacts identified in section 4, we subsequently highlight key stakeholder groups that are impacted by risks occurring at different stages of the phosphorus supply chain, and the transmission of impacts. Finally, we provide examples of potential risk-mitigating measures to demonstrate a diverse range of interventions. The intention of this paper is not to provide a complete identification and management assessment, but rather to open up the debate and make the case for such a comprehensive and collaborative assessment as a way towards better managing phosphorus for food security.

4 Typology of phosphorus supply chain risks and impacts

The international market price of phosphate reflects its economic value as a fertilizer, and, like many other resources, this does not reflect the full sustainability cost of mining and using phosphorus. This section illustrates the spectrum of costs and risks associated with phosphorus fertilizers. These costs and risks are highly diverse, ranging from geopolitical to ecological, global to local, short to long term and with positive to negative impacts, as discussed below.

In Figure 3 we indicate a range of direct costs and externalities to different stakeholders in the phosphorus supply chain, which are described in the subsequent text. Importantly, consistent with Jaffee et al., this takes a whole-of-society approach, as opposed to a narrow single stakeholder perspective.[32]

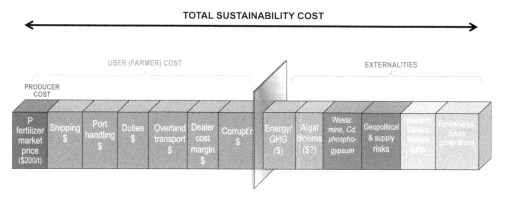

Figure 3. The full sustainability costs associated with phosphate fertilizers, indicating costs to the user (farmer), plus externalities affecting a wider set of stakeholders that are not reflected in transactional prices along the supply chain – environmental and social costs.
Source: Adapted to phosphorus from our sustainability cost framework developed for water (S. Fane, A. Turner, and C. Mitchell, 'The Secret Life of Water Systems: Least Cost Planning beyond Demand Management', in *2nd IWA Leading-Edge on Sustainability in Water-Limited Environments*, ed. M.B. Beck and A. Speers (London: IWA Publishing, 2006).

Externalities are defined as those impacts resulting from transactions that affect third parties not involved in the primary transaction (and those impacts are not themselves traded in markets). Some of these externalities can be costed and internalized, such as life-cycle energy ($/tonne) or algal blooms (as discussed in section 2). For others it may not be appropriate to monetize, but rather require other means of valuing or comparing, such as qualitative risk assessments or multi-criteria assessments that involve deliberative stakeholder engagement, as has been used in the water industry.[33]

---

32 Jaffee et al., 'Rapid Agricultural Supply Chain Risk Assessment'.
33 S. White et al., 'Putting the Economics in its Place: Decision-making in an Uncertain Environment', in *Deliberative Ecological Economics*, ed. C. Zografos and R. Howarth (New Dehli: Oxford University Press, 2008), 80–106.

According to the RapAgRisk framework, major risk categories facing agricultural supply chains include market-related risks, biological and environmental risks, political risks, public policy and institutional risks, weather-related risks and natural disasters, logistical and infrastructural risks, and management and operational risks.[34] In sections 4.1 to 4.4 we use the first four categories to exemplify a range of phosphorus supply chain risks. Overlaps with both logistical and infrastructural risks and management and operational risks are also identified. Implications for specific stakeholders are then highlighted in Table 1 and section 5. Examples are also provided throughout.

4.1   *Market-based risks*

Market-based risks related to fertilizers range from price volatility of raw materials, to high fertilizer distribution costs for some farmers. The phosphate price is affected by typical supply–demand market dynamics and future contracts at negotiated prices with producers.[35] In 2008, the price of phosphate spiked 800% (Figure 4). While there were multiple interrelated causes for this spike – ranging from unforecast demand, capacity constraints, increases in input costs, unfavourable exchange rates and possible speculation[36] – it was largely farmers, the end users, who were affected. While the degree of impact depended in part on farmer purchasing power, it resulted in reduced net profit and/or loss of crop yields.

The farm gate price of fertilizers represents the total cost to the farmer, including the raw fertilizer product price (FOB[37]), plus other distribution costs, such as shipping, port handling, duties, inland transport costs and dealer cost margins (Figure 5). These non-product costs can be highly variable across regions due to geography, state of road and rail infrastructure, local market dynamics, logistics inefficiencies and corruption.[38] This therefore also represents a logistics and infrastructure risk. This higher input cost puts land-locked farmers at greater risk and disadvantage. For example, farmers in some land-locked African countries can pay 2–5 times as much for the same fertilizer product as European farmers, or even countries like Thailand that have more efficient distribution and transparency.[39]

4.2   *Environmental and biological risks*

Environmental and biological risks occur at local to global scales, such as toxic waste generated during fertilizer mining and production, widespread water pollution from farm nutrient runoff, or the global life cycle energy cost of producing and transporting fertilizers.

As with most supply chains, waste is generated at each stage of the phosphorus supply chain. However, for phosphorus this is relatively high: globally, 80% of phosphorus is lost or wasted from mine to fork.[40] These inefficiencies also arise from management-related risks. During mining, phosphorus losses are variable, though can be as high as 30%.[41] As lower grade and more difficult to reach phosphate reserves are mined, more waste is generated per tonne of

---

34   Jaffee et al., 'Rapid Agricultural Supply Chain Risk Assessment'.
35   IFA 'Feeding the Earth: Fertilizers and Global Food Security' (Paris: International Fertilizer Industry Association, May 2008).
36   See section 5 and Figure 7.
37   'Free on Board' at port of loading.
38   IFDC, 'Fertilizer Supply and Costs in Africa'.
39   Ibid.; A. Runge-Metzger, 'Closing the Cycle: Obstacles to Efficient P Management for Improved Global Food Security', in *Phosphorus in the Global Environment: Transfers, Cycles and Management*, ed. H. Tiessen, SCOPE 54 (Chichester: Wiley, 1995), 27–42.
40   Cordell et al., 'The Story of Phosphorus'.
41   M. Prud'homme, 'World Phosphate Rock Flows, Losses and Uses' (paper presented at International Fertilizer Industry Association Phosphates International Conference, Brussels, March 22–24, 2010).

Table 1. Phosphorus supply-chain risks and examples of transmission of impacts to stakeholder groups (*indicates indirect stakeholders).

Location of risk in supply chain (where risk occurs)	Risk and consequences	Stakeholders impacted and nature of expected impact						
		Phosphate industry	Western Sahara*	Farmers	Food consumers	Policy-makers*	Environmental representatives*	Future generations*
1. Phosphate rock mining	**Political risk**: five countries controlling 85% of world's phosphate. Political instability or deliberate market interventions in a producing country can lead to supply disruptions and price fluctuations	Supply delays in the fertilizer production and distribution chain, leading to monetary losses	Resource curse leading to increased social inequity	Farmers unable to afford or access P fertilizers, leading to reduced productivity; in 2008 there were farmer riots and suicides in some countries	Food prices can increase as a result, leading to increased food insecurity	National security risk for importing countries leading to reduced agricultural productivity, affecting both the economy and domestic food security		
	Political risk: Morocco's occupation of Western Sahara and the territory's phosphate rock	Reputation risk for phosphate producers and importers of 'conflict phosphates'	Financial, physical and psychological exploitation of Saharawi people who have legal right to their land and phosphate	Farmers knowingly or unknowingly supporting mining in an illegally occupied territory	Food consumers knowingly or unknowingly supporting mining in an illegally occupied territory			
	Environmental risk: depletion a finite resource, creating an intergenerational risk for future generations.	The quality and accessibility of future reserves are lower than those currently under production, leading to increased production costs in the future						Future generations don't have the same access to a critical resource (or a say in how it is managed today), hence their food security is threatened
2. Fertilizer production and trade	**Environmental risk**: stockpiling radioactive byproduct, phosphogypsum						Toxic material can potentially leach from stacked stockpiles and contaminate drinking water or ecologically sensitive water bodies	

(*Continued*)

Table 1. Continued.

Location of risk in supply chain (where risk occurs)	Risk and consequences	Stakeholders impacted and nature of expected impact						
		Phosphate industry	Western Sahara*	Farmers	Food consumers	Policy-makers*	Environmental representatives*	Future generations*
3. Fertilizer application in agriculture	**Market-related risk**: high and/or variable fertilizer distribution costs, especially for land-locked countries			Reduced farmer purchasing power (e.g. can't afford fertilizers) resulting in lower yields	High fertilizer prices can in turn increase food prices (where farmers are not price takers)			
4. Food production, processing and distribution	**Environmental and Management risk**: huge amounts of food waste generated between farm-gate and consumption means embodied phosphorus is wasted (up to 40%)							More phosphorus wasted now means higher grade phosphate rock is depleted faster and less will be available for future generations (as above)
5. Food consumption	**Market-related risk**: changing dietary preferences can and have dramatically altered (increase) the demand for phosphorus	A lack of long-term planning and foresight can lead to a lagged supply constraint (as per 2008)						

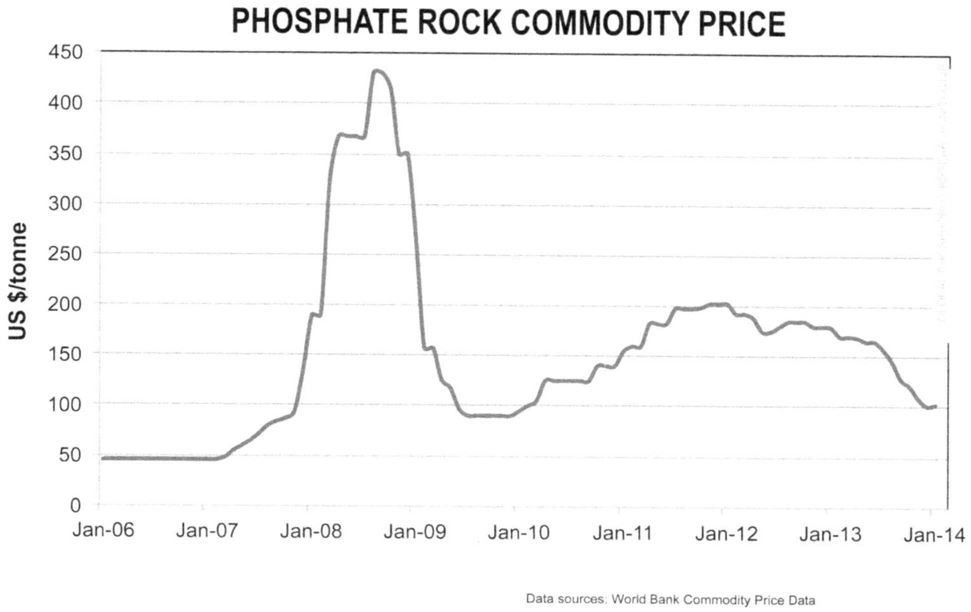

PHOSPHATE ROCK COMMODITY PRICE

Figure 4. Phosphate rock price 2006–14, indicating a 800% price spike in 2008. Data source: World Bank Commodity Price data.

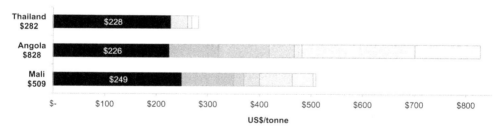

Figure 5. Farm-gate fertilizer costs are highly variable, as indicated by Sub-Saharan Angola and Mali compared to Thailand, largely due to local transport and retail costs.
Data source: IFDC, 'Fertilizer Supply and Costs in Africa' (Chemonics International Inc. and the International Center for Soil Fertility and Agricultural Development, 2007).

phosphate extracted. United Nations Environment Programme (UNEP) has documented the extent of local environmental impacts of phosphate rock mining and processing.[42] During the predominant phosphate fertilizer production process, five tonnes of phosphogypsum by-product are generated for every tonne of phosphate fertilizer.[43] Complicating this picture is that phosphogypsum is deemed radioactive by the US Environmental Protection Agency (EPA), due to the transfer

---

42   UNEP, 'Environmental Aspects of Phosphate and Potash Mining' (Paris: UN Environment Programme & International Fertilizer Industry Association, 2010).
43   Schroder et al., 'Sustainable Use of Phosphorus'.

of radium and thorium isotopes from the phosphate rock stock. Other environmental risks include transfer of heavy metals such as cadmium in phosphate rock to agricultural soils which can be taken up by crops and enter the human food chain.[44] These environmental waste risks can pollute the environment, create expensive management costs, and lead to human health impacts.

The lifecycle energy and greenhouse gas cost of mining and processing lower grade phosphate rock, manufacturing phosphate fertilizers and transporting these commodities from mine to farm gate is not insignificant, estimated at 20 megajoules per kilogram of phosphorus for mining and fertilizer production and trade alone. Phosphate is one of the world's most highly traded commodities at 30 million tonnes a year.[45] The transport fuel used for shipping, rail and road has implications for increasing greenhouse gas emissions that contribute to climate change, and, simultaneously, deplete scarce fossil fuels such as oil and gas. This life-cycle energy consumption also represents a logistical risk.

The ecological cost of eutrophication (nutrient pollution) of the world's rivers, lakes and oceans receives relatively more awareness than other environmental impacts of phosphorus use. Globally, this impact is a consequence of the mobilization of thousands of millions of tonnes of phosphate from the earth's upper crust over the past half-century, 8–9 times the background flow,[46] essentially resulting in the one-way flow of phosphorus from mines to oceans, in turn leading to pollution of the world's aquatic ecosystems,[47] from the Gulf of Mexico to China's Shandong Province to Australia's Great Barrier Reef.

Eutrophication can lead to toxic algal blooms, which can kill fish and entire aquatic ecosystems, pollute drinking water and damage fishing and recreation industries. Globally, the World Resources Institute estimates over 400 'dead zones'.[48] In the US alone the annual cost of algal blooms was conservatively estimated at over US$2.2 billion.[49] In the North American summer of 2014, the drinking water of the US town of Toledo (population 400,000) was rendered toxic from phosphorus pollution associated with algal blooms in the Great Lakes,[50] resulting in the city importing bottled water from interstate. In Australia, floodwaters in Queensland during extreme events carry large volumes of phosphorus-rich sediments from the fertile topsoil of farms to the Great Barrier Reef. This can lead to an irrecoverable loss of valuable nutrients in farmland, and loss of aquatic biodiversity and to fishing, recreation and tourism industries.[51]

Ultimately, resource scarcity of phosphate rock is likely to present the most significant long term environmental risk. As with any critical and finite resource, the quantity of high-concentrate, easy to access phosphate resources have been mined first, leaving behind more expensive, lower-quality and more difficult to access resources, physically, socially and economically.[52] This compromises future generations' ability to efficiently utilize phosphorus resources to support affordable food production and food security.

Phosphate rock has taken hundreds of millions of years to form from under the sea bed to mountains through tectonic uplift. However, a number of recent studies suggest that current

---

44 Ibid.
45 Ibid.
46 J. Rockström et al., 'A Safe Operating Space for Humanity', *Nature* 461 (2009): 472–75.
47 E. Bennett, S. Carpenter, and N. Caraco, 'Human Impact on Erodable Phosphorus and Eutrophication: A Global Perspective', *Bioscience* 51 (2001): 227–34.
48 R. Diaz and R. Rosenberg, 'Spreading Dead Zones and Consequences for Marine Ecosystems', *Science* 321, no. 5891 (2008): 926–9.
49 Dodds et al., 'Eutrophication of U.S. Freshwaters'.
50 D. Mitchell, 'Lake Erie's Green Sludge Highlights our Phosphorus Problem', *Fortune* (August 2014). Available at: http://fortune.com/2014/08/06/peak-phosphorus-toledo-water/.
51 Bennett et al., 'Human Impact on Erodable Phosphorus and Eutrophication'.
52 S. Van Kauwenbergh, 'World Phosphate Rock Reserves and Resources' (Washington, DC: International Fertilizer Development Centre, IFDC, 2010).

reserves are likely to peak mid-century, around 2035–75.[53] Others argue there are 'hundreds' of years remaining.[54] The controversy and inherent uncertainty regarding longevity of phosphate reserves results from differing methods and assumptions underpinning estimates of future demand and supply. For example, the more optimistic studies tend to project static demand into the future, ignoring the significant per capita phosphorus demand increases associated with changing dietary preferences towards more animal protein (particularly in China and India), which require substantially more phosphate fertilizer to support.[55] Further, supply estimates are based on self-reporting by individual companies and/or countries to the US Geological Survey, which collates these figures as a public service without validation of the figures or consistency of underlying assumptions between countries.

This uncertainty and a stark lack of transparency regarding one of the most globally critical resources, coupled with the certainty that we have used up the cheap high-quality phosphate, is enough to warrant some caution when considering availability for future generations.

4.3 *Political risks*

Geopolitical risks carry perhaps the greatest consequences and result from the supply concentration of phosphate producers in potentially politically unstable regions. Although the topic of far less discussion and monitoring, phosphate resources are more geopolitically concentrated than oil. While all countries and farmers need access to phosphorus, only five countries combined control 88% of remaining phosphate reserves.[56] Exacerbating this situation, just one company in one country alone controls 75% of the world's remaining phosphate reserves: the Moroccan kingdom-controlled phosphate company Office Chérifien des Phosphates (OCP). It is predicted that Morocco's market share could increase to 80–90% by 2030.[57] Other countries in the top five include Syria, Algeria, China and South Africa.[58]

The geopolitical risks are both long term, with respect to remaining reserves, and short term, with respect to production. Producing countries (i.e. those countries where phosphate rock is mined and traded) are also concentrated: China, the US, Morocco, Russia and Jordan together hold an 82% market share.[59] Recent civil and political unrest in the Middle East and North Africa has also raised concerns about potential disruptions to phosphate rock supply and capacity development in associated countries.[60]

The implications are potential supply disruptions and price fluctuations. This supply concentration of both producing countries and countries controlling remaining reserves creates both a short-term business risk and a long-term national security risk for importing countries.[61]

---

53 These studies have used post-2010 phosphate reserve data from IFDC 2010 or USGS 2011–13 to calculate supply in different regions. S. Mohr and G. Evans, 'Projections of Future Phosphorus Production', *Philica.com* (2013), http://www.philica.com/display_article.php?article_id=380; P. Walan, 'Modeling of Peak Phosphorus: A Study of Bottlenecks and Implications' (Master's diss., Uppsala University, Sweden, 2013); Cordell and White, 'Life's Bottleneck'.

54 Van Kauwenbergh, 'World Phosphate Rock Reserves and Resources'; D.P.P. Van Vuuren, A.F. Bouwman, and A.H. W. Beusen, 'Phosphorus Demand for the 1970–2100 Period: A Scenario Analysis of Resource Depletion', *Global Environmental Change* 20, no. 3 (2010): 428–39, http://linkinghub.elsevier.com/retrieve/pii/S0959378010000312 (accessed March 18, 2013); D. Vaccari and N. Strigul, 'Extrapolating Phosphorus Production to Estimate Resource Reserves', *Chemosphere* 84, no. 6 (2011): 792–97, http://www.ncbi.nlm.nih.gov/pubmed/21440285 (accessed March 8, 2013).

55 G. Metson, E. Bennett, and J. Elser, 'The Role of Diet in Phosphorus Demand', *Environmental Research Letters* 7, no. 4 (2012): 1–10, 044043.

56 USGS, 'Phosphate Rock', *Mineral Commodity Summaries*, ed. S.M. Jasinski (US Geological Survey, January 2014).

57 J. Cooper et al., 'The Future Distribution and Production of Global Phosphate Rock Reserves', *Resources Conservation and Recycling* 57 (2011): 78–86; HCSS, 'Risks and Opportunities in the Global Phosphate Rock Market.

58 USGS, 'Phosphate rock'.

59 Ibid.

60 HCSS, 'Risks and Opportunities in the Global Phosphate Rock Market.

61 Ibid.

Figure 6. The world's longest conveyor belt transporting phosphate rock 100 km from the Bou Craa phosphate mine in Western Sahara to the port for global export.
Source: Google Maps 2012; Photo credit: Santiago Cordero.

Figure 6 indicates a 'lifeline' of the global food system: the world's longest conveyor belt transporting phosphate rock from Western Sahara 100 km to the Moroccan-controlled port for shipments to Australia, Canada, Lithuania and other importing countries.[62]

Further exacerbating the geopolitical situation is the occupation of Western Sahara. Moroccan forces took control of the territory in 1975 as Spanish colonial powers withdrew.[63] Resource ownership and the legality of the occupation are vigorously contested by Morocco, which claims rightful ownership of the land and resources. However, no other African nation or the UN acknowledge Morocco's claim.[64]

This classic 'resource curse' has led to a concentration of economic/market power and increased social inequity, where Morocco benefits from the processing and trade of the region's phosphate rock, while the Saharawi people are in a situation of social and economic disadvantage. Morocco's state-run phosphate company owns and operates the phosphate mines in the disputed territory, largely employing Moroccan nationals and with profits directly injected into the Moroccan economy, estimated at $4.27 billion over the current life of the mines.[65] While as many as 165,000 Saharawi people live in exile in refugee camps in neighboring Algeria, those in the disputed territory risk persecution, incarceration and have their rights limited.

---

62 WSRW, 'Morocco's Exports of Phosphates from Occupied Western Sahara, 2012 & 2013' (Melbourne: Western Sahara Resource Watch, 2014).
63 Ibid.
64 J. Smith, 'The Taking of the Sahara: The Role of Natural Resources in the Continuing Occupation of Western Sahara, *Journal of Global Change, Peace & Security* (2015).
65 Ibid.

This trade of 'conflict phosphates' implies that importers, distributors, farmers and food consumers in Australia and other importing countries are knowingly or unknowing supporting mining in a disputed territory and therefore potentially illegal trade. Regardless, the direct social impacts result in 'risk transfer' up and down the supply chain, including significant reputational risks for suppliers and consumers associated with a lack of corporate social responsibility.

4.4 *Public policy and institutional risks*

Institutional risks include those that arise from poor governance and can result in a range of consequences, such as increasing the vulnerability of food systems to any unforeseen shock.[66] For example, there are no international bodies responsible for ensuring long-term availability and accessibility of phosphorus for food production.[67] Further, there are no comprehensive, independent, transparent and robust data sets on remaining phosphate rock reserves and trade. Inadequate monitoring, evaluation, forecasting and long-term scenario planning of global phosphate demand can lead to planning errors such as underestimating demand. Further, a lack of policy instruments to stimulate and support effective use of phosphorus means there is little resilience in the system to buffer or mitigate risks.[68]

5   Implications for stakeholders

The implications of not assessing the spectrum of costs, impacts and risks to different sectors are significant for all major stakeholders in the supply chain, whether or not these risks are yet to be realized. Current impacts and potential risks adversely affect direct supply chain participants (such as phosphate producers, farmers, food consumers and policy-makers) and other stakeholder groups (indirect participants), such as the environment, future generations and the Saharawi people of Western Sahara.

The social implications of environmental and geopolitical risks range from local community impacts at mine sites through to indirect impacts further down the supply chain such as the health risk associated with consuming food contaminated with cadmium. Globally, perhaps the most significant single social impact associated with phosphate production is upstream – the social injustice due to the ongoing exploitation and displacement of the Saharawi people whose land and phosphate rock is currently occupied by Morocco.

The case of phosphorus also illustrates the inter- and intra-generational inequity that results when those who gain from resource extraction avoid paying the full costs. Here, the depletion of the resource and the adverse impacts through the supply chain tend to affect the poorest and most vulnerable, as well as future generations.

Table 1 indicates at which stage of the supply chain the risks identified in section 4 occur. It then exemplifies the transmission of these phosphorus supply chain risks and impacts to a range of direct and indirect stakeholder groups. These examples are drawn from our prior research,[69] and are by no means exhaustive. In reality, these impacts will be nuanced and varied between the many actors within each stakeholder group. For example, phosphate industry actors in the global market can be further broken down to include mining companies, fertilizer manufacturers, traders, shipping companies, inspection agencies and banks. Domestic phosphate industry actors

---

66   Cordell and White, 'Phosphorus Security.
67   Ibid.
68   For a fuller description of phosphorus global non-governance and associated vulnerabilities, see ibid. and Cordell and Neset, 'Phosphorus Vulnerability'.
69   E.g. Cordell and White, 'Life's Bottleneck; Cordell and Neset, 'Phosphorus Vulnerability'.

include importers, domestic manufacturers, transporters, banks, port authorities, policy-makers, regulators, wholesalers and agro-dealer retailers.[70]

The transmission or 'ripple effect' from the risk location in the supply chain through to different system stakeholders can be demonstrated by the 2008 price spike. A cocktail of events occurred to that led the 800% price spike (Figure 7). Firstly, the increasing food and agricultural commodity prices meant more farmers were willing to risk purchasing fertilizers to maximize their crop yields and take advantage of high agricultural selling prices. At the same time, a new Ethanol Policy in the US triggered a surge in first-generation biofuel production, which in turn led to a burst of demand for fertilizer to grow biofuel crops.[71] A slower but substantial demand growth was gradually brewing in the background, associated with China and India's increasing appetite for meat and dairy products as a result of increasing affluence, which

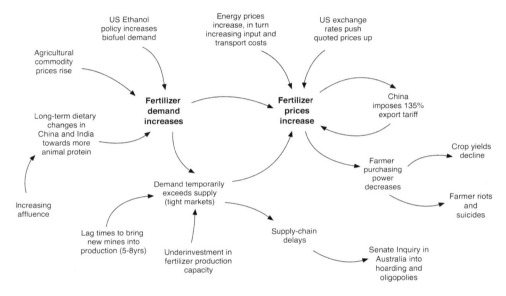

Figure 7: the 2008 phosphate price spike explained, indicating the numerous factors influencing the spike, and examples of negative stakeholder impacts.

results in higher per capita fertilizer demand to support such diets. The few phosphate producers were unable to meet this unexpected demand, in part due to insufficient forecasting, historical underinvestment in fertilizer capacity and lag times in bringing new mines into production.[72]

This temporary supply constraint created tight phosphate markets and led to increasing phosphate prices. Exacerbating these price increases were the spike in energy prices (a key input for phosphate mining, production and transport) and unfavorable US exchange rates pushing up phosphate prices, which are quoted in US dollars.[73] In late 2008, China, one of the major producers of phosphate rock on the market, suddenly imposed a 135% export tariff, further pushing up the price. This unforeseen price spike compounded the food and energy price spikes, leading to farmer riots and suicides in highly vulnerable regions.[74] Even relatively secure countries like Aus-

---

70 IFDC, 'Fertilizer Supply and Costs in Africa'.
71 Cordell, 'The Story of Phosphorus.
72 IFA, 'Feeding the Earth; Cordell, 'The Story of Phosphorus.
73 IFA, 'Feeding the Earth.
74 Cordell and White, 'Life's Bottleneck'.

tralia were affected, triggering a Senate Inquiry into the potential presence of oligopolies and hoarding behavior.[75]

This crisis, although short term, demonstrated how vulnerable the global food system is to even a short-term perturbation in the supply of phosphate. While many factors were unforeseen, there was and still is no transparent international body monitoring long-term phosphorus demand, supply and risk drivers.[76]

The nature and severity of stakeholder impacts can vary within a sector depending on the local sensitivities and local capacity to adapt.[77] For example, extending the case above, farmers who have phosphorus-deficient soils due to geology or mismanagement may be more sensitive to a price spike, while their counterparts working with phosphorus-rich soils might be able to more easily skip a year of fertilizer application and rely on the buffering capacity of their phosphorus soil reserves.[78] However Doody et al. caution that this perceived buffer provided by 'legacy' soil phosphorus from years or decades of fertilizer over-application can also create a leakage risk resulting in loss of nutrient to water bodies, thereby increasing the eutrophication risk.[79]

These impacts can also differ over time: the impact of a tonne of phosphate in the future is greater than a tonne today. For example, as lower grades are mined (containing less phosphorus and more impurities), to extract the same amount of elemental P from ore requires more energy, generates more waste and is overall more costly.

6   Interventions to mitigate and manage risks

Interventions to mitigate or manage risks can enable stakeholders to reduce losses or negative impact by avoiding, coping, transferring, adapting or transforming in response to the risk. The RapAgRisk framework categorizes interventions as technical, market-based, public policy or social in nature.[80] Table 2 provides examples of such interventions to address the different risks identified in Table 1. The text below elaborates on the examples. It is not intended as a complete and systematic analysis of options, but rather to highlight a spectrum of options. In some cases, the same intervention can address multiple risks. In reality, managing risks will need to involve a suite of interventions.

Diversifying input sources is a market-based or public policy strategy that is 'resource responsive' – i.e. responding to external phosphorus supply chain risks.[81] This implies shifting the profile of phosphorus inputs away from dependence on a single or few sources. This can be a public policy decision at the national/regional level – for example the decision of the European Union, a region almost entirely dependent on imported phosphate, to foster markets for domestic recycled phosphate to reduce the region's exposure to geopolitical risks in producing countries.[82] It could also be a business decision for a fertilizer company to source phosphate from diverse phosphate rock producing countries/companies, to reduce the risk of supply disruptions.

---

75   Commonwealth of Australia, 'Pricing and Supply Arrangements in the Australian and Global Fertiliser Market', *Final Report*, Senate Select Committee on Agricultural and Related Industries (Commonwealth of Australia, 2009).
76   Cordell and White, 'Phosphorus Security'.
77   R. Nelson et al., 'The Vulnerability of Australian Rural Communities to Climate Variability and Change: Part I – Conceptualising and Measuring Vulnerability', *Environmental Science Policy* 13 (2010): 8–17.
78   Cordell and Neset identify 26 risk factors leading to phosphorus vulnerability in a national food system, including exposure, sensitivity and adaptive capacity factors. Cordell and Neset, 'Phosphorus Vulnerability'.
79   D.G. Doody, P.J. Withers, and R.M. Dils, 'Prioritizing Water Bodies to Balance Agricultural Production and Environmental Outcomes', *Environmental Science and Technology* 48, no. 14 (2014): 7697–9, http://www.ncbi. nlm.nih.gov/pubmed/24971468.
80   Jaffee et al., 'Rapid Agricultural Supply Chain Risk Assessment'.
81   Matopoulos et al., 'Resource-Efficient Supply Chains'.
82   HCSS, 'Risks and opportunities in the global phosphate rock market; ESPP, 'Special Issue: European Sustainable Phosphorus Conference', 111 (Brussels: European Sustainable Phosphorus Platform, March 2015), http:// phosphorusplatform.eu/images/download/ScopeNewsletter_111_special_ESPC2.pdf.

Table 2.   Examples of sustainable phosphorus interventions to mitigate different phosphorus supply chain risks.

RISKS:	INTERVENTIONS					
	MARKET/PUBLIC POLICY:	MARKET/ PUBLIC POLICY:	PUBLIC POLICY:	TECHNICAL:	TECHNICAL:	SOCIAL:
	e.g. diversifying sources (reduce dependence on imported rock)	e.g. divestments and ethical investments	e.g. future sovereign wealth fund	e.g. increasing efficient phosphorus use by crops	e.g. increasing recycling and reuse of phosphorus	e.g. changing diets towards P-efficient foods
Political risk: market concentration	✪				✪	
Political risk: Western Sahara conflict	✪	✪			✪	
Environmental risk: algal blooms				✪	✪	✪
Environmental risk: resource scarcity			✪	✪	✪	✪
Market-related: risk: High/ variable farm-gate distribution costs	✪			✪	✪	

Divestment strategies can discourage investment in 'conflict phosphates', as has been the case for major Scandinavian funds such as the Swedish government pension fund AP-Fonden, Norway's sovereign wealth fund and Denmark's largest bank, Danske Bank, all of which have divested from or excluded Australian companies Incitec Pivot Limited and Westfarmers, and Canada's PotashCorp which are importing/have imported phosphates from Western Sahara via Morocco's OCP. Upon divesting, Dankse Bank noted '[The company] imports natural resources which are extracted in conflict with human rights norms'.[83]

Another potential public policy intervention is future funds (sovereign wealth funds) that could specifically target phosphorus and food security for future generations. While there are no effective examples for phosphorus, Norway's 'Oil Fund'[84] is a good example that uses profits from oil sales to ensure national economic security to buffer against the depletion of oil and fluctuating prices. However it is crucial that such funds are appropriately governed and managed. The mismanagement of funds from the Nauru Phosphate Royalties Trust is a case in point. The Trust was established in the 1960s to provide reliable national income from foreign mining and export of Nauru's guano phosphate deposits (largely destined for Australia), however corruption and misuse of the funds left the Trust – and the Island State – essentially bankrupt.[85]

Increasing the efficiency of crop phosphorus use is another important strategy and can be achieved through a number of biophysical pathways, including improved fertilizer placement and timing, crop breeding, improved soil composition and the use of mycorrhizal fungi.[86] All of these reduce the need for phosphorus inputs while maintaining crop yields – that is, improving productivity. This not only reduces farmers' input costs, it also reduces the ecological risk of phosphorus erosion and runoff from agricultural fields to rivers and lakes, and can reduce global phosphorus demand and thereby increase the longevity of the world's remaining phosphate rock for future generations.

According to Matopoulos et al., resource sparing in response to resource scarcity is also a means to maintain competitive advantage.[87] Increasing recycling and reuse of phosphorus means recovering phosphorus from all potential losses in the phosphorus supply chain (crop and food waste, animal manure, human excreta) and reusing the recovered phosphorus formally or informally as a renewable fertilizer.[88] In the sanitation sector alone, there are 30–50 technologies for the recovery of phosphorus from wastewater and excreta for reuse in agriculture.[89]

Changing diets refers to a deliberate downward shift in the current high-phosphorus diet economies (such as Argentina or Australia) and contracting the upward trajectory of emerging economies such as China and India with increasingly intensive phosphorus diets, where increasing affluence is increasing demand for meat and dairy foods.[90] Meat- and dairy-based diets are known to require 2–3 times more phosphorus fertilizers than more plant-based diets.[91] Hence a shift to nutri-

---

83 WSRW, 'Morocco's Exports of Phosphates from Occupied Western Sahara, 2012 & 2013'.
84 The Government Pension Fund Global, https://www.regjeringen.no/en/topics/the-economy/the-government-pension-fund/id1441/.
85 J. Garrett, *Island Exiles* (ABC Publishers, 1996).
86 M.J. McLaughlin et al., 'The Chemical Nature of P-accumulation in Agricultural Soils – Implications for Fertiliser Management and Design: An Australian Perspective', *Plant Soil* 349 (2011): 69–87.
87 Matopoulos et al., 'Resource-Efficient Supply Chains'.
88 D. Cordell et al., 'Towards Global Phosphorus Security: A Systems Framework for Phosphorus Recovery and Reuse Options', *Chemosphere* 84, no. 6 (2011): 747–58.
89 C. Sartorius, J. Von Horn, and F. Tettenborn, 'Phosphorus Recovery from Wastewater – State-of-the-art and Future Potential (paper presented at the International Conference on 'Nutrient Recovery and Management 2011: Inside and Outside the Fence', Miami, FL, January 9–12, 2011).
90 N. Alexandratos and J. Bruinsma, 'World Agriculture towards 2030/2050: The 2012 Revision', ESAWork. paper no. 12-03, Agricultural Development Economics Division, Food and Agriculture Organization of the United Nations 2012, http://www.fao.org/3/a-ap106e.pdf

tious diets that depend less on animal protein can substantially reduce global phosphorus demand, and reduce manure generation, which is often responsible for nutrient pollution in countries like Denmark, the Netherlands and the US.

7 Conclusion

Through the lens of a multi-stakeholder supply chain risk assessment framework, this paper has revealed a vast and diverse array of risks and impacts associated with the phosphorus supply chain from mine to fork that together are compromising the achievement of phosphorus security and hence food security. While many of the risks identified are located at the top end of the supply chain (e.g. political and environmental risks occurring in the mining and fertilizer production and trade stages), the negative impacts are transmitted to other stakeholders further down the supply chain, such as farmers and food consumers, and also to non-supply chain stakeholders, such as policy-makers, future generations and the aquatic environment. However, conversely, risks occurring towards the end of the supply chain, such as the changing dietary preferences of food consumers, can have a significant impact on top-end supply chain participants such as mining and fertilizer companies, as was the case in the 2008 price spike where insufficient demand forecasting contributed to price spikes and supply disruptions.

It is hoped that this paper will open up the debate about phosphorus supply chain risks from mine to fork and make the case for a comprehensive, integrated and collaborative assessment that identifies and assesses risks and impacts to all key stakeholders both within and external to the phosphorus supply chain. The RapAgRisk framework has been suggested by way of example; however, other multi-stakeholder agri-food systems frameworks may also be applicable. Undertaking such a comprehensive assessment should also seek to identify a plausible and desirable suite of risk management options to value, mitigate and/or share risks and impacts. Importantly, the phosphorus supply chain and its stakeholders need to be agile and pro-active to manage both known risks and unforeseen shocks. Such risk management interventions can be market-based, policy-oriented, technical, social or hybrid in nature. This in turn can enable policy-makers, industry, investors and the public to make more informed, and socially and environmentally responsible decisions about sourcing and using phosphorus to ensure the global population is fed, farmers and other livelihoods are secure, and waters are free from pollution.

Acknowledgments

The authors would like to thank the two blind peer reviewers for their insightful, thoughtful and constructive comments and suggestions in relation to supply chain risks and ethics that have improved this paper.

Disclosure statement

No potential conflict of interest was reported by the authors.

---

91 Metson et al., 'The Role of Diet in Phosphorus Demand'; Cordell et al., 'The Story of Phosphorus'.

The role of natural resources in the building of an independent Western Sahara

Fadel Kamal

Saharawi Republic Petroleum and Mines Authority, Bir Lahlou, Saharawi Arab Democratic Republic

The Saharawi Arab Democratic Republic (SADR) is a founding member of the African Union (AU) and is the sovereign governing authority in Western Sahara. The SADR government believes that the territory's significant natural resources will play an important part in the development of a viable, self-reliant and democratic nation which will contribute to peace, stability and progress of the Maghreb region. The paper examines the SADR's efforts to manage its natural resources through the establishment of the SADR Petroleum and Mines Authority, the launch of licensing rounds, its claim to an exclusive economic zone in the Atlantic Ocean and the recent enactment of a Mining Code. The paper discusses the SADR's efforts to protect its natural resources in a territory that is under occupation, and examines the SADR oil and gas licensing rounds as an example of SADR's assertion of sovereignty. The SADR natural resources strategy has two basic goals: to deter Morocco's efforts to exploit the country's natural resources and to prepare for the recovery of full sovereignty.

I. Introduction

The organized international community has been successful in a remarkably brief period at the twin projects of ending colonialism and ensuring that the principle of self-determination has taken root, with one notable exception in Africa. Western Sahara, Africa's last colony, remains locked in conflict, its people unable to achieve self-determination while enduring an illegal occupation after the comparable cases of Namibia and East Timor (Timor-Leste) were successfully resolved. The failure to realize the most basic norms of international law, including application of the UN Charter and international humanitarian law in Western Sahara, reveals the limits of international justice and the ability of the United Nations organization to act. The pillage of natural resources from the occupied area of Western Sahara illustrates the aspects of an ongoing denial of self-determination, due to the manner in which the resources are used and the connection they create between the world and Western Sahara. How the Saharawi people govern natural resources in such circumstances is important for the immediate realization of self-determination and the fashioning of an eventual Saharawi state independent in all dimensions.

This paper considers the policy and history of Saharawi governance of the natural resources of their territory, Western Sahara. The development of constitutional and legislative schemes for resource preservation and development, including their intersection with international law, is reviewed. The principal theme of the paper is the national development of natural resources and the prospects they hold for the Saharawi people upon their achieving self-determination. The basis under international law for sovereignty to resources, both under occupation and at independence, receives only limited discussion here, the goal being to consider policy.[1] The activities of the Saharawi Republic's Petroleum and Mines Authority are reviewed as an example of political commitment and capacity to govern natural resources. Finally, prospects for the near-term development of resources and questions about justice in the pillage of those resources from the occupied area of Western Sahara are considered.

II. Pursuing an ideal – Saharawi sovereignty over resources

There are several paradoxes in the Saharawi people's efforts to govern for themselves the natural resources of their country while under occupation and awaiting a UN (and international law) guaranteed right of self-determination. It is useful to understand them in order to acquire a better appreciation of Saharawi government policy. The first is that of the dual roles of the government of the Saharawi Arab Democratic Republic (the SADR) and the Saharawi people's national liberation movement, the Frente Polisario.[2] The mandate and goals of the two entities are complementary when it comes to the natural resources of Western Sahara. A democratically elected government acting through the Saharawi state – that is, the SADR – is responsible for resource development in the liberated area of the territory, including environmental protection, exploration activities and security.[3] The SADR government also assumes a lead role in asserting territorial sovereignty and preservation of natural resources pending the restoration of complete independence through the UN-mandated (and Sahawari agreed) self-determination process. Examples include the engagement of other governments in resource-related matters and the legislation which established the SADR's maritime zones in the Atlantic Ocean.[4] This is governance in the classic sense of mature statehood, not much different from the best current examples in Africa. As a national liberation movement, the Frente Polisario represents the concerns of the Saharawi people about the implications of the pillage of natural resources for self-determination, including externally in their relationship with the United Nations.[5]

---

1 Questions of the sovereignty of the Saharawi people to the natural resources of Western Sahara, while awaiting the exercise of self-determination (as a basic right in international law and specifically assured in their case by the United Nations), have been contentious in recent years. The basis for the Saharawi people to assert resource sovereignty flows from UN General Assembly Resolution 1803 (XVII), 'Permanent sovereignty over natural resources' (December 14, 1962). For a useful discussion of the development of that right in modern decolonization, see Nico Schrijver, *Sovereignty Over Natural Resources: Balancing Rights and Duties* (Cambridge: Cambridge University Press, 1997). The application of international law in this regard to the resources of Western Sahara was the particular concern of the United Nations jurisconsult, Hans Corell, in an opinion to the UN Security Council delivered in 2002, discussed below.

2 *Frente Popular de Liberación de Saguía el Hamra y Río de Oro*; the Popular Front for the Liberation of Saguia el-Hamra and Río de Oro (Frente Polisario). The United Nations deals singularly with the Saharawi people through the Frente Polisario, although it de facto accepts SADR governance in the refugee camps and the liberated zone within Western Sahara proper. Annual reports of the UN Secretary-General to the UN Security Council, read in their entirety, reveal UN policy on Western Sahara. See that for 2015, 'Report of the Secretary-General on the Situation Concerning Western Sahara' (April 10, 2015) UN doc. S/2015/246.

3 Saharawi constitutional norms, the functioning of the state and democratic structures are discussed below. The Frente Polisario and the SADR (its government) may be viewed simply as two entities that for a Saharawi civil society which they represent are concerned with national liberation on the one hand and governance (and the conduct of some international relationships, but not with the UN) on the other. See also the discussion below in footnote 30.
The liberated area east of the separation wall or 'berm' constructed by Morocco in the 1980s extends over a third of Western Sahara's land area of 266,000 square kilometers within territorial frontiers established between 1900 and 1912. The SADR has signed contracts with six oil and mining companies. A mineral company, Hanno Resources, is currently undertaking exploration activities in the liberated area.

4 An example is a letter dated June 12, 2014 from the SADR foreign minister to the foreign minister of New Zealand about the import of Saharawi phosphate rock into the latter country (unpublished, on file with the author). See also Law no. 3 of January 21, 2009 Establishing the Maritime Zones of the Saharawi Arab Democratic Republic, discussed below.

5 The Frente Polisario is the accepted representative organization of the Saharawi people, particularly for those under occupation in Western Sahara, in the refugee camps near Tindouf inside Algeria and among the diaspora. The Sahar-

The second paradox can be appreciated in what is the present program for development of resources, a responsibility of the SADR government, in contrast to the mutual policy position of both the government and the Frente Polisario to preserve the territory's resources until self-determination is achieved and occupation ended. The paradox is resolved geographically. In the liberated area, the SADR government is committed to the present sustainable development of resources, notably minerals. For the occupied area, its position is entirely the opposite, and that is to insist on the complete preservation of resources until self-determination has been realized.[6] While both the government and the national liberation movement accept that the Saharawi people under occupation need access to natural resources and that some activity is necessary to ensure an economy sufficient for their needs, there is great concern that resource activities, especially the fishery and phosphate mining, deepens the occupation and annexation of the territory and therefore delays self-determination. Phosphate rock mining in particular is consistently objected to by the SADR government and the Frente Polisario not only because of the illegality of the act but also due to the fact that the resource is finite (non-sustainable) and less will be available to the Saharawi people in future.[7] Faced with the scale of resource development in recent years, the Frente Polisario has called on the United Nations to administer resources in a manner similar to the two decades of work done by United Nations Council for Namibia, if not directly controlling resource extraction, then possibly accounting for and holding revenues in trust for the Saharawi people.[8]

Two other issues are usefully canvassed. Governments of other states are divided on the status of the Saharawi people and their representative institutions. While on one hand, all member states

---

awi, who were the exclusive inhabitants of Spanish Sahara and when the process for a UN-delivered self-determination referendum began in September 1991, were definitively identified in the UN's December 1999 census-registration. For a useful discussion of the UN census-registration process, see Erik Jensen, *Western Sahara: Anatomy of a Stalemate* (Boulder, CO: Lynne Rienner, 2005).

The Frente Polisario and the SADR government assert sovereignty over all of Western Sahara on several grounds, including the settled rule (*jus cogens*) of international law which confers the right of self-determination (with a choice of independence) on non-self-governing peoples, the declared position of the colonial power, Spain, for Saharawi self-determination (declared in 1974), the Advisory Opinion of the International Court of Justice 1975 on Western Sahara denying any other state title or legal claim to the territory, and the commitments to ensure self-determination made by the United Nations upon entering into the 1990–91 ceasefire and referendum agreement with the Frente Polisario. It is these factors which ground an overwhelming (i.e. legally exclusive) sovereign right to the territory.

The term 'pillage' (interchangeable with plunder) is used here in its ordinary legal meaning, as defined by the Fourth Geneva Convention 1949 and the Rome Statute 1998 of the International Criminal Court. The SADR government employs the term on the basis that a part of Western Sahara is under armed occupation with the International Court of Justice having concluded that the occupying power has no legal claim to the territory. The ICJ's 1975 *Western Sahara Advisory Opinion* is discussed below. The decision of Spanish courts in 2014 and 2015 to apply international humanitarian and criminal law in Western Sahara is also considered below.

6   The SADR government accepts that Saharawi under occupation west of the berm must subsist through some form of a functioning economy. However, the overwhelming participation in the Atlantic fishery, phosphate rock mining and transport, agriculture and aquaculture (at Dakhla) is by a settler population introduced after 1975. For example, in numerous personal conversations with Saharawi from the occupied area and after studying available information, the author concludes that no more than 400 of the 2014 workforce of 2200 persons were Saharawi with some original tie, residency or citizenship in the territory.

7   Phosphate rock mining and exports are controlled through the Office Chérifien des Phosphates SA (OCP SA), a state corporation of the occupying power. In 2014 the company issued a securities financing prospectus which noted that the highest quality top layer of phosphate rock at the Bu Craa mine site would be worked to exhaustion that year. 50 million tonnes of phosphate rock were exported from occupied Western Sahara between 1975 and 2014. Reserves of perhaps 500 million tonnes remain. See OCP SA *Prospectus of 17 April 2014* (debt financing on the Irish Stock Exchange), which may be found with a similar 2015 prospectus at the website of the Irish Stock Exchange, http:// www.ise.ie (accessed July 24, 2015)

8   'We call on the United Nations to establish a UN Council for the Natural Resources of Western Sahara. The UN Council for Namibia which, among other things, legislated for and oversaw the development of natural resources in occupied Namibia until 1990 is a good example and precedent. The UN should retain the revenues received from the exploitation of the natural resources of Western Sahara in trust until the Saharawi people exercise their right to self-determination and decide their future.' Statement by Fadel Kamal, Representative of the Frente Polisario-Western Sahara at the Seminar of the UN Special Committee of Decolonization (C-24) Fiji, May 21–23, 2014.

of the African Union (and many other countries) have recognized the Saharawi state, on the other, most Global North and Asian governments are yet to extend recognition while the Frente Polisario continues as the single representative entity to the United Nations. When it comes to natural resources, this issue is resolved by the fact that it is non-recognizing states which deal in resources exported from the occupied area of the territory, including the European Union in the Atlantic seacoast fishery.[9] Minor exceptions can be found, of course, including small-scale import of phosphate rock by a multinational corporation into a recognizing state (Venezuela) and the failure of the UN Food and Agricultural Organization (the UNFAO) to engage the Saharawi people when it carries out fisheries surveys on the Saharan seacoast.[10] The African Union has long accepted both dualities, treating the SADR as the government of a member state like any other while externally insisting on the Saharawi people's right to self-determination.[11]

Then there is the issue of difficulties that arise in relation to enforcement of settled international law on pillage of resources from territories experiencing conflict. In the case of Western Sahara, the rights of the Saharawi people have proven unrealizable during four decades of occupation and reasons for this are straightforward: (i) the lack of recognition of the Saharawi state which excludes it from the jurisdiction of international legal institutions such as the International Court of Justice; (ii) the general absence of a factual and legal nexus between the occupation of the territory (or export of its resources) and the domestic legal systems of most countries; and (iii) the deferral by states of the 'question' of Western Sahara to a United Nations which has pursued self-determination through negotiation and not by legal remedies. There is also Spain's sidestepping of any singular diplomatic or legal initiatives that it could pursue as *de jure* administering power, for example by bringing the issue before the International Court of Justice, similar to Portugal's action in relation to East Timor from 1991 through 1995.[12] Within both international and domestic legal systems, sufficient measures exist to stop the pillage of Western Sahara's resources.[13]

---

9   The SADR government estimates the current (2014) direct rent (revenue) from the coastal fishery at US$60 million. (The author derives this from personal conversations in 2014 and 2015 with government officials and by reconciling estimates with known payments made by the European Union and Russia to Morocco for fishing in the Saharan Atlantic area.) In September 2014 fishing resumed by European vessels under a renewed EU–Morocco Fisheries Partnership Agreement, by which the occupying power is annually paid €30 million, the remainder being from Russia under an agreement renewed in 2013, a local offshore commercial fishery, and in October 2014 a seasonal tuna fishery conducted by Japanese vessels. Academic commentary on the economic and legal aspects of what in recent years has been a controversial EU fishery remains limited. See notably Jeffrey Smith, 'Fishing for Self-Determination: European Fisheries and Western Sahara – The Case of Ocean Resources in Africa's Last Colony', *Ocean Yearbook* 27 (2013): 267.

10 For current details of phosphate rock exports from occupied Western Sahara, see Western Sahara Resource Watch, *P for Plunder* (Brussels: Western Sahara Resource Watch, 2015). The FAO's Canary Current Large Marine Ecosystem Project of fisheries and ecosystem assessment (and the building of governance capacity in participating states) is detailed at http://www.canarycurrent.org (accessed March 15, 2015).

11 See African Union Peace and Security Council Communiqué of March 27, 2015, AU doc. PSC/PR/COMM./1 (CDXCVI). The Council called on 'the UN Security Council to address the issue of the illegal exploitation of the Territory's natural resources, bearing in mind the call made in the UN Secretary-General report of 10 April 2014, for all relevant actors, in the light of the increased interest in the natural resources of Western Sahara, to "recognize the principle that the interests of the inhabitants of these territories are paramount", in accordance with Chapter XI, article 73 of the Charter' and recommended 'consideration of a strategy of global boycott of products of companies involved in the illegal exploitation of the natural resources of Western Sahara as a way of further sustaining the attention of the international community on the situation in Western Sahara'. Ibid., para. 11.

12 See *Case Concerning East Timor (Portugal v Australia)*, ICJ Reports 1995, 90.

13 The SADR government engages the law where it can, asserting permanent sovereignty of the Saharawi people to their resources under the UN Charter and UN General Assembly Resolution 1803 (XVII), December 14, 1962 (most famously applied by Hans Corell in his 2002 legal opinion for the UN Security Council on the subject of petroleum exploration in Western Sahara), as well as international humanitarian law with its prohibition against pillage under the Fourth Geneva Convention 1949. The Saharawi government also pursues the enforcement of national criminal, civil and regulatory law throughout Western Sahara and accepts that the criminal law of Spain as the colonial-administering power may have a protective role, including after a 2014 *Audencia Nacional* decision concluded that Spanish criminal law has continued in at least the occupied area of the territory. On April 9, 2015, a judge of the same

III. From out of the desert – the Saharawi people and their natural resources

For millennia, what is now called Western Sahara sustained settlement and migration. Ancient paintings in overhead rock galleries located in the liberated area west of Tifariti town depict human uses of the land including pasturing and hunting of animals. The territory has never been heavily populated, at least not until the last years of the twentieth century, and the resources of the land were sufficient for a semi-nomadic society to develop in the centuries prior to colonial contact.[14] Much is made about primary natural resources in Western Sahara, especially the phosphate mining industry and the coastal fishery, together valued at about US$300 million in 2014. However, the greatest resource for the Saharawi people has always been land, and within that, available fresh water which is most abundant as groundwater.[15]

While land is symbolic for Saharawi national identity, including the project to recover the entire territory and thereby bring an end to the legacy of colonialism, there are significant practical matters for the SADR government to address. Foremost is the loss of habitat areas for pasturing and environmental degradation in urban areas and along the length of the berm. Secondary effects from the occupation include loss and disruption of private and communally used land areas, and partitioning of the territory with all the implications for environmental conservation, changed social contact and internal migration, and the problem of the land mine corridor created by the occupying power along the length of the berm.[16] A Saharawi people who come to enjoy independence after self-determination will have a decades-long task to redress the environmental damage which has been caused by the berm.[17] However, a greater concern is the possible overuse and declining supplies of groundwater in the occupied area of the territory.[18] The evidence is incomplete, given the lack of recent studies and record-keeping in the occupied area, and uncertain data about consumption patterns. What is known is that more groundwater is being taken near the principal cities of El Aauin and Dakhla for a growing population of foreign settlers who have migrated into the territory. Water, hardly a commercial resource, is insufficiently valued in its development and delivery cost charges in this setting. Its availability and quality, and future reserves (and aquifer replenishment dynamics) are a continuing problem for the SADR government.[19] Few tangible practical or legal measures are available to ensure water conservation.

---

court determined that a criminal prosecution case on the basis of genocide could be pursued against eight Moroccan military and three civilians for acts in Western Sahara from 1976 to 1991. See Fernando J. Pérez, 'Ruz procesa 11 mandos militares marroquies por genocidio en el Sáhara', *El País*, April 9, 2015.

14 For an historical background, see Tony Hodges, *Western Sahara: The Roots of a Desert War* (Westport, CT: Lawrence Hill, 1983).

15 Western Sahara may be unique among nations in that it routinely has no surficial water courses. Most *wadi* are dry for a majority of the year, and there are no appreciable sized bodies of fresh water.

16 The SADR government considers the construction and continued operation of the berm unlawful, and a criminal act within the relevant provisions of the Geneva and Hague Conventions and the Rome Statute (International Criminal Court). By comparison, the International Criminal Court has concluded that part of Israel's security fence which passes through lands of the State of Palestine to violate international law, concluding that in such places it must be removed. See *Legal Consequences of the Construction of a Wall in the Occupied Palestinian Territory (Advisory Opinion)*, ICJ Reports 2004, 136.

17 Mine action organizations estimate the number of land mines throughout the territory, principally along the inland length of the berm, at more than 7 million. See e.g. http://unrec.org/default/index.php/en/2012-08-14-15-04-20/2013-10-30-09-26-03/conventional-arms-issues (accessed April 7, 2015).

18 The SADR government conducts aquifer studies and regulates groundwater use in the liberated area, which is lightly populated including permanent residents and units of the Saharawi People's Liberation Army as well as, in one location east of the berm, a UN MINURSO site. (Personal conversations and field observations of the author in the presence of Saharawi officials, 2014–15.)

19 The largest use of water in the occupied area is for human consumption, although agriculture applications are considerable, for example in hydroponic farms around Dakhla. Water use for fish processing and phosphate rock washing is comparatively small. In addition to the Saharawi population and around 200,000 Moroccan settlers, there are also over 100,000 occupying troops mostly deployed all along the berm. (Personal conversations of the author with UN officials, Saharawi residents of the occupied part of Western Sahara, and Saharawi officials, 2014–15.)

Western Sahara's secondary (and as yet underdeveloped) resources feature in different ways in the occupation, including as a basis to employ settlers and to ground the pretext of a viable economy. They include ongoing exports of sand (to the Canary Islands for construction and beach development) and salt, as well as hydroponically cultivated vegetables. The exploitation of oil reserves, with no substantial recovery yet achieved, has been the *cause célèbre* in recent years, culminating with test well drilling in 2015. Considerable areas in the occupied zone and the entire continental shelf on the coast of Western Sahara (to an average distance of 100 nautical miles) have been allocated for 'reconnaissance' exploration under petroleum licensing permits from the occupying power's state-owned Office National des Hydrocarbures et Mines (ONHYM). The granting of two of such seabed petroleum permits prompted the UN Security Council in 2001 to seek the advice of the UN's principal jurist, Hans Corell. Mr. Corell evidently concluded that he only needed to consider UN Resolution 1803 before concluding that further petroleum development (exploration or recovery) would violate international law unless done with the consent of the Saharawi people and for their benefit.[20] It was in response to renewed petroleum exploration in 2008 that the SADR government created maritime jurisdiction legislation, bringing it into force in January 2009.[21] Despite this, large-scale and costly seabed exploration has been conducted in two large seabed areas since 2012, with a test well in 2100 meters of water at one site northwest of Boujdour drilled in early 2015.[22] The activity brought a protest from the Frente Polisario Secretary-General to the UN Secretary-General:

> [T]he present petroleum activity is illegal and impedes progress toward the conduct of a 'free and fair referendum' as that has been accepted by the parties. (See report of Secretary-General 18 June 1990, UN document S/21360, paragraph 47(g).) The activity underscores to the Saharawi people that a violation of well-settled, universally [accepted] rules of international law is allowed to continue. That suggests the organised international community is unwilling to ensure the paramount obligation of self-determination flowing from Article 73 of the UN Charter.[23]

The goal of the SADR government is to preserve petroleum, which is a finite resource, until complete independence has been achieved. The making of timely protests to the United Nations and

---

20 Letter dated January 29, 2002 from the Under-Secretary-General for Legal Affairs, the Legal Counsel, addressed to the President of the Security Council, UN doc. S/2002/161. The letter is routinely misquoted by petroleum companies and corporations which purchase phosphate rock. The operative conclusion and therefore legal guidance to the Security Council is at paragraph 25: '[I]f further exploration and exploitation activities were to proceed in disregard of the interests and wishes of the people of Western Sahara, they would be in violation of the principles of international law applicable to mineral resource activities in Non-Self-Governing Territories.' This requirement has its origins in UN General Assembly Resolution 1803 of December 14, 1962 declaring the right of non-self-governing peoples to sovereignty over their natural resources.

21 The Maritime Zones statute, above, was remarked upon by the UN Secretary-General in his 2009 report to the Security Council and appears to have caused the EU Parliament to reconsider the 2007 EU–Morocco Fisheries Partnership Agreement, resulting in its rejection in December 2011. See Johann Schoo, 'Letter – Fisheries Partnership Agreement between the European Community and the Kingdom of Morocco – Declaration by the Saharawi Arab Democratic Republic (SADR) of 21 January 2009 of jurisdiction over an Exclusive Economic Zone of 200 nautical miles off the Western Sahara – Catches taken by EU-flagged vessels fishing in the waters off the Western Sahara' (European Union/Commission Legal Service Opinion), July, 13 2009. The letter was made public in February 2010 and can be found on the website of Western Sahara Resource Watch, http://www.wsrw.org.

22 The two areas are from Dakhla south to the Cape Blanc peninsula (Groupe Total SA) and the Boujdour Offshore Block (Kosmos Energy Ltd.) where the *Gargaa/El Khayr* website was drilled in Q1 2015. The Saharawi government protested to both companies.

23 Letter of January 26, 2015, http://www.spsrasd.info (accessed March 2, 2015). The UN Secretary-General noted the protest in his annual report to the Security Council, 'Report of the Secretary-General on the situation concerning Western Sahara' (April 10, 2015) UN doc. S/20-15/246, para. 62. And see para. 80: 'In the light of increased interest in the natural resources of Western Sahara, it is timely to call upon all relevant actors to "recognize the principle that the interests of the inhabitants of these territories are paramount", in accordance with Chapter XI, Article 73 of the Charter of the United Nations.'

others helps to underscore the political and economic risks faced by the corporations involved.[24] For the present, such risks have joined with depressed market prices for petroleum to make petroleum development unattractive.

Exploration for minerals other than phosphate rock has been pursued in the occupied area of Western Sahara, notably since 2004. Despite seemingly good prospectivity for metal ores in numerous locations, no commercial extraction is in the works. The most valuable resources in Western Sahara remain those when Spain departed in 1975, the Atlantic fishery and phosphate rock, not yet eclipsed by mining and petroleum extraction. With high market values for each, the revenues from them even in recent years of record phosphate prices have been used to offset the costs of the military occupation. The occupation of Western Sahara was costing Morocco during the years of war an estimated $1.9 billion a year.[25]

IV. Toward a just future – the role of resources in Saharawi self-determination

Western Sahara's natural resources have important implications for an eventually independent Saharawi nation. The cornerstone of Saharawi government policy is to ensure availability of the resources as one basis for economic development, including through creation of employment, secondary market and services activities, and taxation revenues. A balance of resources (and public transparency in their development) are features of avoiding the 'resource curse' of excessive reliance on a single high-value (and non-renewable) commodity such as petroleum.[26] Finally, with resources comes trade, and that is an important dimension of how the Saharawi state will interact with others in the international community.

The prospects for economic returns from the territory's resources are promising. With a small population and an abundance of natural resources, the future independent SADR will be a viable and a flourishing nation that will be a factor of stability and peace in the Maghreb region and an example of a modern and democratic nation in North Africa, one tolerant and willing to interact with all its neighbors and with the international community. Such a state is keen to attract investment in a transparent and open manner and for the benefit of all.

It is estimated that the annual revenue streams from Saharawi resource commodities is likely to be US$1260 million (2015).[27] The combined taxation and commodity (rent) return to

---

24 In January 2014 the SADR detailed a compensation claim to the largest purchaser of Saharawi phosphate, Potash Corporation of Saskatchewan Inc., noting the claim then to be a minimum of US$400 million. (A copy of the Saharawi Republic's unpublished letter is on file with the author.)

25 'Burden or Benefit? Morocco in the Western Sahara', lecture given at the Middle East Studies Centre, Oxford University, February 18, 2005 by Toby Shelley (author of *Endgame in the Western Sahara:What Future for Africa's Last Colony?* (London: Zed Books, 2004)). The text of the lecture is available at http://www.arso.org/TSh180205.htm (accessed April 8, 2015).

26 Energy security in a future Western Sahara has been studied by the SADR government with a view to alternative energy sources given the cost of petroleum and desired national contributions to reducing greenhouse gases from the use of fossil fuels.

27 This is the author's calculation, arrived at through the following methodology. The net present annual revenue-taxation return from the territory's present four leading resources is calculated over a 25-year period. 250 million barrels of petroleum is assumed to be available at a market price of US$60 per barrel and extracted at 10 million barrels annually, for a revenue stream of $600 million per annum. The second resource, the fishery, is accepted as having a $60 million taxation (rent) revenue, unchanged from 2014 when EU fishing resumed. The amount is then doubled to account for secondary economic production in the sector, notably processing and services to vessels, for a fisheries sector total of $120 million. Third, phosphate mineral rock exports are put at 2.5 million tonnes per year, up slightly from the five-year average (2010–14) of 2.1–2.2 million tonnes, at $120 per tonne for a total market (commodity) payment to government of $300 million annually. (From this amount would be deducted the cost to operate the mine and transport infrastructure, about $100 million per year.)

It is the fourth resource, iron ore, that has the greatest variability in making estimates. Details about the volume and quality of reserves in the occupied area are not available or lack credibility. However, enough is known from the experience of the high value site at *Kedia d'Idjil-Zouerate* nearby in Mauritania and recent prospecting in the liberated

government would be less than half this amount, perhaps $300 million (as a matter of expected royalty and taxation in an independent SADR). The contribution of the primary resources to the Saharawi economy is understood by calculating gross domestic product (GDP) in comparison to other countries.

The SADR government's natural resources policy – applicable throughout all of Western Sahara – has important economic and legal dimensions, together with the engagement of the Saharawi people for a viable future. The Saharawi people will proceed through self-determination with a substantial endowment of resources and, equally importantly, with an increasingly sophisticated and democratically accountable governance of them.

The SADR aims to adopt a prudent, far-sighted strategy with regard to the management of the natural resources.[28] The goal is for resources to be used for the benefit of the Saharawi people while also contributing to the prosperity of the Maghreb region. The intention is also that resources play a role in the peaceful resolution of the conflict and become a factor of peace and stability in the region. Hence, the 2007 Proposal of the Frente Polisario for a mutually acceptable political solution provides that '[t]he guarantees to be negotiated by the two parties would [include] agreement on equitable and mutually advantageous arrangements permitting the development and the joint exploitation of the existing natural resources or those that could be discovered during a determined period of time'.[29]

V.   Of states and sovereigns – the SADR and its resource governance policies

The Saharawi people govern their natural resources in a manner which is unique in the era of decolonization achieved in the aftermath of General Assembly Resolution 1514. Their leading political institutions, the Frente Polisario and the SADR state, are democratic, they govern themselves in refugee exile, and, through the SADR itself, hold a part of Western Sahara.[30] Moreover, they have the advantage of settled international law when it comes to proposed resource activities in the liberated area and to constrain the pillage of resources in the occupied area west of the berm (even as that law goes unenforced). The Saharawi government is conscious of the imperative to

---

area that estimates can be done with confidence. A future iron ore mine with reserves of 300 million tonnes yielding recoverable ore at 35% and an annual net production of four million tonnes at $60 per tonne results in revenue of $240 million.

The four annual revenue streams total ($600 million + $120 million + $300 million + $240 million) US$1260 million.

28   Examples of this policy stance include legislation and governing mechanisms for resource development in the liberated zone, the general maintenance and improvement of rule of law measures in the SADR government such as initiatives for transparency in decision-making and civil society participation in resource planning, the call for United Nations involvement in current resource exports, and continual protests over the taking of resources (and environmental protection concerns) in the occupied area of Western Sahara.

29   'Proposal of the Frente Polisario for a mutually acceptable political solution that provides for the self-determination of the people of Western Sahara', UN doc. S/2007/210 (April 16, 2007), at para. 9.3.

30   The political economy of the Saharawi state must be considered in the context of the setting of the Saharawi refugee camps and the pursuit of national liberation through the Frente Polisario. The SADR assumes a form closest to a classically Western (i.e. Global North) democratic ideal in the electoral mandate it receives to govern for the maintenance of civil society in the camps. That mandate, when it comes to self-determination, and engaging external entities such as the United Nations, is conferred through the Saharawi parliament (the National Council) upon government for exercise by the Frente Polisario. 'The Sahrawi National Council is the legislative organ of the SADR. Its fifty-three members are elected each eighteen months. The council meets in two annual sessions with commissions functioning between times. It considers the programme put forward by the government and if two-thirds of the members consistently oppose it, the head of state must choose between dissolving the council or choosing a new cabinet. The council can censure the government. Along with the prime minister, deputies of the National Council can propose legislation.' Shelley, *Endgame in the Western Sahara*, 183. For a discussion of governance in Saharawi refugee camps see Stephen Zunes and Jacob Mundy, *Western Sahara: War, Nationalism, and Conflict Resolution* (Syracuse, NY: Syracuse University Press, 2010).

balance such matters, and to put them in proper context given the overarching goal of self-determination and the restoration of independence.

The focal point of government policy for natural resources is the SADR Constitution.[31] Apart from allocating authority to government for the administration of resources, democratic norms are established by the Constitution which require stewardship of resources in the national interest. This includes a high degree of consensus among legislators and, in crucial matters, the whole Saharawi population. The Constitution, last amended in December 2011 by the 13th Saharawi National Congress, draws upon modern liberal concepts and Islam as a source of law, and it is accepted that environmental conservation principles flow from the Qu'ran.[32] Article 17 provides that natural resources ('public goods') are the 'property of the people, consisting of mineral riches, energy resources, the resources of the seabed and territorial waters, and other resources defined by law'.[33] Article 18 requires that resources be defined and managed in accordance with national law. In general, it falls to ministers of the SADR government (and, in a general executive context, the SADR president) to properly manage resources under Articles 64–74. The Saharawi legislature (i.e. parliament, the National Council) has authority in respect of legislation through which government officers act, as detailed in Articles 75–123.[34] Although a state institution, the Saharawi judiciary is formally independent of the two branches of government. Because the courts act in the name of the Saharawi people and government must comply with their decisions, judicial review of government decision-making about natural resources and environmental matters is possible, although no case has yet been pursued.

Similarly, the Constitution guarantees private property rights, at Article 35. The question of such rights and the development of natural resources, for example the state licensing of mineral exploration in areas that include privately owned real property is an ongoing policy topic, although no conflict in practice has yet emerged. The SADR government has considered how private property interests in the occupied area will be accommodated after that area is restored to the state.[35] An example is the allocation of petroleum exploration areas on the Atlantic coast, which extend seaward from the low-water mark; 'public lands' under the Constitution, so designed to ensure a demarcation with upland private holdings (and to be consistent with the practice of states generally). Current policy planning includes how mineral and groundwater access development exercised by the Sahawari state can reconcile private property interests, including through a scheme of expropriation compensation, social and environmental impact assessment, and judicial review. The question of private property has been engaged in the liberated area in limited instances though not much land has been given over to private uses or settlement.[36]

---

31 An Arabic language version of the *Constitution* is available at http://www.20may.org/ar/wp-content/uploads/2014/06/للجهة-13-المؤتمر-عن-الصادر-الديمقراطية-الصحراوية-العربية-الجمهورية-دستور.pdf (accessed March 5, 2015).Accountability of the Saharawi government to its citizens is realized for the most part through the dialogue and review of government programs and decisions by the National Council, as noted above. There is not a tradition of judicial review of executive action or government decision-making, or commentary by third parties including external entities such as the Office of the UN High Commissioner for Refugees. Human rights organizations are routinely invited into the refugee camps for open-access visits, such as a delegation from the Robert F. Kennedy Center in the summer of 2012, but they have not considered governance institutions or the adequacy of democratic norms in Saharawi society.

32 The just allocation of water in a society (*Qu'ran* 16:65) and the conservation of resources from past generations for future ones (*Qu'ran* 89:19) are relevant tenets of Islam.

33 SADR Constitution, Article 17.

34 Ibid., Articles 75–123.

35 The experience of Timor-Leste after 24 years of occupation during which there were significant changes of property ownership (and expropriation by the occupying state) is instructive.

36 The SADR government is sensitive to cultural heritage, and has studied and regulated the protection of historic sites in the liberated zone, for example the rock gallery paintings west of Tifariti. Provisions of the 2014 Mining Code restrict government grants of mining license areas ('Tenements') over certain types of private property and provide for expropriation compensation.

While there are various legislative initiatives for environmental protection and to regulate (including by application of criminal law) the removal of natural resources from Western Sahara, the most recent 'projects of law' have been the 2009 Maritime Zones Act and the 2014 Mining Code. The constitutional basis for resource development in the two statutes is territorial sovereignty: in classical terms, the Saharawi state's assertion of sovereign, original and indivisible title from which rights and obligations for resources may be identified and transferred to others. Article 4 of the Maritime Zones Act continues such sovereignty into the offshore consistent with the 1982 UN Convention on the Law of the Sea, which includes possession and territorial rights seaward to 12 nautical miles and to the resources of the sea within a 200 NM exclusive economic zone and, further seaward, the resources of an extended continental shelf. The dual aspects of the development and preservation of resources until independence is restored through self-determination can be appreciated in the following provisions of Article 8 of the Act, Article 8(3), allowing the Saharawi government the flexibility to permit exploration and development to proceed or to take a preservationist stance in light of the occupation:

Rights and Obligations

1. In the exclusive economic zone, the Saharawi Arab Democratic Republic has sovereign rights for the purpose of exploring, exploiting, conserving and managing the natural resources, whether living or non-living, of the sea-bed and subsoil and the superjacent waters, and with regard to other activities for the economic exploitation and exploration of the zone, such as the production of energy from water, currents and winds. …

3. There shall be no exploration or economic exploitation of the natural resources of the exclusive economic zone by persons or vessels other than nationals of the Saharawi Arab Democratic Republic … unless such activity has been authorized by the Government of the Saharawi Arab Democratic Republic.

The Mining Code was several years in the making. There were a number of reasons for this, including the need to consult widely in Saharawi civil society and to ensure a framework that would provide confidence for mining exploration firms that would remain uninterrupted through self-determination and make for seamless application thereafter through all of Western Sahara.[37] The Mining Code governs mineralogical exploration and extraction and is distinct from the petroleum survey-production sharing regime which has been in place since the opening of a first licensing round in May 2005. A useful precursor was the evaluation of a Technical Cooperation Agreement that had operated from 2007 through 2011 for a mining exploration firm to conduct surveys in the liberated area.[38]

The Mining Code defines the terms of exploration permits, mining permits, small-scale mining permits and infrastructure permits. Exploration permits allow for the exclusive exploration of all minerals within a designated area. An exploration permit may comprise an area of up to 2000 km^2 with any one person or entity able to be granted up to 10 permits. A permit is valid for an initial period of three years, renewable twice each for further three-year terms. After demonstrating an economically viable mineral deposit, the exploration permit holder can apply to convert their rights in the deposit area by the grant of a mining permit valid for 30 years, renewable twice each for a further 10 years. These provisions are thought by Saharawi officials to make for good governance and to be consistent with best regulatory practice in Africa.

---

37 Law No. 02/2014. The Code was adopted on May 26, 2014 after considerable review by elected legislators and revisions to satisfy their public policy concerns. It had latterly been revised by the Economic Committee of the National Council after consultation with the SADR executive branch. A principal goal was a statute drafted to international standards including with the assistance of legal firms with extensive experience in advising governments on mining law. See http://www.sadrpma.com (accessed March 2, 2015).

38 In July 2011 Hanno Resources Limited (formerly Excalibur Resources Group Limited) presented the results of its work under the Technical Cooperation Agreement (TCA), noting that Western Sahara is highly prospective for iron ore, gold, base metals and uranium. The results of more detailed assessments were provided in March 2015 and are discussed below.

Actual mining activity is to be carried out under establishment and infrastructure licenses. Establishment agreements require feasibility studies of the proposed mining operation by independent third party experts, as well as an acceptable plan to work and eventually decommission (i.e. remediate) a mine site, together with measures to comply with environmental protection controls. An important part of establishment licenses is the implementation of 'community development agreements' which are intended to mitigate the adverse effects of mining operations by sustaining economic and social viability of local population centers, and ensuring the protection of cultural sites. Establishment permits also contain extensive provision for the free import and use of equipment and matériel for mining operations, payment of rent taxation to the SADR government, arbitral dispute resolution, and compliance measures with labor standards, and occupational health and safety regulations. Infrastructure licenses may be thought of as a 'global building permit', within which a mining company may 'construct and maintain buildings, roads, pipelines, powerlines' and 'things incidental' to mining operations. The framework of the Mining Code is designed to balance state and social requirements for sustainable extraction of mineral resources having a high degree of environmental protection and Saharawi civil society 'social license' with commercial efficacy including an acceptable return for mining companies for their initial exploration and capital development costs.[39]

Mining activities, including administration of the Mining Code and the granting of petroleum exploration permits throughout Western Sahara is presently the responsibility of the SADR Petroleum and Mines Authority (the PMA). The Authority is designated as the Mining Department under the Code, and reports to the Saharawi government through a chief executive and a responsible minister. In addition to administrative and technical (e.g. geological survey) work, the PMA also has the dual roles of overseeing environmental protection in the occupied area of Western Sahara, that is, gathering data and providing policy advice to Saharawi leaders about environmental impacts and resource depletion in the area west of the berm, and coordinating responses to the illegal extraction and export of resources under occupation.[40]

VI.   The future arrives – the potential of Saharawi resources

The SADR government, from an initial foray into regulating resource development activity, has for more than a decade issued petroleum exploration permits for the seabed of Western Sahara.[41] With the advent of mining regulation, this is intended to set the stage for resource development, with a diminishing requirement that independence (or the 'restoration of full independence' as the usual employed phrase) must first result. The territory's petroleum and mining areas can be broadly divided into two general geological parts: the 'El Aauin basin' extending inland from the Atlantic coast, and the interior Reguibat Shield, which is highly prospective for iron ore, gold and base metals, part of the regional pre-Cambrian 'West Africa Craton' shield.[42] This is something of a simplification, although a dividing line can be seen on political maps of the territory, namely the berm which through much of its course follows ridge elevations between the two areas, except in the far northeast in

---

39   The Mining Code also establishes the state royalty on extracted, marketable minerals. It was first thought that royalty rates should be governed though a flexible scheme of government regulations and ministerial directions; however, the need for commercial certainty under a National Council (parliament) created statute was eventually preferred.

40   This role extends to the fisheries although shared with the SADR Ministry of Foreign Affairs because of the international relations implications of European and other states' treaty fisheries on the Saharan coast.

41   The SADR government granted a Technical Cooperation Agreement to Fusion Oil and Gas in 2000 which enabled that company to assess the potential of the territory.

42   The El Aauin basin is also known as the Coastal basin. See Nasser Ennih and Jean-Paul Liégeois, *The Boundaries Of The West African Craton, With Special Reference To The Basement Of The Moroccan Metacratonic Anti-Atlas Belt* (London: Geological Society, 2008) and Jean Fabre, *Géologie du Sahara occidental et central* (Tervuren: Musée royal de l'Afrique centrale – Belgique, 2005).

the inland Tindouf Basin, which it traverses. It is in the El Aauin basin that the extensive deposit of phosphate mineral rock at Bu Craa is found. This area consists of sediments, including the seabed offshore, and is accordingly considered to have the best petroleum prospectivity. The area is under the control of the occupying power and therefore access and credible data about the possible presence of minerals is incomplete. Tiris Iron Ore Province extends northwest from the Zouerate Mining Complex in neighboring Mauritania, with multi-billion tonne iron ore potential demonstrated in the SADR. Visible gold in quartz veins and numerous significant gold and base metals anomalies have also been identified in greenstone belts within Western Sahara proper. In recent years a Canadian mineral exploration company has carried out field and aerial surveys in the central south, around Auserd and Tichla, but has not made its findings public.[43] Offshore petroleum prospectivity is similarly obscured by a lack of disclosure from the two leading enterprises involved, both of which conducted extensive seabed seismic surveys during the summers of 2012, 2013 and 2014.[44]

The PMA has divided the offshore and onshore prospective oil and gas basins of Western Sahara into 18 license blocks. The SADR has engaged a number of independent advisors to develop agreements that are competitive and typical of the region. This professional counsel has included independent oil and gas consultants, academic experts and legal professionals, all of whom have a wealth of international oil industry and contractual experience.

In May 2005 the SADR government announced an inaugural oil licensing round in London and agreements are now in place with four international companies in eight permit areas. The exploratory rights are contracted under assurance agreements that will convert to production sharing contracts following any UN resolution which provides for (i.e. assures the immediate realization of) the Saharawi people's right to self-determination. The aim of the assurance agreements is primarily to create a low-cost option over exploration areas ('acreage' in regulatory usage) until such time as the sovereignty issue is resolved. The PMA does not require the assurance agreements to be worked by active exploration given the considerable presence of armed forces throughout the occupied area of Western Sahara.

Mining development in the liberated area of the territory has proceeded only after detailed appraisals under the 2007 Technical Cooperation Agreement.[45] It was only in 2014 that government arrangements were considered satisfactory to begin issuing mineral exploration permits.[46] In October 2014 the SADR government signed seven Exploration Permits with Hanno Resources. The company is now advancing in its exploration of the permit areas.[47]

The SADR PMA continues to assess how to undertake mining operations and extract minerals in the liberated area east of the berm. The SADR PMA and its foreign partners are in discussion on how to overcome logistical hurdles to the extraction and export of minerals, including

---

43　See http://metalexventures.com (accessed March 1, 2015). The company claims possible deposits of gold, zinc, lead and other metals, and diamonds in kimberlite in what is the Mauritanides Thrust Belt of the Reguibat Shield which extends 50–80 km west of the berm.

44　The PMA has assessed data made available to it, and accepts a general statement made in 2014 by Kosmos Energy Ltd. that the Boujdour Offshore permit area may contain up to 1 billion Barrels of Proved Oil Equivalent (BPOE). Following the decline in petroleum prices in the second half of 2014, the PMA assigned a figure of $70 per barrel as the threshold for return of viable deepwater petroleum recovery on the Saharan coast.

45　The SADR entered into a TCA with Hanno Resources in March 2007. Under the terms of the agreement Hanno undertook to provide a technical appraisal of the mineral potential of the SADR. See http://www.hannoresources.com/ (accessed July 24, 2015)

46　Much of the liberated area was surveyed in the seven years of the TCA, including assessments of how extracted ore can be transported for export. A significant challenge was ensuring the safety of prospecting teams working near unmarked, unexploded munitions, particularly land mines deployed by the occupying power east of the berm. Studies to assess mineral deposits in the occupied area continue, including literature surveys, analysis of satellite data, and appraisal of samples.

47　The exploration permits cover the Oum Abana Greenstone Belt, an area highly prospective for gold and base metals, and the Tiris Iron Ore Province noted above as prospective for iron ore.

transportation to the coast or a seaport for export.[48] The commodities most likely to be developed first are gold and iron ore, because they are concentrated in readily accessible deposits. The area of present iron development is the Tiris Iron Ore Province described above, near the semi-circular border with Mauritania in the southeast, with the 2014 prospecting licenses described above within a 100 km radius.[49] The area is relatively distant from population centers in the liberated zone and government support, with prospecting teams (mixed Saharawi and foreign nationals from the contracted company) necessarily operating with a high degree of autonomy but receiving support of the Saharawi military regions situated throughout the SADR's liberated area. Government planning for urban development and the availability of workers for possible mines in this area after self-determination has extended to assessments of infrastructure in nearby towns in the occupied area; Guelta Zemmur, Bir Anzarene and Auserd.

The current mineral prospecting licenses are intended to advance several policy objectives of the SADR government. Foremost is an accessible commercial and regulatory regime for mining companies and investors to begin mineral development. With acceptable environmental protection measures and civil society involvement, it was time for the Saharawi state to pursue resource development, particularly with other resources such as the Atlantic fishery being out of reach. Taxation-rent revenue is an important feature of this development, in part because the Saharawi people in their refugee exile depend greatly on external aid, and to better pursue the development of financial regulation and transparency within the SADR government.

An important secondary objective of present mining policy is the growth of institutional and intellectual capacity in the Saharawi state. This entails the development of a professional cadre of geologists, technicians, economists, planners and policy analysts equipped to deal with the complexities of a new resource regime that is intended to expand for all activities in Western Sahara once self-determination is realized. Advanced graduate education of geologists at leading African and European universities is an example. So, too, is the explicit policy of obtaining advice from third party governments and mining enterprises on regulating mining and measures to ensure social responsiveness of the Saharawi government to its people.

Mining activities and the granting of *in futuro* petroleum prospecting licenses in the Saharan offshore are a part of the expression of Saharawi aspirations to self-determination and the *effectivités* of demonstrating territorial sovereignty.[50] While the objective of such an expression is to couple sovereignty to natural resources to the right of self-determination, and to underscore the fact of an illegal occupation, it has the result of highlighting the ongoing pillage of primary resources from Western Sahara. Overlapping or ostensibly competing seabed petroleum licenses, for example, are useful to illustrate the fact of an occupying state taking resources without a legal basis.[51] The Saharawi government has considered how fishing rights could be exercised, conclud-

---

48 Nouadhibou is a possible industrial harbour for exports, located on the Cape Blanc peninsula, the seaward side of which is the southernmost part of the SADR liberated area, including the town of Laguera.

49 Four of the licenses are in the ore province, and three are 60–80 km to the north.

50 The SADR government and the Frente Polisario have noted for decades that Saharawi territorial integrity is settled, in part by customary international law through the *uti posseditis* principle and the African Union Charter, and by the conclusion of the International Court of Justice in 1975 that neither Mauritania nor Morocco had any tenable claim to the territory of the then Spanish Sahara. See *Western Sahara Advisory Opinion*, ICJ Reports 1975, 12 at para. 162.
    While no court of competent jurisdiction has declared Western Sahara to be occupied as such, the combination of the ICJ's 1975 opinion, resolutions of the UN General Assembly which declare the territory to be occupied, the positions of neighbouring states such as Algeria and Mauritania, and, crucially, the facts on the ground (a sustained armed occupation and the military partitioning of the territory by construction of the berm) make clear the legal status of the territory. Moreover, it must be recalled that the occupying power has always committed to relinquishing possession of Western Sahara on the completion of a referendum for self-determination of the Saharawi people, should they choose independence. The commitments made by the occupying power under the 1990–91 UN sponsored ceasefire and referendum agreement remain unchanged.

51 Two sources of law apply to the pillage of resources from Western Sahara: Resolution 1803 permanent sovereignty rights (requiring consent and benefit of resource extraction exclusively to the Saharawi people) much discussed after

ing that a similar approach of offering future access to the fishery is impractical because of the commercial nature of the industry and the possibility to re-engage the European Union after self-determination.[52]

There is, finally, the important project of advancing and demonstrating a viable rule of law in the Saharawi state and its governing institutions. All countries have an interest in the development of their resources as a vehicle or basis to foster the rule of law. This is true of the SADR, for the expected reason of sound democratic governance and for the crucial matter of ensuring the understanding across Saharawi society that government transparency and accountability will successfully transpose into a post-self-determination setting. The present development of Saharawi resources through the SADR PMA offers an opportunity to assess such obligations.

VI.   Conclusion: resources, sovereignty and statehood

It remains a daunting prospect for the Saharawi people to move to what they call the 'restoration of their independence'. A Saharawi state with sovereignty over all of Western Sahara will have diverse natural resources. The lessons from Namibia and Timor-Leste suggest this will be a good thing, Namibia having diverse natural resources with an economy not bound to rents alone from them, and Timor-Leste conversely with an overwhelming reliance on petroleum revenues into the state. The particular challenge, therefore, will be the effective governance of such resources.[53] This will be crucial to demonstrate to an organized international community that has invested much, including political capital, in support of newly created and emergent states such as South Sudan and Timor-Leste in recent years that a self-determined Saharawi people have the social, institutional and economic capacity to succeed in the project of independence. Establishing a present framework for future resource development is a stark lesson drawn from the successes (and failures) of recent self-determination cases. The careful approach to the creation of a mining regime by the SADR government, coupled with its policy-making while under occupation for the Atlantic fishery and seabed petroleum exploration in recent years augur well for robust governance.

At the same time, the singular pursuit of a resource-dependent or -oriented post-independence economy will not be a panacea. Resource extraction and, where possible, processing, can never entirely assure employment and just social conditions in a post-occupation society. Even if considerable wealth is immediately realized from the Saharawi people's national resources, the policy choice is to avoid an over-reliance on that sector in state building. A Saharawi economy and labor market (and thus the services related to them, including education) must necessarily have a diverse foundation. The present policy of preparing to govern resources for the future is an attempt to realize this.[54]

---

the 2002 Corell–UN Security Council opinion, and international humanitarian law with its criminal law prohibition on pillage except for resources for the needs of a civil population under occupation. The SADR government routinely asserts both sources of law in its protests about resource development and exports. Letters of protest are occasionally made public, such as that of January 26, 2015, referred to above.

52   The Frente Polisario is presently challenging the legality of the EU–Morocco Fisheries Partnership Agreement in the European Court of Justice, in part on the basis that the 2009 Treaty on the Functioning of the European Union prohibits an arrangement contrary to international law. See EJIL Talk (blog of the *European Journal of International Law*) 'Trade Agreements, EU Law, and Occupied Territories – A Report on EU Council' (July 1, 2015) at http://www.ejiltalk.org (accessed July 3, 2015).

53   The challenges to transparent, accountable and democratic control of resources in post-conflict states are manifold, and go to the core of establishing the rule of law. The design of institutions, the reviewing role of courts, and then engagement of civil society in resource planning are a part of this. For extensive useful commentary in the case of Timor-Leste after that country's 2002 independence, see the website of the Timor-Leste Institute for Development Monitoring and Analysis, http://www.laohamutuk.org (accessed April 1, 2015).

54   SADR PMA executives and others in Saharawi civil society, galvanized after 2012 by the prospect of petroleum in the Saharan seabed, have started to consider how a permanent, transparent and well-governed sovereign resource fund can be created along the lines of those in Norway and Timor-Leste. The policy analysis about that has usefully informed appeals for UN oversight or trust administration of resources while under occupation.

In many respects, the natural resources of Western Sahara mirror the circumstances of the Saharawi people themselves. In the 50 years since the organized international community has pursued the self-determination of colonized peoples, the legal principles toward that end together with those for the protection of sovereign rights to natural resources have become increasingly settled. Few can doubt that the Saharawi people will capably manage the transition from self-determination to a fully restored independence. That is now increasingly true when it comes to the governance and accountability in relation to development of natural resources in a liberated Western Sahara.

Acknowledgments

The author gratefully acknowledges the comments of Jeffrey Smith, barrister, on drafts of this paper.

Disclosure statement

No potential conflict of interest was reported by the author.

Independence by *fiat*: a way out of the impasse – the self-determination of Western Sahara, with lessons from Timor-Leste

Pedro Pinto Leite

Secretary, International Platform of Jurists for East Timor

Western Sahara and Timor-Leste (East Timor) are twin cases marking an incomplete end to the era of decolonization. The two are remarkably similar: they are former European colonies with peoples who had been promised self-determination only to be invaded within weeks of each other in late 1975 by neighboring states, themselves recently decolonized. Decades would pass while the international community stood by. The people of Timor-Leste eventually achieved freedom against the odds while most of Western Sahara and half the Saharawi people remain under foreign occupation, the scene of established human rights violations and the ongoing export of natural resources. For 25 years, Morocco has refused the Saharawi people a referendum, with the United Nations organization unable to respond as a result of a threatened veto by some permanent members of the Security Council. However, a Saharawi state arguably has come into being, enjoying popular legitimacy, governing institutions and accepted control over a part of Western Sahara. Moreover, regionally and within the African Union, the Saharawi Republic enjoys broad recognition and advocacy for its people. While drawing on lessons from the comparative experience of self-determination in Timor-Leste, this paper contends that the UN should follow the example of the African Union and welcome the Saharawi Republic as a member state. To achieve that result, a wider recognition among states is needed. The UN General Assembly, by employing its 1950 Uniting for Peace resolution, can decide to 'consider the matter immediately' and compel a breakthrough which the Security Council has so far not been able to deliver.

Introduction

The brave era of decolonization has all but passed. 2015 is a time to recall the successes of humanity's most important modern project: the universal realization of human rights through the emancipation of peoples worldwide under colonial domination. The year marks 55 years since the United Nations under the General Assembly's leadership declared the right to self-determination in Resolutions 1514 and 1541; 45 years since the UN took charge of the difficult case of Namibia;[1] 40 years since the International Court of Justice affirmed for the Saharawi people their right of self-determination in the *Western Sahara* Advisory Opinion,[2] and 20 years since the same result from the Court for the East Timorese people in the *Timor Gap Treaty (Portugal/Australia)* decision.[3] The shared values among states and the nature of international law in this landscape have never been clearer. And yet the Saharawi people – half refugees in exile in desert camps and half under military occupation – are among the last of all peoples awaiting the right to self-determination, the support of which right is the paramount obligation of all

---

1 'Namibia – UNTAG Background', United Nations, New York, http://www.un.org/en/peacekeeping/missions/past/untagFT.htm (accessed August 10, 2015).
2 *Western Sahara, Advisory Opinion*, ICJ Reports 1975, 12.
3 *East Timor (Portugal* v. *Australia), Judgment*, ICJ Reports 1995, 90.

members of the organized international community, including the United Nations.[4] Despite a formal process for their self-determination established nearly a quarter of a century ago, it is a right that continues to be denied to them. The international community has deferred to a United Nations unable to break the impasse over Saharawi self-determination because of a Security Council that is unwilling to act and a General Assembly which has relinquished its successful historical role in decolonization.

Two fundamental obligations of international law, namely the prohibition against aggression and the outlawing of territorial conquest, continue to be violated in Western Sahara. These obligations are the basis for peace and stability in the modern order among nation-states. There are other continuing violations, of course, ones routinely noted by outside commentators, for example human rights abuses and the stripping (pillage) of resources.[5] The norms of international law have apparently been forgotten in the Sahara, the resulting impunity enjoyed by Morocco being an objectionable precedent and a phenomenon that arguably damages international law. The case of Western Sahara could not be more compelling, whatever one's perspective, including as a matter of international relations, law, the social and economic development of northwest Africa, and justice itself. Jacob Mundy, an American scholar who writes about Western Sahara, has expressed the circumstances as follows:

> The [International Court of Justice's 1975] opinion on Western Sahara is most often cited as proof definitive that Western Sahara is owed a referendum on self-determination. However, this claim is based upon a half-reading of the *summary* of the Court's opinion. A full reading of the Court's entire opinion shows that the ICJ was very clear that the sovereign power in Western Sahara was and is the native Western Saharans [the Saharawi people]. The purpose of a self-determination referendum in Western Sahara is not to decide between competing sovereignties, whether Moroccan or Saharawi, but to poll the Saharawis as to whether or not they wish to retain, modify or divest their sovereignty. We need to stop talking about self-determination as an act that constitutes sovereignty in Western Sahara. Sovereignty is already constituted in Western Sahara. As the ICJ said, Western Sahara has never been *terra nullius*.[6]

With such reasoning as a starting point, and given the stalled dynamic of realizing the Saharawi people's rights and resolving their circumstances, this paper examines the issue of self-determination which has been the single demand of the Saharawi people as the path to decide their political and legal status including perhaps as an independent state. The analysis takes regard of the close parallel to the successful realization of self-determination for the people of Timor-Leste in 1999. A proposal to overcome the impasse is then advanced.

Decolonization's promise and precedent

The historical circumstances that led to the Saharawi people being offered a United Nations administered referendum to resolve their status in the post-colonial world as a non-self-

---

4 'Saharawi' refers to the name of the original people of the territory of Western Sahara which was known as Spanish Sahara until 1975. The Saharawi population as an identifiable ethnic, cultural and linguistic group is about 350,000 people: 160,000 in the refugee camps at Tindouf, 120,000 in occupied Western Sahara and a diaspora concentrated in Mauritania and Spain. On 27 February 1976 the Saharawi Arab Democratic Republic was proclaimed, the act later ratified by the Saharawi electorate in the acceptance of a national constitution.

5 See most recently the annual report of the UN Secretary-General to the UN Security Council, 'Report of the Secretary-General on the situation concerning Western Sahara' (April 10, 2015), UN doc. S/246/2015. The Secretary-General is properly oblique about the application of international law in its various forms to Western Sahara, consistent with the wider UN organization's characterization of the matter not as conflict or territorial occupation or, for the most part, a matter of decolonization, but in anodyne terms as 'the question' of Western Sahara. Annual Secretary-General Reports on Western Sahara can be found online at http://www.un.org/en/peacekeeping/missions/minurso/reports.shtml (accessed July 26, 2015).

6 Jacob Mundy, 'The Question of Sovereignty in the Western Sahara Conflict' (presentation at the IAJUWS conference 'La Cuestión del Sáhara Occidental en El Marco Jurídico Internacional', Las Palmas, Canary Islands, June 27–28, 2008).

governing people have been addressed at length elsewhere.[7] A United Nations administered referendum for the Saharawi people is to be the same in the substance of elective choices as was successfully delivered by the UN in Namibia in 1989 and Timor-Leste (East Timor) a decade later.

The case of Timor-Leste is particularly instructive in relation to Western Sahara. Both Spain and Portugal were in the process of ending their colonial ventures by the mid-1970s and in both Timor-Leste and Western Sahara neighboring powers invaded, in 1975, before the colonization process was completed. In both cases, the United Nations recognized the former colonial power to have maintained continuing legal authority pending formal decolonization and in both cases occupation by the invading neighboring power – Indonesia in the case of Timor-Leste and Morocco in the case of Western Sahara – has not been recognized under international law.

Through a confluence of circumstances, including international pressure on continuing human rights abuses (highlighted by the Santa Cruz Massacre of 1991), the cost of occupation, a change of regime in Indonesia and Portugal's continuing advocacy, the UN brokered a 'popular consultation' among East Timorese people (as defined by the UN) on the question of whether the territory would remain as an autonomous part of Indonesia or whether it would move towards independence. Amid widespread pro-Indonesia violence and destruction, on 30 August 1999 the vote in favor of independence was carried by 78.5% of the voting population.[8] This result then spurred a further wave of pro-Indonesia violence and destruction, leading the UN to mandate the intervention of a peace-keeping force and to apply a UN interim administration ahead of elections and independence on 20 May 2002. Although Spain has not actively represented Western Sahara in the UN and the pressures on Morocco differ, the UN could legally assume advocacy for such a ballot in the occupied territory, applying the same process of transitional administration should the ballot similarly decide in favor of independence.

Having noted that, the majority of decolonization cases, especially in Africa, were accomplished without such a consultative act. But the difficult cases suggest that the organized international community confers the realization of self-determination upon the neutral implementing organization which the UN is perceived to be and it is delivered through a formal democratic, transparent process. These requirements are sufficient and they have been at the heart of the impasse over Western Sahara.

A few observations can be made about a referendum for Saharawi self-determination. An inconvenient legal fact is that a self-determination referendum, which is a consultative electoral choice by the legitimate inhabitants of a colonized territory to settle their political status, is not required generally under international law or as a matter of the UN decolonization resolutions, General Assembly Resolutions 1514 (XV) and 1541 (XV) of 14 December 1960. The requirement for a referendum, regardless of who was to arrange it, has never been UN policy or otherwise compulsory (such as, for example, by operation of customary international law) in decolonization cases. Electoral consultation did not occur in the majority of instances during the era of decolonization in the 1950s and 1960s. Of course, a referendum would confer legitimacy on a United Nations organ-

---

7   See Tony Hodges, *Western Sahara: The Roots of a Desert War* (Westport, CT: Lawrence Hill, 1983); Jeffrey Smith, 'State of Exile: The Saharawi Republic and its Refugees', in *Still Waiting for Tomorrow: The Law and Politics of Unresolved Refugee Crises*, ed. Susan Akram and Tom Syring (Newcastle upon Tyne: Cambridge Scholars, 2014, 25–53); Stephen Zunes and Jacob Mundy, *Western Sahara: War, Nationalism, and Conflict Irresolution* (Syracuse, NY: Syracuse University Press, 2010); Karin Arts and Pedro Pinto Leite, eds., *International Law and the Question of Western Sahara* (Leiden: IPJET, 2007).

8   For useful histories of the invasion of Timor-Leste and the 1999 referendum see James Dunn, *East Timor: A People Betrayed* (Milton, Queensland: Jacaranda Press, 1983); Carmel Budiardjo and Liem Soei Liong, *The War Against East Timor* (London: Zed Books, 1984); Irena Cristalis, *East Timor: A Nation's Bitter Dawn*, 2nd ed. (London: Zed Books, 2009); and Richard Tanter, Mark Selden, and Stephen R. Shalom, eds., *Bitter Flowers, Sweet Flowers: East Timor, Indonesia, and the World Community* (Oxford: Rowman & Littlefield, 2001).

ization which by its current presence in Western Sahara has the self-assumed obligation to ensure orderly and democratic self-determination as it did in Timor-Leste. The form of realizing self-determination – the process of ensuring a colonized people have before them a truly elective choice – is less important than the substantive right to be decided upon, be it continuing colonization (incorporation into the colonizing state), association with the former colonizing state, or independence. The UN has been clear such outcomes are to be always available to non-self-governing peoples, even as the number of cases dwindles. And it has assured the Saharawi people that such a range of elective choices will be available to them. There seems to be little choice for the UN in the matter, after the International Court of Justice (ICJ) confirmed the expansive scope of self-determination in its 2010 *Kosovo* Advisory Opinion:

> During the second half of the twentieth century, the international law of self-determination developed in such a way as to create a right to independence for the peoples of non-self-governing territories and peoples subject to alien subjugation, domination and exploitation ... A great many new States have come into existence as a result of the exercise of this right.[9]

Of course, the UN Security Council has noted Morocco's pursuit of its 2007 autonomy referendum proposal, which would retain the territory within Morocco as its so-called Southern Provinces, to be 'serious and credible'.[10] The conduct of a referendum by the UN as a neutral interlocutor can allow for a more politically acceptable outcome for the occupying state, as with Indonesia in Timor-Leste. (Although hardly a 'just' result, the acquiescence of the occupying state to self-determination can serve to absolve it in part of the wrongful annexation of a territory, extending even to crimes committed during an occupation, as was the result for an *apartheid* South Africa in Namibia.[11]) Moreover, the important factor of political recognition of a new state – if the choice of a self-determining people is for independence – in the organized international community is a useful advantage. The need to promote peace, community order and social development in a newly independent former colony, after a period of annexation, where peoples from the occupying state may choose to remain is helped by a transparent, externally assured and democratic process.[12]

The roots of a referendum

The issue of independence and the subsequent act of self-determination of a colonized people is the responsibility of the decolonizing power, in this case of Spain as the colonizing state in Spanish Sahara. Then and now, international law did not allow the obligation to be cast aside, even by Spain's agreement in November 1975 with Mauritania and Morocco to jointly administer the territory under a vague promise that the three parties would somehow see to Saharawi self-determination.[13] The UN's intervention would come more than a decade later, drawing on the

---

9 *Accordance with International Law of the Unilateral Declaration of Independence in Respect of Kosovo, Advisory Opinion*, ICJ Reports 2010, 403, para. 79.
10 This began with UN Security Council 1754 (2007) (April 30, 2007) and has continued, for which see now UN Security Council Resolution 2218 (2015) (April 28, 2015). The Security Council resolutions have also reflected the change in the UN organization's position that there be a 'just and lasting' resolution of the question of Western Sahara, to one that is 'just, lasting and mutually acceptable'.
11 See United Nations Security Council Resolution 435 Namibia, July 27, 1978.
12 This might be called *civil society consensus*, a shared values structure that was important in Timor-Leste given the legacy of violence during the occupation of that territory, and the challenges of reconciliation after the August 1999 referendum.
13 For a discussion of the 1975 agreement, the Madrid Accords, see Hodges, *Western Sahara*. The crucial obligation to ensure for the Saharawi people a referendum was assumed by the UN in 1991, in agreement with Morocco and the Saharawi people (acting through their national liberation movement the Frente Polisario), the terms of which are in two reports of the UN Secretary-General to the Security Council in 1990 and 1991.
In November 1975 Spain legislated an end to its colonial responsibility for the Sahara, the position of successive governments since. However, Spanish criminal law (and by incorporation international criminal law under the Rome

work of the Organization of African Unity (OAU, now the African Union – AU) which after 1984 culminated in a 1988 settlement proposal accepted by Morocco and the Frente Polisario in the form of measures adopted by the Security Council in 1990–91. The agreement came at a vital moment.[14] Mauritania had earlier abandoned its claim to the territory and recognized the Saharawi Republic.[15] In the aftermath of Mauritania's 1979 peace treaty, which contained the admission that it had conducted an 'unjust war', the Saharawi people had only a single occupier with which to contend. In this era, the Moroccan army sustained heavy losses and therefore the 'berm', the sand wall that now partitions the territory, was constructed.[16] By the late 1980s an active end to hostilities spurred peacemaking efforts and allowed Morocco to consolidate its occupation, both demographically by the settlement of its nationals and on the world stage.[17]

Arrangements for peoples in territories under occupation to exercise their right of self-determination tend to come with complications. In retrospect, the 1988–91 agreement for an act of self-determination for the Saharawi people was flawed because of the lack of capacity bestowed upon the United Nations Mission for the Referendum in Western Sahara (MINURSO). MINURSO was unable to ensure impartial and accurate registration of Saharawi nationals for the referendum and to effectively ensure public order and the protection of human rights in the occupied part of the territory prior to a referendum.[18] Such shortcomings were also evident in Timor-Leste's referendum for independence in 1999, from which the UN could have applied its lessons to help ensure that a referendum would proceed in Western Sahara. Instead, compromise demanded that Morocco be allowed flexibility to challenge voter identification and add people to the register for the referendum. The result was that the kingdom demanded the acceptance of large numbers of persons with limited or no connection to the Saharawi people and their territory. This pattern of events continued until the referendum registration process ground to a halt in 2004.[19] The result has been that, during the active years of the UN's administration of the referendum process, Morocco boycotted meaningful voter identification and insisted on adding large numbers of its nationals, thereby ensuring postponement of the referendum.[20] It should be recalled, however, that MINURSO did complete voter registration. Nearly a decade after it came into being, MINURSO identified 86,386 Saharawis as eligible. Morocco, perhaps fearful of defeat in a referendum to follow, contested the result.[21]

Statute 1998 of the International Criminal Court) applies in Western Sahara as a matter of recent decisions by the appeals court the Audencia Nacional (July 2014 and April 2015).

14 The Settlement Plan, built on the earlier peace proposal of the Organization of African Unity, became effective in September 1991 with a ceasefire and measures to prepare for a referendum. MINURSO, the United Nations Mission for the Referendum in Western Sahara, was established by UN Security Council Resolution 690 (April 29, 1991) with a mandate to monitor the ceasefire and conduct the referendum.

15 Mauritania signed a peace treaty with the Frente Polisario in August 1979 and recognized the SADR in February 1984.

16 This was acknowledged by independent observers and also Morocco. See e.g. 'Desert War Flares Anew', *Chicago Tribune*, October 6, 1988, http://articles.chicagotribune.com/1988-10-06/news/8802050099_1_polisario-front-morocco-moroccan (accessed April 2, 2015).

17 See also Jacob Mundy, 'Morocco Settlers in Western Sahara: Colonists or Fifth Column', *Arab World Geographer* 15 (2012): 95.

18 See the statement of former US Ambassador Frank Ruddy, a former senior official with MINURSO, to the United States Congress on January 25, 1995 at http://www.arso.org/06-3-1.htm (accessed April 2, 2015).

19 The berm in its successively built segments is longer than 2400 kilometres. It remains heavily fortified, the largest minefield in the world, with perhaps 65,000 Moroccan FAR soldiers stationed along it. The berm was reportedly constructed with the assistance of Israel, the USA and Saudi Arabia, although few details are available. Following the ICJ's reasoning in its 2004 *Palestine Wall* Advisory Opinion, it can be safely concluded that construction of the berm violated international law.

20 Ruddy's report, above, denounced the obstacles put by Morocco to MINURSO's work. Francesco Bastagli, who in 2005 was appointed UN Special Representative for Western Sahara, strongly criticized UN inaction on Western Sahara and resigned in protest in 2006.

21 This was the voter registration figure on 30 December 1999. The Identification Commission announced the result on 15 January 2000 and the Secretary-General reported it to the Security Council that 17 February. See UN doc. S/2000/

The former United States Secretary of State, James Baker, appointed in early 1997 as the UN Secretary-General's Personal Envoy for Western Sahara, offered a proposal to overcome these problems. It was labeled the Framework Agreement and informally known as Baker Plan I.[22] The plan for a path out of the impasse did not allow for independence as an option[23] – only autonomy within Morocco[24] – and it was therefore contrary to international law which stipulates that the people of a non-self-governing territory can only be said to have achieved self-government if they have available all options to be an independent state.[25] As has been observed, the norm is the core of the right of peoples to self-determination, with a quality of (sometimes debated) *jus cogens* and one to be supported in principle (if sometimes not in practice) by all states as an obligation *erga omnes*.[26] The Saharawi people had always favored independence, expressing that ambition through the Frente Polisario to the UN and in the work of their social and government institutions, and therefore it surprised no one that they rejected the first Baker Plan.[27]

As a result, Baker pursued a second plan for self-determination. It provided for Saharawi self-rule under a 'Western Sahara Authority' to operate for a transitional five years then followed by an independence referendum. The 'Baker Plan II' guaranteed that Moroccan settlers, who by 2000 began to outnumber Saharawis in the occupied part of the territory, would be permitted to vote. This was, again, contrary to norms of self-determination.[28] By comparison, in Timor-Leste's 1999 referendum, Indonesian settlers were disqualified from voting. Nevertheless the Security Council endorsed Baker Plan II. The Frente Polisario reluctantly – even 'surprisingly' according to some observers – accepted the plan.[29] The Saharawi leadership endorsed it, confident of an outcome where Moroccan settlers would reliably choose independence – a remarkable thing

---

131 (February 17, 2000). 'From Morocco's point of view, the numbers indicated total defeat'. Zunes and Mundy, *Western Sahara*, 215.

22 *Framework Agreement on the Status of Western Sahara*, Annex I of UN Secretary-General Report S/2001/613 of June 20, 2001.

23 UN Secretary-General Kofi Annan may have instructed his personal envoy to go no further than autonomy for Western Sahara within the Moroccan state. Marrack Goulding, a former UN Undersecretary-General, said that Annan asked him 'to go to Houston to persuade James Baker III to accept an appointment as Special Representative and try to negotiate a deal based on enhanced autonomy for Western Sahara within the Kingdom of Morocco'. Marrack Goulding, *Peacemonger* (London: John Murray, 2002), 214–15.

24 Timor-Leste's 1999 referendum had two options: autonomy within the state of Indonesia, and independence. Under the Western Sahara Framework Agreement autonomy would be imposed on the Saharawi people. This is contrary to Principle IX of Resolution 1541 (XV): '[I]ntegration should be the result of the freely expressed wishes of the Territory's peoples acting with full knowledge of the change in their status, their wishes having been expressed through informed and democratic processes impartially conducted and based on universal adult suffrage'.

25 'A Non-Self-Governing Territory can be said to have reached a full measure of self-government by: (a) Emergence as a sovereign independent State; (b) Free association with an independent State; or (c) Integration with an independent State.' Resolution 1541, Principle VI.

26 'The exceptional importance of the principle of the self-determination of peoples in the modern world is such that today the principle has been held to constitute an example of jus cogens, that is, 'a peremptory norm of general international law', to quote the expression used in article 53 of the Vienna Convention on the Law of Treaties'. Hector Gros Espiell, *The Right to Self Determination: Implementation of United Nations Resolutions*, study prepared by the Special Rapporteur of the Sub Commission on Prevention of Discrimination and Protection of Minorities, E/CN.4/Sub.2/405/Rev.1, 1980.

27 During the time of Baker's appointment until his second plan, the people of Timor-Leste completed their self-determination and achieved independence. The Saharawi people were certainly aware of the rapid progress and eventual successful result of independence under UN administration of the self-determination process in Timor. The two states recognize each other, exchange diplomatic representatives and have some social and cultural contacts.

28 Even the New York City Bar Association has noted that 'the right to self-determination under international law pertains to the indigenous inhabitants of a Non-Self-Governing Territory – in this case the Saharawis who inhabited the territory – and cannot be invoked by non-indigenous settlers'. *The Legal Issues Involved in the Western Sahara Dispute – The Principle of Self-Determination and the Legal Claims of Morocco* (New York: New York City Bar Association, Committee on the United Nations, June 2012), 94.

29 Tobey Shelley, 'Behind the Baker Plan for Western Sahara', *Middle East Research and Information Project*, August 1, 2003

given the uncertain prospect of Saharawi rule.[30] Moreover, Morocco feared that democracy during the five years of transitional administration leading to the referendum might 'infect' the kingdom.[31]

Since 2002, Morocco has rejected the idea of a self-determination referendum in Western Sahara – regardless of the population accepted as eligible to participate. Despite the commitments of Morocco's Hassan II to the UN's 1990–91 settlement terms and the 1997 Baker process, his successor Mohammed VI has rejected a referendum except for the narrow option of a circumscribed regional autonomy, declaring as irrevocable Morocco's claimed sovereignty over the Southern Provinces.[32]

To maintain the perception of a Morocco willing to engage the 'question' of Western Sahara, in April 2007 the kingdom's government transmitted to the new UN Secretary-General Ban Ki-moon a proposal for the territory's autonomy. The 'Moroccan initiative for negotiating an autonomy statute for the Sahara region' was put forward as 'a basis for dialogue, negotiation and compromise'.[33] The Frente Polisario had anticipated the move, delivering a day earlier to the Secretary-General its 'Proposal for a Mutually Acceptable Political Solution Assuring the Self-Determination of the People of Western Sahara'.[34] Later that same month the Security Council issued Resolution 1754, urging Morocco and the Frente Polisario to 'enter into direct negotiations without preconditions and in good faith'.[35] Discussions between the two, which have been overseen by successive personal envoys of the Secretary-General, began that June in Manhasset, New York. Numerous rounds have since been held in various locations. While these negotiations, led in recent years by the well-regarded former US diplomat Christopher Ross, have forced Morocco to deal with the Frente Polisario as an equal, there has been effectively no progress since the two parties' 2007 proposals, referred to above. Discussions during a 2011 session in Geneva on the subject of natural resources in Western Sahara proved fruitless, as have efforts in recent years to create a role for MINURSO to observe and report on human rights conditions, the only UN mission of its kind without such a mandate.[36] This lack of a human rights mandate is indicative of the weakness of the overall mandate of MINURSO in Western Sahara and illustrates the lack of commitment to resolving the impasse. From the standpoint of the involvement of the UN and the organized international community, the impasse following Baker's resignation from the process in 2004 continues and there has been no reconciliation or common negotiating space

---

30 Statement by Emhamed Khadad, member of the National Secretariat of the Frente Polisario and coordinator for MINURSO, at a meeting on Western Sahara at the University of Utrecht, March 25, 2002.

31 On the response of the Saharawi people and Morocco to Baker Plan II see Zunes and Mundy, *Western Sahara*, 234 ff.

32 In March 2006 during a visit to the territory Mohammed VI declared: 'Morocco will not cede a single inch, nor a grain of sand of its dear Sahara'. See the statement at http://www.arso.org/01-e06-1314.htm (accessed July 26, 2015).

33 See http://w-sahara.blogspot.com/2007/04/moroccos-plan-full-text.html (accessed April 4, 2015). Frank Ruddy described the proposal as 'the latest in a long line of illusions that Morocco has created over the years to distract world attention from the real issue', adding 'The Moroccan limited autonomy plan for Western Sahara ... might sound like a step forward, at least until one reads the not-so-fine print. Article 6 of the plan provides that Morocco will keep its powers in the royal domain, especially with regard to defense, external relations and the constitutional and religious prerogatives of his majesty the king. In other words, the Moroccans are offering autonomy, except in everything that counts. It gets even more disingenuous where the Moroccans say their plan will be submitted to a referendum, but fail to provide details'. 'Foreword' in Arts and Pinto Leite, *International Law and the Question of Western Sahara*, 12.

34 The Proposal is at http://www.arso.org/PropositionFP100407.htm#en (accessed April 5, 2015). The Frente Polisario restated its acceptance of Baker Plan II, held out the prospect of citizenship to Moroccan settlers at independence, and waived reparations claims between the two states. The Frente's 2007 Proposal remains its formal position as well as a commitment to a 'genuine referendum'.

35 Resolution 1754 (2007) adopted by the Security Council at its 5669th meeting, April 30, 2007.

36 See e.g. the 2012 annual report of the Secretary-General to the Security Council, 'Report of the Secretary-General on the situation concerning Western Sahara' (April 5, 2012), UN doc. S/20121/197, paras. 72 ff. See also 'Preliminary Observations: Robert F. Kennedy International Delegation Visit to Morocco Occupied Western Sahara and the Refugee Camps in Algeria' (September 3, 2012), http://rfkcenter.org/images/attachments/article/1703/Final091012.pdf (accessed April 1, 2015).

resulting from the parties' 2007 proposals. While such a status quo is regarded as unacceptable, the community of states defers wholesale to the UN's conduct of the matter and that, in part, has perpetuated the stalemate.

Impasse in the desert

Almost a quarter of a century on, it would appear that the prospect of a legitimate process of self-determination for the Saharawi people is as remote as it ever has been. This is the result of the inability of the parties to transform or step away from closely held positions. For its part, the Frente Polisario is perceived to be intransigent in its demand for a referendum that includes the option of independence, and less the question of who is qualified to vote or how human rights and protection of the territory's natural resources from pillage should be resolved in the run-up to a referendum. Insisting on a Saharawi climb-down is difficult because of the close identification by the Frente Polisario with and understanding of what international law guarantees them. For the Saharawi, the success of the East Timorese people in their 1999 referendum and the ICJ's *Kosovo* Advisory Opinion in favor of independence[37] are sources of inspiration. While it cannot be said that the Saharawi people were deceived when they agreed to a ceasefire and referendum process that was to begin in the second half of 1991, what was promised has since been denied to them. Further, there has been no challenge to that principal foundation of peace and security – territorial integrity – even as the ICJ uniquely concluded among all its decolonization decisions that Morocco had no basis for a territorial claim. None of this should be surprising when it is recalled that the organized international community at large, the UN or Spain as the colonial power responsible have not sought to ensure the protection of the Saharawi civil population, which suffers documented war crimes while under occupation.[38] The parallels with Timor-Leste from 1975 until 1999 are close, given the lack of commitment by the international community to find a solution to Indonesia's occupation of and war crimes in East Timor (until international opinion began to turn after a military massacre of civilians in Dili in 1991 and the collapse of the Indonesian economy and subsequent resignation of authoritarian President Suharto in 1998).

There are two other things about the impasse over Western Sahara that are to be regretted, namely the diminished role of the African Union as a respected interlocutor to the 'question' of Western Sahara and the failure of the Security Council to act to resolve the matter under its 1990–91 agreement commitments and the UN Charter.[39] The second of these is the more ominous in light of the UN, led by the Security Council, being successful in arranging referenda on self-determination for the peoples of Namibia and Timor-Leste. For the Saharawi people who have relied on the assurances of the organized international community acting through the UN, the possibility of their referendum appears to have been deferred indefinitely.

If the delay in resolving the issue of Western Sahara has resulted from a now entirely stalled process to arrive at a self-determination referendum for the Saharawi people, then the means by which the referendum process was arrived at and pursued must be critically questioned. The ICJ confirmed in its *Western Sahara* advisory opinion that 'the application of the right of self-determination requires a free and genuine expression of the will of the peoples concerned'.[40] This is an

---

37 *Accordance with International Law of the Unilateral Declaration of Independence in Respect of Kosovo, Advisory Opinion*, ICJ Reports 2010, 403

38 Ali Lmrabet, 'Un responsable marroquí reconoce crímenes de guerra en el Sahara', *El Mundo*, June 17, 2008, see also 'Morocco', *Country Reports on Human Rights Practices*, Bureau of Democracy, Human Rights, and Labor, US State Department, February 23, 2001.

39 The AU has been a consistent supporter of the Saharawi state. On 27 March 2015 the AU Peace and Security Council issued a *communiqué* to the UN Secretary-General insisting on Saharawi self-determination and calling the export of natural resources from Western Sahara 'illegal exploitation'. See http://www.peaceau.org (accessed April 15, 2015).

40 *Western Sahara, Advisory Opinion*, para. 55.

acknowledgement, even as the practice of the UN in the three cases that followed was for a formal referendum, of the importance of a credibly expressed popular choice. The people of Western Sahara were understood by the UN's visiting mission in May 1975, a group of General Assembly diplomats, to overwhelmingly want independence. The release of the mission's report that October,[41] within a day of the ICJ's advisory opinion, could have been the entire end of the matter. The need to account for the collective will of a colonized people does not necessarily turn on that consensus being expressed through an externally administered plebiscite, meaning that Western Sahara could have, and could still be, recognized as independent by the UN without further discussion. This is where the UN in Western Sahara has by its conduct de facto limited the options for self-determination.[42] Such conduct, of course, is the failure of the UN to see through a referendum on terms it committed to during the process from 1988 to 1991.

It is useful at this point to return to what had become accepted practice in the organized international community in the legitimate cases of decolonization. The majority of them in the busy years of decolonization reveal the acceptability of peoples exercising the right to self-determination and accession to independence without referenda. Among these can be counted all former Portuguese colonies with the exception of Timor-Leste (and perhaps Macao).[43] The risk of carrying out a less than fully credible (or democratic) referendum in Western Sahara should be considered carefully. A sham process, with unforeseen consequences for the creation of the new state, could harm the Saharawi people and damage international law, as the fraudulent consultative exercise in West Papua, the 1969 'Act of Free Choice', has demonstrated.[44] A UN administered referendum conducted in Western Sahara would now most likely include Moroccan nationals although settled illegally by Morocco in the territory.[45] Hence, the UN could and arguably should simply declare Western Sahara to be independent.

The parallels of Timor and the Sahara

To consider the case against an externally conferred referendum, it must be remembered that the Saharawis exercised for themselves their right of self-determination when they constituted the Saharawi Republic in February 1976. That event and the later ratification of it by the Saharawi in later years seems to have been credible – that is, acceptable in law and by democratic decision.[46] However, when it comes to the close historical and legal parallels between Timor-Leste and Western Sahara, an important difference must be noted. For the Timorese a referendum was arguably necessary because, while there had been a declaration of independence and Timor

---

41 Dietrich Rauschning, Katja Wiesbrock, and Martin Lailach, *Key Resolutions of the United Nations General Assembly 1946–1996* (Cambridge: Cambridge University Press,1997), 186.

42 'The validity of the principle of self-determination, defined as the need to pay regard to the freely expressed will of peoples, is not affected by the fact that in certain cases the General Assembly has dispensed with the requirement of consulting the inhabitants of a given territory. Those instances were based either on the consideration that a certain population did not constitute a "people" entitled to self-determination or on the conviction that a consultation was totally unnecessary, in view of special circumstances' (*Western Sahara, Advisory Opinion*, para. 59).

43 During the era of decolonization after 1960, Africa saw few formal acts of self-determination. The 1956 referendum in French Togoland was not about self-determination per se, because it did not include the option of independence and would be later rejected by the UN General Assembly. The 1989 and 2011 referenda in Namibia and South Sudan were done with all parties having agreed that a choice for independence would be accepted. The 1993 referendum in Eritrea served to confirm a de facto independence because Eritrea had successfully broken away from Ethiopia, its referendum done to gain UN and OAU recognition.

44 See Esther Heidbüchl, *The West Papua Conflict in Indonesia: Actors, Issues and Approaches* (Berlin: Verlag, 2007).

45 Apart from the positions of the parties, there remains the problem of establishing a current (accurate) voter roll for self-determination. Arguably, the UN remains responsible for that as a matter of its commitments in the 1990–91 referendum and ceasefire agreement. But it is difficult to envision the UN having liberty of action in Western Sahara to conduct an objective registration. The problem is alleviated, of course, if the referendum is on those terms proposed by Morocco in 2007. Completeness of registration matters less where independence is not at stake.

46 Saharawi vote each four years for local government in the 'independent' zones of the territory, and in self-administering camps in Algeria.

briefly met the conditions for statehood under the Montevideo Convention and customary international law, when it was invaded by Indonesia the Timorese people lost governance and territorial control.[47] The short-lived Democratic Republic of East Timor achieved only limited recognition from 11 states. The regional organization, Association of Southeast Asian Nations (ASEAN), sided with Indonesia. In addition, the exiled East Timorese leadership did not attempt to govern from exile, instead adopting the narrative of a non-self-governing and occupied people. This was reinforced by a Portugal that maintained it was the *de jure* colonial administering power. It demonstrated this by challenging the 1989 Australia–Indonesia Timor Gap Treaty for seabed petroleum and through becoming a party to the 1999 agreement with Indonesia for a referendum in the territory.[48] Finally, following the initial referendum of 1999, a UN administered referendum was needed to promote the consensus within East Timor that the UN could legitimately govern the territory and to create institutions of state until independence in May 2002.[49] The utility of a legitimate consultative plebiscite can be seen at present in Kosovo and was an important culminating step in South Sudan's long campaign to secede.

The Saharawi people find themselves in manifestly different circumstances. It seems clear that, however limited in financial resources and suffering the constraints of being operated from a refugee exile inside Algeria, the Saharawi Arab Democratic Republic (SADR) is a state. The criteria for such a legal existence are well established: (i) a people culturally and linguistically different from those of Morocco;[50] (ii) a defined territory within colonially prescribed and universally accepted boundaries, one-fifth of which is under its control;[51] (iii) a government with exclusive jurisdiction over a substantial part of the Saharawi population in the liberated area of Western Sahara and the refugee camps at Tindouf; and (iv) the capacity to enter into relations with other states, the SADR having been recognized by more than 80 states (and conducting diplomatic relations with 40 of them, with embassies in 18 capitals).[52] In addition, the SADR was admitted in 1982 to the regional organization, the OAU (something that resulted in Morocco quitting the organization) and is a founding member of OAU's successor, the African Union.[53] The qualification is that, while it is recognized as having statehood status, at the time of writing, no external power, including the UN, was prepared to use force to expel Morocco from the territory.

While it is true that the larger urban and economic heart of the territory is controlled by Morocco, illegal occupation cannot by itself terminate statehood.[54] Indeed, as Kuwait's 1990 invasion by Iraq demonstrated, there is an obligation under international law expressly to maintain (or restore) territorial integrity in cases of annexation. An additional factor is the absence of an engaged colonial administering state. International law and widespread state practice is clear

---

47 Article 1 of the *Montevideo Convention on the Rights and Duties of States* (December 26, 1933) 165 LNTS 19: a permanent population, a defined territory, a government, and capacity to enter into relations with the other states.

48 Although it did not recognize the Democratic Republic of East Timor after its unilateral declaration of independence in November 1975, Portugal severed diplomatic relations with Indonesia after the invasion.

49 Or, more accurately, the restoration of independence or 'realization of full independence'.

50 The Saharawi speak Hassaniya, a distinct Arab dialect.

51 After Morocco completed the berm in the late 1980s, the Saharawi acquired control to the east of it, confirmed by the 1990–91 UN ceasefire and referendum agreement together with free passage to the area allowed by Mauritania and Algeria.

52 These figures were obtained in interviews with SADR officials at international conferences, including in Algiers in December 2012 and Abuja in May 2015. Algeria's position in international law appears to be unique: it recognizes the SADR and accords it a refugee and government-in-exile presence within its territory. "Security Council Extends Western Sahara Mission until 30 April 2016, Unanimously Adopting Resolution 2218" (2015), April 28, 2015.

53 In July 2002 SADR President Mohamed Abdelaziz was elected vice-president of the African Union at the new organization's inaugural summit. Morocco is the only African state not a member of the organization.

54 Ian Brownlie, *Principles of Public International Law*, 3rd ed. (Oxford: Clarendon Press, 1979), 83. Similarly, Hector Gros Espiell (*The Right to Self-Determination*, para. 45) notes that the 'foreign occupation of a territory – an act condemned by modern international law and incapable of producing valid legal effects or of affecting the right to self-determination of the people whose territory has been occupied – constitutes an absolute violation of the right to self-determination'.

that a colonizing state continues in the obligation to ensure the self-determination of a subject non-self-governing people, however much that state may have attempted to relinquish the responsibility. Spain's abandonment of Western Sahara can be viewed not as any recognition of a Saharawi state but of the reality that all other options for self-determination have been exhausted.[55] The problem with the existence of the Saharawi state is two-fold: the requirement for recognition by all states as a political act whatever the material-factual existence of the Saharawi Republic, and the deference to the UN in resolving the 'question' of Western Sahara exclusively within the construct and norms of self-determination and not – as recently with Kosovo and South Sudan (and, in a somewhat different context, Palestine) – a new state emerging into the organized international community.

The problem with accepting an existing, functional Saharawi state may be the result of confusion over what has come to be a desired single standard of the international community, visible in the recent cases of secession, that peoples who wish to create a new state for themselves must pursue equivalent legitimacy requirements including a credible democratic choice for independence, and obtain the consent of the former colonial or occupying state.[56] However, the better reason for the lack of acceptance of the Saharawi state is the reluctance of the organized international community to disturb the status quo of a claim clearly rejected by the ICJ but which continues to be persisted in by Morocco. Whatever the overarching norms of international law, deferring the matter to the United Nations has contributed to the impasse.

Occupied with a referendum

It is clear that a referendum for self-determination arranged for the Saharawi people is not a mandatory requirement of international law, state practice or UN norms. If the *right* to self-determination is accepted – and it almost universally is by states in the case of Western Sahara – it can be accomplished by other means. The overwhelming precedent is that of colonized peoples simply being allowed their independence, of moving directly to it (unlike East Timor which underwent a referendum on the question). The Saharawi people have been resolute about their choice for independence. This is why all efforts to negotiate a compromise since 2007 have ended in failure. No serious argument, much less any credible evidence, can be asserted that the Saharawi people favor anything less than outright statehood. That part of their population which has been in self-governed exile and therefore able to express a consensus has demanded it continuously. The problem that confronts the organized international community in accepting Saharawi statehood, in other words recognition of the SADR, is not of tolerating a Saharawi state so much as the reluctance to confront an illegal occupation. There is also the understandable concern about the implications for a Morocco that has constructed a national identity with considerable reliance on its annexation project – what it calls the 'national question'. In any event, a UN administered referendum offered as the sole route to self-determination, whether in a non-self-governing or secessionary context, establishes a norm that may be unworkable in future cases where an occupying state's cooperation and consent is considered necessary to the exercise.

---

55 Hans Corell, the former UN Under-Secretary-General for Legal Affairs, describes the Madrid Accords in these terms: 'The Madrid Agreement did not transfer sovereignty over the territory, nor did it confer upon any of the signatories the status of an administering power; Spain alone could not transfer that authority unilaterally. The transfer of the administration of the territory to Morocco and Mauritania in 1975 did not affect the international status of Western Sahara as a Non-Self-Governing Territory. On 26 February 1976, Spain informed the Secretary-General that as of that date it had terminated its presence in Western Sahara and relinquished its responsibilities over the territory, thus leaving it in fact under the administration of both Morocco and Mauritania in their respective controlled areas.' Hans Corell, 'Western Sahara – Status and Resources', *New Routes* 4 (2010): 10–13.

56 Hector Gros Espiell reasoned that: 'the right of peoples to self-determination has lasting force, [and] does not lapse upon first having been exercised to secure political self-determination ... ', *The Right to Self Determination*, 45.

We should ask why if, when it comes to the Saharawi people, a referendum is not required under the law or in practice there remains such insistence on it. After all, there is not much doubt, and seemingly less than in the cases of Namibia and Timor-Leste, that independence would be overwhelmingly chosen. This said, it should be accepted that the Saharawi people would benefit from the perception of an externally administered referendum. Nothing, as the case of Timor-Leste after 1999 has shown, engages the support of the organized international community quite like the perception of legitimate resolution. Even the Saharawi accept this; in the language of the UN in recent years, the 'question' of Western Sahara must be resolved in a manner that is 'just, lasting and mutually acceptable'.[57] A referendum would more readily bring universal recognition by states and the further legitimization of the Saharawi statehood project by the participation of the whole of Saharawi society. As with Timor-Leste, a useful result of a referendum would be to eliminate obstacles in the SADR's new relationship with more powerful states such as France and to a certain extent the United States that have resulted from their support to Morocco.

Can justice be achieved through the Security Council?

Within the UN the 'question' of Western Sahara has become almost exclusively the preserve of the Security Council. The role of the General Assembly, in its idealized best during the 1960s and 1970s to end the occupation of Namibia – including the creation of a council to govern the territory in absentia – has faded in the decades since. Annual resolutions of the General Assembly received from the Special Political and Decolonization Committee which restate the right of self-determination are of little consequence to the Security Council.[58] The discussion in UN corridors is a wearied acceptance of Morocco as a proper party, to be dealt with as if it had a legitimate claim over Western Sahara or to be present in the territory.

There is also the fact of Western Sahara's continuing inclusion on the UN's list of Non-Self-Governing Territories conferring a degree of protection not so much to the Saharawi people as to the one right they nominally possess.[59] For years there has been a concern among Saharawi leaders that emphasizing an existing statehood would put that fragile consensus of the right to self-determination at risk.[60] This must be the reason the SADR government has not pursued a more active diplomacy beyond Africa and the AU, quietly staying away from UN organizations such as the UN Food & Agriculture Organization which carries out fisheries research in Saharan coastal waters without Saharawi participation.[61]

---

57 Resolution 1813, 'The Situation Concerning Western Sahara', United Nations Security Council, New York, April 30, 2008.

58 The 2014 resolution of the General Assembly was formulaic, unchanged in its preamble and operative recitals from those of the past decade. See UN General Assembly Resolution, 'Question of Western Sahara', A/Res/69/101 (December 5, 2014) at para. 2: '[The General Assembly] *Supports* the process of negotiations initiated by Security Council resolution 1754 (2007) and further sustained by Council resolutions 1783 (2007), 1813 (2008), 1871 (2009), 1920 (2010), 1979 (2011), 2044 (2012), 2099 (2013) and 2152 (2014), with a view to achieving a just, lasting and mutually acceptable political solution, which will provide for the self-determination of the people of Western Sahara, and commends the efforts undertaken by the Secretary-General and his Personal Envoy for Western Sahara in this respect'.

59 A protection, however, that cannot be taken for granted when the case of West Papua is considered. Although the 'Act of Free Choice' was fraudulent (admitted as such by the then UN Under-Secretary-General Chakravarthy Narasimhan and confirmed recently by the Dutch academic Pieter Drooglever), West Papua was removed from the UN's list of non-self-governing territories and has since been considered part of the Republic of Indonesia. See Pieter Drooglever, *An Act of Free Choice: Decolonisation and the Right to Self-Determination in West Papua* (The Hague: Institute of Netherlands History, 2009).

60 Personal communication with senior Saharawi officials in 2012 and 2015. The present inchoate form of Saharawi statehood appears to have been a successful effort, alongside maintaining the Frente Polisario as the Saharawi people's national liberation movement. Comporting itself as a state has gained the SADR acceptance in AU circles and serves to valuably prepare the state for what is referred to as the 'restoration of full independence'.

61 See the Food and Agriculture Organization of the United Nations (FAO)/ United Nations Environment Programme (UNEP) 'Canary Current Large Marine Ecosystem Project' at http://www.canarycurrent.org/ (accessed April 1, 2015).

We can diagnose the situation as a kind of schizophrenia. The Saharawis conduct their affairs as a state, at least for that part of the population in exile that can do so, while much of the community of states is not willing to accept the legal existence of such a state.[62]

Out of the impasse – a consideration of options

When it comes to the Saharawi people, the insistence of the UN and those states concerned about a referendum has been a pragmatic choice. But that insistence has allowed the underlying right of the people of Western Sahara – the ability to actually achieve their desired status – to be frustrated. It would be different if a referendum were imposed or could be organized by Saharawi acting collectively on both sides of the berm. Neither is likely. Morocco suppresses all efforts at public dialogue in the matter by both censoring alternative opinions within its own media and arguing strongly against dissenting views in public forums. The UN, for its part, is very unlikely to act unilaterally, especially when it cannot even assure a basic level of human rights protection in a territory for which it is responsible, as reflected in the lack of a human rights mandate for MINURSO. And therefore the long-running demand on some kind of process not only obscures the desired right, it has obstructed its realization.

So how might the present situation be addressed? What innovative approaches are available, especially by those states and organizations concerned and which, through the UN, exercise a power dynamic to determine the fate of the Saharawi people and their territory. To that we turn.

In considering an alternative to a referendum, the UN Charter offers a useful place to start. Several prescriptions are available.[63] In the event of territorial annexation – and for years there has been no clearer case than Morocco in Western Sahara – the Security Council is able, through one or some combination of the rules in Chapters VI and VII of the Charter, to act on and resolve this matter. Despite the unstated conclusion that the impasse over Western Sahara will not soon be resolved (leaving aside the sheer illegality of its initial occupation and annexation) there has been no serious consideration of applying the Charter's compulsory provisions. This is, of course, a reflection of the prevailing status quo.

What clearly engages the UN Charter, assuming the legitimacy of decolonization and the broad recognition of SADR, is the violation of Western Sahara's territorial integrity. The right to self-determination of the Saharawi people having been denied by the invasion of their territory, such an act must be ended by the withdrawal of Moroccan government control from the territory.[64] The Security Council had an accurate understanding of this at the material time when it demanded in Resolution 380 of 6 November 1975 that 'Morocco immediately ... withdraw from the Territory of Western Sahara ... '[65] How can the Security Council be compelled to act?

A coordinated campaign for recognition of the Saharawi Republic by UN member states is now timely. It has been given impetus recently by the AU Council for Peace and Security's

---

62 The status of Saharawi diplomats reflects this. Ubbi Bachir and Ali Mahamud Embarek, formerly Frente Polisario representatives in The Netherlands were later SADR ambassadors in Nigeria and Panama, respectively.

63 The former United Nations juris consult Hans Corell, in his private capacity, has recently suggested alternatives to a UN directed referendum. See 'The Responsibility of the UN Security Council in the Case of Western Sahara', *International Judicial Monitor* (Winter 2015): 1. He posits three options, namely: (i) a mandated governing presence for the UN in Western Sahara, similar to that in Timor-Leste during its post-referendum transition to independence; (ii) Security Council direction to Spain to resume its responsibilities as the colonial administering state; and (iii) recognition of the Saharawi Republic. Corell recognizes the options could be combined. '[Recognizing] Western Sahara as a sovereign state ... should be acceptable from a legal point of view. It would not deprive the people of Western Sahara from seeking a different solution to their self-determination in the future, if they so wish.' Ibid., 2.

64 See Susan Marks, 'Kuwait and East Timor: A Brief Study in Contrast' (in Arts and Pinto Leite, *International Law and the Question of East Timor*, 174–9), comparing the invasion of Kuwait by Iraq with the Indonesian invasion of Timor. For the reasons outlined above, her conclusions apply *a fortiori* to the Moroccan invasion of Western Sahara.

65 At paragraph 2 of the resolution. Article 25 of the UN Charter obligates members of the United Nations to implement decisions of the Security Council.

2015 resolution.[66] An example of the appetite for recognition can be seen in the 2004 letter from the President of the Republic of South Africa, Thabo Mbeki, to Morocco's Mohammed VI, explaining the colonial legacy underpinning South Africa's decision to recognize the Saharawi Republic.[67] Further afield, political parties in Austria, Brazil and Denmark pursued initiatives for governmental recognition of the Saharawi state in 2014. Of course, as a matter of contemporary international law, recognition is not strictly necessary for the existence of statehood because it has a limited declaratory value. But international politics is something else and here the concept matters. So it is worth repeating that the SADR has been recognized widely and participates extensively in the African Union.[68]

In recent years, apart from being recognized by a few states *ex novo* (most recently South Sudan) and establishing diplomatic relations with others sometime after recognition (most recently Guyana), the SADR has managed to reverse the position of eight states that had suspended or 'withdrawn' recognition: Nicaragua, El Salvador, Ecuador, Paraguay, Chad, Uganda, Sierra Leone and Vanuatu. There are also indications that states in the Global North are considering recognition, for example Sweden, where the Parliamentary Committee on Foreign Affairs approved a resolution in November 2012 calling on that country's government to extend recognition.[69]

It is in this endeavor – a campaign for universal recognition of the Saharawi state – that solidarity groups have a vital place. What is needed across transnational civil society is to coordinate action among the many groups concerned. The necessary umbrella organization does not yet exist and the need for it is increasingly obvious.[70] As an example, when it comes to protecting the resources of the territory from ongoing pillage, the Brussels-based Western Sahara Resource Watch pursues campaigns that are coordinated across several countries and languages.[71] External NGO (non-governmental organization) monitoring and action over human rights in occupied Western Sahara is nearly as sophisticated, with the Geneva-based Bureau International des Droits pour le Respect humains au Sahara Occidental (BIRDHSO) created in 2002.[72] A newly created NGO, Western Sahara Human Rights Watch (WSHRW), has the broader self-declared

---

66   See the March 27, 2015 Peace and Security Council of the African Union (AU PSC) *communiqué*.

67   'For us not to recognise SADR in this situation is to become an accessory to the denial of the people of Western Sahara of their right to self-determination. This would constitute a grave and unacceptable betrayal of our own struggle, of the solidarity Morocco extended to us, and our commitment to respect the Charter of the United Nations and the constitutive act of the African Union.' Letter of August 1, 2004 at http://arso.org/MBK.htm (accessed April 1, 2015).

68   Even as the organized international community will not urge the UN to act on the 'question' of Western Sahara, no state publicly supports Morocco's territorial claim to the Sahara. The kingdom's isolation was highlighted in 2011 when South Sudan achieved independence, joined the AU and established diplomatic relations with the SADR. There has been a campaign in recent years by Morocco to promote withdrawal of recognition of the SADR by states in the Global South, with mixed success. Commentators agree that withdrawal of recognition does not signify or hasten the end to a state's formal existence, for which see article 6 of the Montevideo Convention. Such 'withdrawals' have bordered on the absurd, for example Guinea-Bissau's first recognizing the SADR in 1976, withdrawing recognition in 1997, again extending recognition in 2009 and withdrawing it in 2010.

69   See 'Committee on Foreign Affairs at the Swedish Parliament Calls on the Government to Recognize SADR', Sahara Press Service, November 15, 2012, http://www.spsrasd.info/en/content/committee-foreign-affairs-swedish-parliament-calls-government-recognize-sadr (accessed April 11, 2015).

70   Stephen Zunes has compared solidarity movements in the causes of Timor and Western Sahara, and noted this is a 'factor working against Saharawi independence ... despite their impressive efforts at building well-functioning democratic institutions in the self-governed refugee camps where the majority of their people live, the Saharawis have never had the degree of international grassroots solidarity that the East Timorese were able to develop, which eventually eroded support of the Indonesian occupation by Western powers'. See http://www.spectrezine.org/resist/wsahara.htm (accessed April 2, 2015). 'Though an international solidarity movement does exist for Western Sahara, primarily in Europe, it pales in comparison with the movement in support of East Timor, which grew dramatically in the 1990s, and helped encourage greater media coverage on the human rights situation.' (East Timor and Western Sahara: a Comparative Analysis on Prospects for Self-Determination, Presentation to the Conference on International Law and the Question of Western Sahara, Institute of Social Studies, The Hague, October 27–28, 2006).

71   See http://www.wsrw.org (accessed April 7, 2015).

72   See http://www.birdhso.org (accessed April 7, 2015).

task 'to promote and support campaigns for the defense of human rights in the Western Sahara, civil and political, as well as economic or cultural'.[73] The space for coordinated action remains open for the vital work of a single competent and respected organization. It would need to have regard for and even work loosely alongside Saharawi public diplomacy.

It is also clear that the Saharawi Republic must increasingly create institutions as if it were a state on the global stage, including the pursuit of deeper (if informal) relationships with Global North states and to prepare governance capacity in anticipation of the restoration of full independence. Timor-Leste offers an example of the steps that might have been taken over 24 years of occupation, given the challenges faced there by the UN and the first government after independence to build civil society organizations and democratic institutions. On the narrow issue of asserting territorial sovereignty, the SADR has from time to time acted with sophistication, for example by its 2009 creation of ocean jurisdiction legislation which would later influence the European debate over the acceptability of fishing arrangements with Morocco on the coast of the occupied territory.[74]

None of this is to suggest that the Saharawi people and their leadership – both in exile at Tindouf and inside occupied Western Sahara – should maintain anything less than an outspoken demand for the exercise of self-determination. Such an option must always necessarily remain available along with, in theory – if only because it is legal within international law – the resumption of armed hostilities.[75] However, the time has come for the most tenable and at least equally acceptable option to be advanced, and that is greater recognition of the Saharawi Republic. What is to result is no more of an uncertain or damaging prospect for international relations, political stability in the states concerned, and the maintenance of the international legal order than has resulted from the present circumstances.

Determining the future

A campaign for recognition of the Saharawi Arab Democratic Republic will need to articulate the goal of achieving a majority of approving member states in the UN General Assembly. For practical purposes, recognition means acceptance as a UN member state and therefore the support of the Security Council. Hans Corell has explained it as follows:

> In view of the fact that the issue of Western Sahara has been on the agenda of the United Nations for four decades, the solution may be a … more radical option, namely that the Security Council recognises Western Sahara as a sovereign state. Also this option should be acceptable from a legal point of view. It would not deprive the people of Western Sahara from seeking a different solution to their self-determination in the future, if they so wish.[76]

Subject to the specific requirements of the UN Charter for the SADR's membership in the UN, two things would result: (i) the extension of formal relationships by previously uninterested states, and (ii) a putting into perspective for possible action by the UN and the organized international community the problem of the illegal occupation of Western Sahara and continuing aggression of that act revealed in the carrying out of the annexation, including human rights abuses, settler in-migration and the pillage of natural resources.

---

73 See http://www.wshrw.org (accessed April 7, 2015).
74 Law 03/2009 of January 21, 2009 Establishing the Maritime Zones of the Saharawi Arab Democratic Republic. The legislation resulted in the European Parliament reviewing the EU–Morocco 2007 Fisheries Partnership Agreement, which had allowed European fishing in the coastal waters of Western Sahara. The EU Parliament rejected such fishing in December 2011 which resumed in 2014 under revised arrangements with Morocco.
75 The use of force against colonial or otherwise illegal armed occupation is permissible under international law. In its resolution 'Importance of the universal realization of the right of peoples to self-determination' (December 3, 1982), UN doc. A/RES/37/43, the General Assembly affirmed 'the legitimacy of the struggle of peoples for independence, territorial integrity, national unity and liberation from colonial and foreign domination and foreign occupation by all available means, including armed struggle'.
76 Corell, 'The Responsibility of the UN Security Council in the Case of Western Sahara', 1.

The General Assembly has previously assumed the leading role for decolonization and the creation of states, the best example being that of its work for the Namibian people. While the UN Charter and precedent confer sufficient authority, it should be recalled that the General Assembly's 1950 Uniting for Peace resolution can also be invoked, Western Sahara being an instance where the Security Council, because of a

> lack of unanimity of the permanent members, fails to exercise its primary responsibility for the maintenance of international peace and security in any case where there [is a] breach of the peace, or act of aggression, the General Assembly shall consider the matter immediately with a view to making appropriate recommendations to Members for collective measures ... to maintain or restore international peace and security.[77]

There may be no better example of the intended use of the resolution than the long-running and unjust case of Western Sahara.

Even the casual observer must conclude that there is little prospect of the Saharawi people being offered in the years to come a self-determination referendum that has much credibility or acceptability. Only a determinedly new approach by the UN Security Council or fundamental political change in Morocco can apparently change the impasse. Neither seems likely. With an organized international community more concerned with the aftermath and complex problems that have resulted from the 2011 Arab Spring, there is a reluctance to act when it comes to Western Sahara. The status quo may continue to prevail. And therefore the time is right to recall that the Saharawi people are the sovereigns of their territory, and the fact of their state is well established. From such a place there should be little distance to travel to a completed and universally accepted statehood, and that is by the path of recognition.[78] The Saharawi people, their international supporters and the member states of the General Assembly each have a role in the achievement of that goal.

Acknowledgments

I am grateful to several reviewers who offered comments in the preparation of this paper. All errors remain mine.

Disclosure statement

No potential conflict of interest was reported by the author.

---

77 UN General Assembly Resolution 377 A (November 3, 1950). See Jean Krasno and Mitushi Das, 'The Uniting for Peace Resolution and Other Ways of Circumventing the Authority of the Security Council', in *The UN Security Council and the Politics of International Authority*, ed. Bruce Cronin and Ian Hurd (London: Routledge, 2008), 173–95.

78 The emergence of a fully independent Saharawi state will engage the question of Morocco's presence in Western Sahara. The case of Timor-Leste suggests acceptance in the face of such a *fait accompli*.

Saharawi conflict phosphates and the Australian dinner table

Erik Hagen

Board Member, Western Sahara Resource Watch

This article describes how the investor community has intervened vis-à-vis the global fertilizer companies sourcing phosphate rock from occupied Western Sahara. The territory holds large phosphates deposits, and the export of such rock constitutes the biggest source of income for the Moroccan government in the territory it has annexed. Due to the particular nature of the conflict in that territory, such practice is associated with concerns of human rights breaches, international law violations and political controversy. A dozen companies purchase these phosphates from the Moroccan government, while their traditional and legal owners are increasingly active in trying to stop the practice. Investor engagement and company improvement are discussed with a particular focus on Australia. By the end of the 1980s, 39% of all phosphate rock in Western Sahara ended up in Australia. After a massive shareholder campaign directed at the Australian importers, the country has basically ended its dependence on such phosphate rock. The article also looks at import cases in North America. The article outlines the different arguments and strategies of investors, based on public statements and on internal dialogues between international investors and the civil society organization Western Sahara Resource Watch over the last decade.

Introduction

Sourcing phosphate rock from a Moroccan state-owned company operating a mine in occupied Western Sahara is associated with numerous ethical, political and legal concerns. The exports of Western Sahara phosphate is Morocco's biggest source of income in the territory, and the trade is regarded by many as complicating the finding of a solution to the Western Sahara conflict.

This article places a particular focus on Australia, which for decades was one of the leading importers of phosphate rock from Western Sahara. Such rock is crucial to Australia's agricultural industries after being turned into fertilizers in Australian fertilizer plants. It is due to these fertilizers that Australia has become a global producer of meat, wheat and wool, and is able to engage in large-scale farming for domestic and international consumers. After two decades of heavy dependence on this rock, two of the three importing companies in Australia de facto ceased to import, with only one producer remaining today.

This article sets out to describe how the investor community has intervened vis-à-vis the global fertilizer companies sourcing phosphate rock from occupied Western Sahara. Investors, both in Australia and globally, have been a key force in guiding the companies towards behaving better. In fact, the investor community has become an important player in the world community's approach to the conflict.

Investors' concerns can be traced back to a legal opinion prepared for the UN Security Council in 2002.[1] Western Sahara is a territory rich in resources and in 2001 Morocco issued

---

1 United Nations, 'Letter dated 29 January 2002 from the Under-Secretary-General for Legal Affairs, the Legal Counsel, addressed to the President of the Security Council', S/2002/161, 2002.

the first oil licences to foreign companies in Western Sahara. The UN Security Council responded by asking its legal office whether such a move was legal. In his response, the UN Legal Counsel concluded that any further oil exploration or exploitation in Western Sahara would be illegal if the indigenous Saharawis did not consent to it and also if they did not benefit from it. The argument was deduced from the rights of the people of the territory to self-determination, and the legal status of the territory not having completed the process of decolonization.

Yet the oil companies proceeded with further oil exploration, without seeking the consent of the Saharawi people. Large bulk carriers transporting phosphate rock from the occupied territory also kept up the same pace of exporting as they had previously done.

On this basis, in response to the companies' continued activities in Western Sahara, civil society groups, governments and investors responded. The international non-governmental association Western Sahara Resource Watch (WSRW) emerged in part because of these events. WSRW, established in 2004, investigates the companies and governments that choose to enter into deals with the Moroccan government for resources located in Western Sahara. WSRW confronts each of the companies with an essential question: did they check with the owners of the resources, or did they only consult the Moroccan government? Their answers vary, although the WSRW has found they generally avoid responding to the question altogether.

WSRW exposes this corporate behaviour to the media, through which international investors then learn of it. The WSRW also nurtures contact directly with the investors outside of the public realm. Some elements in this article regarding the investors' behaviour are based on general observations that the author and WSRW has made from its decade-long dialogue with investors.

The companies involved in the trade have become increasingly well prepared, notably by having elaborate answers to send to concerned investors. The documents look impressive enough and it takes time to discover the flaws in their presentation. Yet some investors take time to study these replies in detail. These investors make assessments of the international and human rights law and decide on that basis whether they will continue to engage or to divest, with some not accepting the arguments provided by the companies and thus divesting.

Controversial industry

Only weeks after the 1975 invasion of what was then Spanish Sahara by Morocco, the phosphate rock of the Bou Craa mine in Western Sahara was being exported to fertilizer companies overseas. Now controlling the Bou Craa mine and the exports was the Office Chérifien des Phosphates SA (OCP), Morocco's national phosphate company.

Phosphates de Boucraa SA (Phosboucraa) is a fully owned subsidiary of OCP. Its main activities are the extraction, so-called beneficiation, transportation and marketing of phosphate ore from the Bou Craa mine, as well as operating a treatment plant located on the Atlantic coast, at El Aaiún. OCP puts production capacity in Western Sahara at 2.6 million tonnes annually. Though OCP claims that the Bou Craa mines represent only 1% of all phosphate reserves exploited by Morocco, no less than a quarter of its exported phosphate rock departs from El Aaiún.[2] The exceptionally high quality of Western Sahara's phosphate ore makes it a much-coveted commodity for producers of fertilizers.

However, that export process could be coming to an end. The Bou Craa phosphate deposit consists of two layers. So far, only the first, top layer has been mined. This particular layer contained phosphate rock of the highest quality across all of the reserves controlled by OCP. In 2014, Bou Craa phosphate mining moved on to the second layer, which is of lower quality. Morocco has

---

2   OCP SA, 'Prospectus', April 17, 2014, http://www.ise.ie/debt_documents/Base%20Prospectus_b81be83f-8e8f-43ef-85d9-cc5a4ae0277a.PDF?v=402015.

now sold all of the high-quality phosphate that ought to have been available to the Saharawi people upon realizing their right to self-determination.

OCP claims that Phosboucraa is the largest private employer in the wider Bou Craa area, with around 2200 employees. More than half of those are claimed to be locally recruited. It also claims that Phosboucraa is a major provider of economic viability and well-being for the region's inhabitants. OCP equally boasts of the social impact of Phosboucraa, in terms of providing pensions to retirees, and medical and social advantages to employees, retirees and their families. OCP presents the purported economic and social benefits as a justification for its exploitation of phosphate mines outside of Morocco's internationally recognized borders.

The illegally exploited phosphate rock is the Moroccan government's main source of income from Western Sahara, which it continues to occupy contrary to international law. Representatives of the Saharawi people have been consistently outspoken against the trade, both in the UN, generally, and to specific companies. The refugees from Western Sahara, representing half of the Saharawi people, do not see any benefits from the trade, having been forced to flee as Morocco invaded the territory. Some Saharawis had worked at the phosphate production unit up until the Moroccan invasion.

Morocco uses the Bou Craa phosphates for its political lobbying to gain the informal acceptance of other countries for its illegal occupation. An official Moroccan document leaked in 2014 explicitly states that Western Sahara's resources, including phosphate, should be used 'to implicate Russia in activities in the Sahara'. The document goes on to say that 'in return, Russia could guarantee a freeze on the Sahara file within the UN'.[3] This corresponds to other statements from the Moroccan government. A former fisheries minister once stated that Morocco's fisheries agreement with the EU was more of a political agreement than a financial one.[4] Morocco's current Minister of Communication has been quite outspoken in this regard. He declared that all agreements that do not exclude 'the Moroccan Sahara' from their application prove that the area is Moroccan.[5] With control over not only its own, but also Western Sahara's phosphorous reserves, Morocco has placed itself in a very important position geopolitically. Approximately 75% of global phosphate reserves are now controlled by the Moroccan government. Importantly, phosphate is a mineral containing the element of phosphorous which is fundamental for all living cells.

Massive trade

WSRW tracks all shipping traffic in the waters of Western Sahara on a daily basis, and routinely publishes reports on Moroccan exports from the occupied territory, identifying all shipments of phosphates taking place. The latest report, *P for Plunder 2014*, was issued in March 2015.[6]

WSRW believes that it has detected, tracked and accounted for all vessels departing from El Aaiún harbour since the second half of 2011. For 2014, the total exported volume from Western Sahara was calculated by WSRW at 2.1 million tonnes, shipped in 44 bulk vessels. That constitutes a slight decline in sales from 2013.

The amount of phosphate loaded into a ship is ordinarily calculated to be 95% of the ship's overall cargo capacity. In cases where ships had a cargo carrying capacity of less than 40,000 tonnes, the 95% factor was reduced to account for a higher relative amount of fuel and provisions. Ships are then tracked and confirmed to have arrived at stated destinations. Where possible,

---

3 WSRW, 'Morocco Admits to Using Saharawi Resources for Political Gain', November 25, 2014, http://www.wsrw.org/a105x3070.

4 Mohamed Boudarham, 'Accord de pêche: naufrage polisarien', *Aujourd'hui Le Maroc*, May 24, 2006, http://www.aujourdhui.ma/maroc/societe/accord-de-peche-naufrage-polisarien-41767.

5 Al Hayat, وزير الاتصال المغربي لـ«الحياة»: الجزائر و«بوليساريو» يمنعان إحصاء اللاجئين في مخيمات تيندوف January 14, 2013, http://www.alhayat.com/Details/472155.

6 WSRW, *P for Plunder 2014* (2015), http://www.wsrw.org/a105x3185.

estimated loaded amounts were checked against shipping documents, including bills of lading and port arrival receipts.

As has been noted, phosphate rock is the biggest financial engine for Morocco's settlement project in Western Sahara. In recent years, global phosphate prices have increased exponentially. For decades, the price for phosphate remained stable at around $40–50 per tonne. However, in the last decade there have been fluctuations in price. It peaked briefly in 2008, at around $500 a tonne. Since then it has stabilized between $200 and $100 a tonne. In 2014, it averaged at around $110. For our calculations, phosphate prices are obtained from the commercial commodities pricing website 'Index Mundi' and checked against other sources.[7]

The Moroccan state earns massively from the mine it controls in the occupied territories. The volume exported would be an estimated US$230 million for 2014. In comparison, the value of the annual multilateral humanitarian aid to the Saharawi refugee camps is approximately €30 million.

WSRW's *P for Plunder 2014* report attributes the purchased phosphate to nine identified and one unknown importers in nine countries internationally. There is little change from year to year in the customer pattern. Of the nine identified importing companies in 2014, five are listed on international stock exchanges or are majority owned by enterprises which are listed. All of these have been subject to blacklisting by ethically concerned investors due to this trade.

The report reveals that between them, the Canadian company Agrium Inc. and the Lithuanian company Lifosa AB in 2014 accounted for 58% of all purchases from Western Sahara.

The Australian imports

The Australian farming industry is dependent on phosphate imports to fertilize pastures for livestock and for agriculture. There has always been a domestic production of phosphates in Australia, but the industry remains heavily reliant on imports. Three companies control the Australian market of so-called 'super phosphates' fertilizers – Wesfarmers Ltd, Incitec Pivot Ltd and Impact Fertilisers Pty Ltd.

Throughout the twentieth century, the major share of Australia's phosphate demand was supplied from large deposits on Christmas Island. From 1981 to 1987, this mine was operated by the Australian Phosphate Corporation (APC), a government-owned entity. By 1987–88, the transports from Christmas Island to Australia had come to a complete stop, except for a limited resumption of trade from the mid-1990s onwards. These Christmas Island phosphates were mostly replaced with imports from Nauru, Western Sahara and a few other sources, Australian import statistics show.

From what WSRW has been able to establish, APC started importing on a massive scale from the occupied territory of Western Sahara in 1987. During that calendar year, APC received 292,000 tonnes of phosphate rock from Boucraa, corresponding to 39% of the total Boucraa production of that year. The following years, the APC imports declined steadily, and from 1992 APC did not itself import phosphates, as other Australian importers took over.[8]

By 2006, Incitec Pivot imported a probable 238,010 tonnes, Wesfarmers 105,200 tonnes and Impact 50,350 tonnes, totalling 424,710 tonnes. These figures, from calculations of shipments from Bou Craa, correspond more or less with the import statistics from Australian official databases. 2006 was a year of particularly high phosphate exports from Bou Craa, and the Australian imports amounted to around 14% of the total production in the occupied territory.[9]

---

7 Index Mundi, http://www.indexmundi.com/.
8 http://www.businessofaustralia.com/c/b/australian-phosphate-corporation-limited/005788072 (accessed August 10, 2015).
9 http://www.iama.org.au/sites/default/files/Australian%20Fertilizer%20Industry%20Value%20and%20Issues%20August%202010.pdf (accessed August 10, 2015).

During the financial year 2005/6, the rock, which according to Australian trade statistics originates from 'Morocco', accounted for 62% of all Australian phosphate imports. At the time, WSRW found that the importers and the investor community had very shallow knowledge about the concerns related to the phosphate exports from Western Sahara.[10]

Around this time, the Australian government also formulated its opinion on the matter of the plundering of the territory. The main approach is to recommend that Australian companies seek independent legal advice.[11] At one point, in 2010, the Australian government was placed in a position where it had to clarify its policy: an Australian company had requested the government to produce a letter of support which it could in turn send to Morocco. The company had been invited by the Moroccan government to take part in a tender for an exploration permit in Western Sahara for a 'potentially world class multi-commodity (uranium, rare earths, tantalum and iron) project'.[12] There was a particular interest in the uranium extraction.

The government concluded that it could not comply with the request. The government stated that '[g]iven the status of Western Sahara, we do not consider it appropriate for the Australian Government to assist [and to] write a letter of support', and 'a letter of support may prejudice Australia's position on the conflict, which strongly recognises the UN-mediated process and advises companies of the international law considerations of operating in the region'.[13]

The Fertilizer Industry Federation of Australia (FIFA) has, for its part, systematically defended the imports of phosphates. Its members cover basically the entire market of fertilizer produced, imported and sold on the Australian market. In a communication, FIFA noted that '[t]he resolution of the long-running dispute between Morocco and the Polisario in relation to the sovereignty of the area known as Western Sahara is, and should be, in the hands of the international community, not individuals or companies'.[14]

Eight years later, in 2015, two of the three importers have de facto stopped purchasing from Western Sahara, and the imported volume to Australia has reduced to a fourth of that of 2006. In the following paragraphs, the involvement of the three companies Incitec Pivot, Wesfarmers and Impact Fertilisers are discussed.

Incitec Pivot (IPL)

Incitec Pivot Ltd, also referred to as IPL, is an Australian multinational corporation that engages in the manufacturing, trading and distribution of fertilizers. The company's fertilizer segment includes Incitec Pivot Fertilizers (IPF), Southern Cross International (SCI), and Fertilizers Elimination (Elim).

IPL has been importing from Western Sahara for the past 30 years. The company is headquartered in Melbourne, Australia, and is registered on the Australian Securities Exchange. In 2015, Incitec Pivot was the largest supplier of fertilizer products in Australia, but it also markets its products abroad, such as in India, Pakistan and Latin America. IPL manufactures a range of fertilizer products, but uses the Saharawi phosphate for its so-called superphosphate products produced at plants in Geelong and Portland.

---

10 Ibid.

11 Australian Department of Foreign Affairs and Trade, 'Important Information on Western Sahara', http://www.dfat. gov.au/geo/morocco/Pages/important-information-on-western-sahara.aspx.

12 Australian Department of Foreign Affairs and Trade, various declassified files and correspondence, 2007–10: 238–45, http://www.wsrw.org/files/dated/2015-05-04/dfat_australia_docs_2007-2010.pdf.

13 Ibid.

14 FIFA, 'Phosphate Rock imports from the Western Sahara', December 12, 2007, http://www.wsrw.org/files/dated/2015-05-03/fifa_13.12.2007.pdf.

In February 2015, IPL confirmed to WSRW that it received three shipments of phosphate rock from Western Sahara in 2014, a total volume of 94,600 tonnes.[15] This volume corresponds to the cargo capacity of the three bulk carriers received that year.

IPL's sustainability report provides a good summary of the company's arguments and approach to the topic.

> The situation regarding the Kingdom of Morocco and the status of the Non Self Governing Territory of Western Sahara is a complex one, managed under the auspices of the United Nations … We remain satisfied that we are not in breach of either Australian law or International law, as there has been no determination by the UN or any other competent legal authority that the production and use of phosphate from the Non Self Governing Territory of Western Sahara is in violation of any applicable law or the Geneva Convention [sic]. Over many years IPL has engaged in dialogue and enquiry with many parties on this matter. In particular, IPL meets periodically with the Australian Department of Foreign Affairs and Trade, and has had discussions with Office Cherifien des Phosphates, its supplier of phosphate rock from the Non Self Governing Territory of Western Sahara, as well as with Australian ambassadors to the Kingdom of Morocco.[16]

Although IPL fully consulted Australian and Moroccan authorities in this instance, it has never responded to a central question asked by WSRW: 'What steps, if any, has IPL taken to assure itself of the continuing consent of the Saharawi people to such purchases, consistent their right to self-determination, the 2002 UN Legal Opinion (S/2002/161) and international humanitarian law?'[17]

Impact Fertilisers

Impact Fertilisers (Impact), based in Hobart, Tasmania, imported phosphates from Western Sahara from about 2002 until 2013. It is not possible to accurately conclude what caused Impact Fertilisers' exit from Western Sahara. However, from 2010, a Swiss trading company Ameropa AG became majority owner, and the company was shortly after pressured by Swiss parliamentarians to halt the trade.[18] In 2013, the company announced that it had ended the imports. WSRW observed the last shipment to Impact in August 2012. Before then, the company's response to WSRW's query regarding trading in Western Sahara phosphates was that it had 'a contrary view and advice to that expressed by you regarding the legitimacy of the trade'.[19] In particular, the company had said:

> Whilst we continually review our rock sources based on suitability and cost for our production system, this source remains a key and viable source for our production requirements. In relation to your assertion that if all Australian importers were to act together to cease this trade it would alter the issues or referendum, this is fundamentally flawed. Australia is a relatively small proportion of the trade from Western Sahara and any void left would soon be filled by other purchasers.[20]

Wesfarmers CSBP

Wesfarmers Limited is one of Australia's largest public companies, headquartered in Perth, Western Australia. The company is listed on the Australian Securities Exchange. Its fertilizer

---

15 Incitec Pivot to WSRW, February 13, 2015, http://www.wsrw.org/a240x3172.
16 Incitec Pivot, *Sustainability Report 2013* (2014), http://www.incitecpivot.com.au/~/media/Files/IPL/Sustainability/2013%20Sustainability%20Report.pdf.
17 WSRW letter to Incitec Pivot, February 6, 2015, http://www.wsrw.org/a240x3171.
18 WSRW, '8 Swiss Parliamentarians Protest Ethics of Tasmanian Company', September 9, 2010, http://www.wsrw.org/a105x1585.
19 Impact Fertilisers to WSRW, May 12, 2008, http://www.wsrw.org/a128x718.
20 Ibid.

subsidiary, Wesfarmers CSBP, was a major importer of phosphates from Western Sahara for at least two decades.

The earliest known imports of Saharawi phosphates by CSBP date back to 1990. Wesfarmers used to import between 60% and 70% of its phosphates from Western Sahara. The imports to CSBP/Wesfarmers probably amounted to between 63,000 tonnes and 159,000 tonnes during the years 1992–97, corresponding to 4% to 10% of the entire annual production from the Bou Craa mine.

However, it was not concerns over international law that first drew attention to Wesfarmers' involvement in Western Sahara phosphate imports. In November 2005, two stowaways were found dead in the vessel *Furness Karumba* as it arrived in Australia from Western Sahara with phosphates for Wesfarmers. From then on, the media became more interested in the matter, and, on 7 November 2005, Wesfarmers for the first time sought advice from the Australian government:

> The Australian Government has not imposed any trading restrictions with Western Sahara. CSBP is satisfied that it is not in breach of international law and will continue to be guided by the Australian Government's position on trade with the region.[21]

As will be discussed below, Wesfarmers has now de facto halted its purchases, at least temporarily.

How the investors argue

The reasons why investors engage with the fertilizer companies vary greatly, and the highly diverse ethical policies and guidelines of each investor is a major factor in this variation. The arguments of each investor are mainly founded in human rights, international law or overall ethical principles established in their respective responsible investment guidelines. Some employ a legalistic approach, concluding that the operations in Western Sahara violate the law, and that the investors cannot be the owners of such companies.

Numerous studies seek to address to what extent ethical fund management is less or more profitable than fund management which does not take ethical considerations into account. This article does not seek to explore that discussion. It is worth noting, however, that some shareholders declare that there is a real financial risk in maintaining their ownership in companies associated with this controversial trade. For example, one Canadian investor noted that '[r]eputational and political risks brought on through Agrium's business relationship with the Moroccan government-owned phosphate company (OCP) has the potential to negatively impact shareholder value'.[22]

When analysing corporate behaviour in light of investors' ethical standards, a hierarchy is applied to the issue of responsibility, with certain types of involvement being considered as having more serious implications than others. A company's majority ownership in a controversial licence is considered more serious than in the cases where the company has a minor stake. An operator exploiting the resources is more involved than the client of the plundered goods. A long-term customer with a ten-year supply contract from Bou Craa is seen as much more involved than one purchasing a random shipment from Bou Craa on the spot market. Shipping companies transporting the phosphate rock with a long-term transport agreement with the importer are seen as more involved than shipping companies taking an accidental load on the spot market. Contractors helping with infrastructure, consultancy or seismic studies, for example, are seen as even less involved. Yet companies engaged in all such activity have been approached by ethical investors.

---

21 Wesfarmers to Norwegian Support Committee for Western Sahara, February 15, 2012, http://www.wsrw.org/files/dated/2012-10-05/wesfarmers-skvs_15.02.2012.pdf.

22 Vancity, *2014 Shareholder Engagement Report* (2015), https://www.vcim.ca/pdfs/2014ShareholderReport.pdf.

However, the level of shareholder engagement, and the probability of exclusion, follows the pyramid: the more involved companies are, the more likely they are to receive concerned calls from their investors.

Active ownership and exclusions are confidential matters for many banks and investors. They often do not want to reveal which companies they are in dialogue with, which companies they have divested from, or the value of the shares they have sold in divestment cases. It is thus not normally known which investors have blacklisted companies involved in Western Sahara, or the value of these divestments. There are exceptions: some investors publish press releases of their divestments as they happen, while others declare these decisions in the annual reports. Others describe their active ownership processes in various company responsibility reports. The largest known single exclusion incident was around US$350 million.[23]

A common argument against excluding a company breaching ethical standards is stated as follows: 'When we blacklist a company, we lose the opportunity to influence them positively'. WSRW considers this an exaggeration because it appears that divestors are well able to maintain a dialogue with the companies even after they have been blacklisted, being clear that they will reinvest once the operation in question has been halted. The threat of exclusion is only a real threat if exclusions are routinely carried out.

A common denominator in the investor–importer relationship is the two criteria established in the UN 2002 legal opinion.[24] This asks whether the Saharawi people wish for the trade to take place and, if so, whether they benefit from it. The investors highlight either one or both of these criteria in their dialogue with the involved companies. Some investors conclude on the compliance with these two principles simply by looking at the political infrastructure of Western Sahara. As long as Morocco does not seek the consent of the Saharawi refugees, and as long as neither Morocco nor the companies seek the consent from any Saharawi group seeking self-determination, it is clear that the exploitation and trade cannot take place in line with the wishes of the people of the territory. Even if Morocco had wanted to seek consent from the Saharawis in Western Sahara, it would be impossible to do so as the political infrastructure imposed by the Moroccan government would not allow it. For instance, groups advocating for self-determination are actively undermined.[25] By concluding the argument already at that stage, these investors do not even start assessing the question of benefits to the Saharawis.

The following arguments are used by investors.

(a) *Violation of international law due to failure to seek consent*

Upon exclusion of PotashCorp and Incitec Pivot from its portfolios, the Swedish government pension fund AP-Fonden stated:

> Western Sahara has been under Moroccan occupation since 1975 and is on the United Nations' list of non-self-governing territories that should be decolonised. The UN's legal counsel stated in January 2002 that exploration of mineral resources in Western Sahara without local consent would be in breach of the International Covenant on Civil and Political Rights and the International Covenant on Economic, Social and Cultural Rights.[26]

---

23 Norwegian Ministry of Finance, 'Government Pension Fund Global: Two Companies Excluded from the Fund's Investment Universe', news release, June 12, 2011, https://www.regjeringen.no/en/aktuelt/government-pension-fund-global-two-compa/id665637/.

24 United Nations, 'Letter dated 29 January 2002 from the Under-Secretary-General for Legal Affairs, the Legal Counsel, addressed to the President of the Security Council', S/2002/161, 2002.

25 Human Rights Watch, *World Report 2015: Morocco/Western Sahara* (2015), http://www.hrw.org/world-report/2015/country-chapters/morocco/western-sahara.

26 WSRW, 'Swedish Government Pension Fund Blacklists Sahara Importers', September 30, 2013, http://www.wsrw.org/a217x2664.

The latest exclusion from this particular investor was announced in the fund's annual report 2014, published in 2015.[27]

(b) Violation of international law due to failure to guarantee local benefit

The Norwegian company KLP stated, regarding its divestments from Wesfarmers, Incitec Pivot, PotashCorp and FMC Corp in 2010:

> The company is thus indirectly funding Morocco's illegal occupation of the territory. In an opinion, issued in 2002, by the UN Under-Secretary General for Legal Affairs, the exploitation of natural resources in colonized territories, Western Sahara in particular, was declared illegal if it is not to the benefit of the people of the territory.[28]

(c) *Violation of human rights norms*

'[The company] imports natural resources which are extracted in conflict with human rights norms', noted the largest bank in Denmark, Danske Bank, upon divesting from PotashCorp, Wesfarmers, FMC Corp and Incitec Pivot.[29]

(d) *Violation of fundamental ethical norms*

Upon the divestment from PotashCorp and FMC Corp, the Ethical Council of the Norwegian sovereign wealth fund stated:

> Since this concerns non-renewable resources, these will be lost to the exiled local population, even if the territory's status at some time in the future should change and the exiled local population is able to return. The view of the Council on Ethics is therefore that OCP's activities in Western Sahara must be considered grossly unethical.[30]

Similarly, Norwegian investor KLP stated that purchase of phosphates from Western Sahara 'via a long-term contract with the state-owned Moroccan company Office Chérifien des Phosphates (OCP), is deemed to represent an unacceptable risk of contributing to violations of basic ethical norms, and therefore contravenes KLP's guidelines for responsible investment'.[31]

(e) *Violation of UN Global Compact principles*

Both Innophos Holdings and PotashCorp have been excluded for being in breach of the Global Compact principles by the American SRI Fund of the BrownAdvisory.[32]

(f) *Illegality*

'Illegal exploitation of natural resources', stated the Luxemburg pension fund Fonds de Compensation commun au régime général de pension upon blacklisting all the involved phosphate companies.[33]

How the investors act and succeed

Multinational companies on the international stock exchanges are often 'ownerless', in that they are owned by everyone but not necessarily by a single major shareholder. Institutional investors, such as a national pension fund holding 1–2% of the shares in a company, could be among the biggest investors in that company. Those owners often administer the savings of millions of

---

27 WSRW, 'Swedish Government Fund Excludes Agrium over Western Sahara Imports', April 10, 2013, http://www.wsrw.org/a105x3208.

28 KLP, *Responsible Investments, SRI Report June 2010*, June 1, 2010, https://www.klp.no/polopoly_fs/1.10504.1359544017!/menu/standard/file/sri_report_june_2010.pdf.

29 Danica Pension, 'Ekskluderte selskaper', http://wsrw.org/files/dated/2010-12-18/danica_webpage_17.12.2010.pdf.

30 WSRW, 'European Banks Divest from Unethical Sahara Fertiliser Industry', November 30, 2010, http://www.wsrw.org/a159x1704.

31 KLP, 'Exclusion from Investment Portfolios', news release, December 1, 2014, http://english.klp.no/polopoly_fs/1.29227.1417436404!/menu/standard/file/Agrium%20decision%20to%20exclude%2001122014%20ENGLISH.pdf.

32 BrownAdvisory, 'October 2014 Factsheet', http://www.brownadvisory.com/LinkClick.aspx?fileticket=iobRki8gxSc%3D&tabid=383.

33 WSRW, 'Luxembourg Pension Fund Blacklists Six Firms over Saharan Imports', November 19, 2014, http://www.wsrw.org/a106x3065.

people. The problem is who will call the management and board of the companies to account if they behave irresponsibly when no owner controls more than a small proportion of the shares?

The only way an investor can get any leverage with a company they partly own is if other owners do the same. It is in these joint efforts, coordinated or uncoordinated, that we see the full force of change in corporate behaviour in relation to the Western Sahara phosphate trade. This was noted by one head of responsible investments at Finnish investor Ilmarinen: 'We hope to see more investors join us in urging companies linked to the territory to act responsibly and help Western Sahara get the attention it needs'.[34]

Together with other Nordic investors, Ilmarinen has carried out engagement with companies in Western Sahara over a number of years, assisted by the Swedish screening company GES Investment Services. Among the companies that have been approached are PotashCorp, FMC Corp, Incitec Pivot and Wesfarmers. On this engagement, the Ilmarinen Director said:

> Although Western Sahara has not attracted as much media attention as some other conflict areas, this does not mean that it is not of importance to investors. The latest UN reports strengthen the case for investors to engage with companies operating in this area to improve the situation'.[35]

In other words, the investors have not only a responsibility to act, but also possibilities for action which are very different from the behaviour of states or civil society, which until now have been considered the main actors in the issues relating to basic human rights and self-determination in Western Sahara.

There are limitations, of course. First of all, not all of the companies involved in Western Sahara are appropriate for investors to approach on the international stock markets. In general, and perhaps naturally, the investors are mainly interested in engaging those companies that they have themselves invested in. There are some exceptions to this: for instance, investors who want to keep engaging companies which they have already divested from. Some also seek to engage companies in which they could potentially invest in the future. In terms of the Western Sahara phosphate trade, this automatically excludes some of the importers from the reach of the players on the global stock market.

Another hurdle for the investors is the lack of documentation. The reports coming out of Western Sahara are inherently biased one way or the other. No state in the world functions as the administrative power of Western Sahara vis-à-vis the UN today, meaning that no state takes on the obligation for reporting on the well-being or self-determination process of the people of Western Sahara. As noted in the UN Legal Opinion, Morocco is not the administrative power of the territory, and even refuses to characterize itself as such.[36] Morocco also denies any ability on the part of the UN Mission for Referendum in Western Sahara (MINURSO) to observe and report on the human rights situation. The companies involved are sometimes also not keen to provide detailed reports about their activities. Most importantly, they fail to answer how the trade is carried out with respect for the wishes of the people. Some do not respond at all. The best-known case of a totally silent company is Innophos Holdings, the parent of an importing subsidiary in Mexico. Such silence makes it harder to verify the company's participation in trade. 'A company we invest in should not be rewarded by keeping quiet when we confront them with our concerns', stated one investor regarding Innophos.[37]

---

34 WSRW, 'Investors Calling on Company Responsibility', June 20, 2012, http://www.wsrw.org/a214x2343.
35 Ibid.
36 United Nations, 'Letter dated 29 January 2002 from the Under-Secretary-General for Legal Affairs; Morocco World News, 'Full Text of King Mohammed VI's Speech on 39th Anniversary of Green March', November 6, 2014, http://www.moroccoworldnews.com/2014/11/143369/full-text-of-king-mohammed-vis-speech-on-39th-anniversary-of-green-march/.
37 Interview with investor, 2014. None of the investors that the author and WSRW have been in contact with have ever received an answer from Innophos. WSRW letters remain unanswered. An example of the lack of response can be seen in Council of Ethics for the Norwegian Government Pension Fund Global, 'Recommendation 26 September

In practical terms, it is sometimes complicated to exercise the actual power inherent in the ownership. The owners are not always investing in the companies directly, but via external fund managers. These managers handle the capital of numerous clients. The challenge emerges then if one of the dozens of companies in that particular fund starts dealing with Western Sahara phosphates. The composition of the fund would in such a case no longer comply with the ethical guidelines of the investors. 'Either you remove that company from the fund you are selling us, or we have to find another fund or manager', would be an expected response from the investor. Needless to say, some of the larger investors could have remarkable leverage on the fund managers. A company like the Kempen Capital Management (KCM) from the Netherlands notes that it has both possibilities at the same time: it can influence the importer directly, and it can try to engage the manager.[38] In 2010, the importer FMC Corp was present in one fund which JPMorgan managed for KCM. The Dutch company then engaged JPMorgan to act.[39] On the other hand, some fund managers could decide not to engage in the behaviour of companies represented in the portfolio of a particular fund. The investor would then need to decide whether to abandon the fund or the fund manager altogether. This is normally associated with great administrative and financial costs. Some accept that cost for the sake of an ethically tidy portfolio.

Making the contact

As the investors make contact with the involved fertilizer producers, they quickly receive a ready-made answer package. The packages typically contain two types of documentation. The first goes into the operations on the ground, detailing what social programmes and employment conditions exist, and the investments which the Moroccan state-owned phosphate company, OCP, has carried out in the territory. The second type of documentation contains legal opinions written for OCP, analysing and supporting the legality of the trade. These documents are all readily distributed by OCP to the importing companies, and the importing companies in turn distribute them under strict confidentiality to their investors. Ideally, what is required at this stage is for investors to engage in their own investigations around related ethical and legal issues before making a decision on the trade. The question is to what extent does the material received contain any substance? Do the reports really answer the concerns of the Saharawi people or the criteria outlined in the UN Legal Opinion? The ethical investors mentioned in this article believe that this is not the case, and that the conclusions drawn by those directly involved in the trade are not well enough proven.

The on-the-ground analysis has been done by OCP itself, helped in recent years by the audit company KPMG. The conclusion of the reports – none publicly disclosed or viewed by the author – is said to be that the local population benefits.[40] But what was really the question which led to that conclusion? As the report is not published, it is impossible to know what terms of reference or research questions the study used. All Saharawi groups which are critical of the Moroccan presence in Western Sahara have confirmed to the author that they were not involved in the study. Indeed, all known Saharawi civil society groups and their government in exile have consistently rejected the benefits of the trade.

2014 to Exclude Innophos Holdings Inc', September 26, 2014, http://www.etikkradet.no/en/recommendation-26-september-2014-to-exclude-innophos-holdings-inc/.

38 Kempen Capital Management, *Annual Report 2012, Sustainability Report* (2013), http://www.kempen.nl/uploadedFiles/Kempen/01_Asset_Management/Specialismen/Duurzaam_beleggen/Annual%20report%202012%20sustainability.pdf.

39 Ibid.

40 WSRW contact with all investors confirms this trend. An indication of the content of the analysis is to be found in a statement by the importer PotashCorp: 'Phosphate Rock from Western Sahara', August 2014, http://www.wsrw.org/files/dated/2015-07-26/potashcorp_rock_position_aug2014.pdf.

The legal opinions commissioned by OCP, on the other hand, were prepared by three international law firms: one opinion has been drafted by the US company Covington and Burling LLP, which has been actively representing OCP for a number of years.[41] Another legal opinion was produced by DLA Piper in collaboration with Spanish firm Palacio y Asociados. These documents, all commissioned by the Moroccan operator of the mine, is that its operations are in line with international law, fulfilling the requirements that the UN Legal Office has set forward.

None of these firms, or the importers, want to disclose the opinions, as they are said to be the property of OCP. Based on statements from the importing companies, the legal opinions appear to come to the same conclusion: that the trade in Western Saharan phosphate rock through OCP is acceptable under international law, citing benefits to the 'local population' as validation for the exploitation and subsequent export to take place.[42]

OCP has not replied to questions regarding the trade, whether from WSRW or from concerned Saharawis. One Saharawi has on numerous occasions tried to obtain the opinions from the management of OCP, but without success.[43] When she posted a video on YouTube about how she wanted to get access to the document, an entity called 'OCP Maroc' tried to have her videos removed.[44] If the dialogue between the importers and their investors gets serious, the importing company calls in the lawyers Covington and Burling to pay the investors a visit.[45]

These interactions between the importing companies and their investors take different routes, and the outcomes vary accordingly, influenced by many different factors. On one hand, it depends on the characteristics of the importer, including the company's dependence on the Boucraa rock, whether it purchases the phosphate on the spot-market or through long-term contracts, and the duration of the contract. On the other hand, it also depends on the investor's dispositions – for example, the nature of their investment guidelines, their capacity, their partnerships with other investors, if they have invested themselves or via fund managers. Lastly, the dynamics take different routes depending on the national government policy on Western Sahara and the media or civil society pressure in the home countries of the investor and of the importer.

In the following, three different cases will be presented, where in each case the interaction ended with a different result. Each case illustrates investors willing to go to great lengths to improve the behaviour of the importers.

CASE A: Mosaic Co., the easy way out

The Swedish bank Nordea in its 2010 annual report accounted for its successful active ownership process with one of the importers. The company was the Florida-based fertilizer producer Mosaic Co. WSRW had during the period from 2001 to 2009 documented 15 shipments from Western Sahara to its plant in Tampa, USA.

> Nordea's engagement with the Mosaic Company (US) was successfully ended in June 2010. Mosaic has now disclosed that they have discontinued their purchase of phosphate from Western Sahara, which also has been independently confirmed. The company has acknowledged the human rights issues involved with importing phosphate from Western Sahara.[46]

Some years later, Mosaic confirmed that the reason behind its decision to halt Western Sahara imports was 'because of widespread international concerns regarding the rights of the Sahrawi

---

41 WSRW, 'US Law Firm Continues Pro-occupation Lobby', December 8, 2013, http://www.wsrw.org/a204x2181.

42 WSRW, *P for Plunder 2014*.

43 WSRW, 'OCP Refuses to Respond to Saharawi Refugee', March 4, 2015, http://www.wsrw.org/a105x3169.

44 WSRW, 'This Video is Too Tough for OCP, Tries to Stop Youtube Stunt', November 16, 2013, http://www.wsrw.org/a217x2704.

45 Norwegian Government Pension Fund, Council on Ethics, 'Recommendation', October 15, 2010, https://www.regjeringen.no/globalassets/upload/fin/etikk/2011/rec_phospahte.pdf.

46 WSRW, 'European Banks Divest from Unethical Sahara Fertiliser Industry'.

people in that region', a Mosaic spokesman stated to Bloomberg.[47] The news service clearly juxtaposed Mosaic's responsible approach to the contrary behaviour of its North American competitors, still involved in the trade. Mosaic also confirmed in a letter to WSRW that in 2009 it had received its last shipment from Western Sahara and that it 'had no plans' to import again.[48]

Luxembourg-based Sparinvest group noted that

> Mosaic was held up as an example of good ... practice when (in contrast to its competitors) it immediately terminated involvement with the Non-Self-Governing Territory of Western Sahara once alerted to the fact that it was against international norms to exploit the natural resources of a territory with unresolved sovereignty.[49]

Another successful shareholder engagement was by the Norwegian insurance company Storebrand in 2008, when the latter used its ownership to make Chinese shipping company Jinhui to terminate its transports from Western Sahara to New Zealand. Storebrand stated Jinhui's operations had been 'in conflict with Storebrand's company standards'.[50] Only two weeks after Storebrand made Jinhui aware of the breach, the shipping company stated it would 'quit this business'.[51] Jinhui confirmed to local Chinese media it would not do 'any more business out of there'.[52]

CASE B – Wesfarmers, the hard way out

What happened in the case of Wesfarmers' imports of Western Sahara's phosphates into Australia was unique. Through an investment in its processing plant in Perth, the company de facto changed its supply chain and started taking in all its phosphates from elsewhere. Although it might not represent a particular response on the global scene of investor engagement and company response, it does stand out among the Western Sahara phosphate importers. A multitude of shareholders pursued engagement with the company, and the outcome can serve as an example for other importers of how to solve the dilemma.

Two years after the media's interest was drawn to Wesfarmers' imports due to the two dead stowaways on the *Furness Karumba*, investors from all over the world were making both coordinated and uncoordinated requests to Wesfarmers. The Australian pension fund Christian Super became aware of Wesfarmers' involvement in the trade in 2009. At the time, Wesfarmers represented the tenth largest holding of Christian Super. The CEO of Christian Super even travelled to Wesfarmers' headquarters to discuss the issue, together with other investors. Christian Super also visited the company's fertilizer production facilities to better understand the nature of the operations.[53] The dialogue lasted for three consecutive years, and Christian Super acted as a representative of several investors. 'Because we were local, we could speak to the company', the CEO Tim Macready stated.[54]

---

47   Christopher Donville, 'Agrium Was No. 1 Buyer of Phosphate From Western Sahara', *Bloomberg*, March 13, 2015, http://www.bloomberg.com/news/articles/2015-03-13/agrium-was-no-1-buyer-of-phosphate-from-western-sahara.

48   WSRW, 'No More Mosaic Phosphate Imports from Western Sahara', August 26, 2010, http://www.wsrw.org/a159x1568.

49   Sparinvest, 'Sparinvest Responsible Investment Review', July 2014, http://www.sparinvest.co.uk/~/media/international/downloads/ri/jul2014_sparinvest%20responsible%20investment%20review.ashx.

50   WSRW., 'The Jinhui Decision to Stop Shipping Western Sahara Phosphate Rock', April 24, 2015, http://www.wsrw.org/a128x3216.

51   Gerald Hayes, 'Conquering the World or Baby Steps? SRI's Puzzling Progress', Global Capital, September 9, 2013, http://www.globalcapital.com/article/jbxq1jtctxz6/conquering-the-world-or-baby-steps-sris-puzzling-progress.

52   Ivan Broadhead, 'A Line in the Sand', *South China Morning Post,* May 11, 2008, http://www.scmp.com/article/637220/line-sand.

53   UNPRI, *Report on Progress 2010* (2011), http://2xjmlj8428u1a2k5o34l1m71.wpengine.netdna-cdn.com/wp-content/uploads/2010_Report-on-Progress.pdf.

54   Rachel Alembakis, 'Christian Super Engaging with Companies on African Assets', *The Sustainability Report*, October 12, 2014, http://www.thesustainabilityreport.com.au/christian-super-engaging-with-companies-on-african-assets/.

This was only one of many engagements with the company whereby shareholders acted more formally together. A partnership of North European investors, the Nordic Engagement Cooperation, was in close dialogue with Wesfarmers from 2008.[55] Another instance of formal cooperation, through the UN-supported Principles for Responsible Investment initiative, outlined that Wesfarmers's involvement may 'unwittingly aggravate the conflict or become complicit to the oppression' occurring in the area; it was signed by many shareholders.[56] One of those joining that initiative, the Australian equities manager Northward Capital, separately met with the company in 2009. 'Trade in phosphates from occupied Western Sahara is a violation against international law', Northward stated.[57]

The main problem for Wesfarmers' subsidiary CSBP[58] was that its plant could smell bad, literally. The local neighbours of the production plant suffered from the smell of the production whenever the phosphate rock was sourced from places other than Bou Craa. Phosphate rock has numerous qualities, and in order to fix the odour issue regarding non-Bou Craa rock, Wesfarmers had to make investments in the plant. In October 2009, Wesfarmers CSBP announced it was willing to accept the financial cost to source the rock from somewhere other than Western Sahara.

'Following several years of research, CSBP announced an investment of almost $5 million in a regenerative thermal oxidiser (RTO) that will oxidise waste gas to address odour issues associated with processing phosphate rock from new sources', Wesfarmers noted.[59]

'The RTO will enable CSBP to broaden supply options … and reduce dependence on phosphate rock from Western Sahara. If CSBP did not invest in the RTO, it would not be able to use alternate product', Wesfarmers said, noting that it had been 'in dialogue with interested parties regarding the importation of phosphate rock from Western Sahara such as ethical investment funds, Wesfarmers shareholders, the Australian Western Saharan Association, and other interested members of the public'.[60]

The news was very well received in the investor community. 'Christian Super congratulates Wesfarmers for its willingness to listen and act upon concerns raised by its stakeholders', said CEO of Christian Super, Tim Macready. 'This course of action is encouraging for the whole ethical investment industry, as it demonstrates that a respectful dialogue with companies can lead to a change of behaviour, which in turn helps companies and its investors mitigate risks', Macready stated.[61] F&C Asset Management and the Swedish bank Folksam both underlined the importance of the joint investor initiatives for the success.[62] Folksam hinted that Wesfarmers might be re-included in the portfolios. 'Imports from Moroccan-occupied Western Sahara led to a decision by Folksam to dispose of its holding in Wesfarmers in 2008. If these imports stop, it will be possible for Folksam to reconsider its decision'.[63] As seen, investors can exert pressure even after they have disposed of shares in a company.

Folksam still keeps Wesfarmers on its list of excluded shares, because Wesfarmers has never committed categorically to halting the imports.[64] The lack of clear promises is particularly visible

---

55 UNPRI, 'PRI Reporting and Assessment Survey 2010, Full Responses', Your Organisation: Folksam, http://unpri. org/report10/2010_PDFs/PRI%202010%20-%20Full%20Responses%20for%20publication%20-%20Folksam% 20%280017000000N7cw1%29.pdf.
56 Northward Capital, 'Environmental Social and Governance News', February 2012, http://www.northwardcapital. com/sites/default/files/ESG%20Update%20Feb%202012%20FINAL_1.pdf.
57 Ibid.
58 This is the formal name of the company, rather than being the company's initials.
59 Wesfarmers to Norwegian Support Committee for Western Sahara, February 15, 2012, http://www.wsrw.org/files/ dated/2012-10-05/wesfarmers-skvs_15.02.2012.pdf.
60 Ibid.
61 Rachel Alembakis, 'Christian Super Engaging with Companies on African Assets'.
62 F&C Investments, 'F&C Portfolios Fund Interim Period ending 31 March 2013', www.fandc.com/documents/ portfolios-fund-reo-report-q1-2013/.
63 UNPRI, 'PRI Reporting and Assessment Survey 2010, Full Responses'.
64 Folksam, 'Företag i vilka vi inte placerar' [Companies in which we do not invest], http://omoss.folksam.se/ varthallbarhetsarbete/varaplaceringskriterier/uteslutnaforetag (accessed July 20, 2015).

in correspondence between the company and a Western Sahara solidarity association in 2011.[65] So far, the company has still only said it would 'reduce its dependence' on the imports, and it seems to leave open the possibility that the imports could continue, albeit to a limited degree, depending on price and availability of alternative sources.[66] From daily observations of the ship traffic in Western Sahara in October 2012 until August 2015, WSRW has not identified a single shipment to Wesfarmers.

CASE C – PotashCorp, no way out

The Canadian/US company PotashCorp has the longest track record of importing from Western Sahara. The company has imported since 1996 when it acquired another company that had already been sourcing its rock in Bou Craa since the 1980s. Because of its massive imports and long-term strategic contract with OCP, PotashCorp was the first company in the sector to be scrutinized by the investor community. From the early days, the trade was well documented not only through shipment monitoring, but also through the transparent reports issued by the US Customs service. PotashCorp is also represented in very many funds internationally, as a consequence of being the world's biggest fertilizer company.[67] These factors probably explain why this particular company received more and earlier attention than the other companies importing such phosphates.

PotashCorp today appears among the standard 'blacklists' of ethical investors globally. A French study from 2013 looked into 19 ethical investors in Holland, Belgium, Luxembourg and Scandinavia, with a combined investment portfolio of €1500 billion. Of these funds, seven investors had excluded PotashCorp, while many had also excluded other companies involved in the Western Sahara trade.[68] Similarly, a research paper from the Dutch Association of Investors for Sustainable Development in 2011 found that one-fifth of 25 pension funds reviewed in the Netherlands had excluded PotashCorp from their portfolios.[69] There is reason to believe that the number of funds blacklisting PotashCorp internationally has increased considerably since then.[70]

In order to justify its ongoing purchases, PotashCorp has published a number of position statements on Western Sahara imports entitled 'Phosphate Rock from Western Sahara'.[71] Shareholders who have divested from PotashCorp have found these documents offer inadequate explanation.

---

65 WSRW, *P for Plunder. Morocco's Exports of Phosphates from Occupied Western Sahara, 2012 & 2013* (2014), http://www.wsrw.org/a228x2905.
66 Ibid.
67 PotashCorp, 'PotashCorp Confirms Friendly Proposal to K+S', news release, June 25, 2015, http://www.potashcorp.com/news/2034/.
68 Novethic, *Entreprises controversées, Les listes noires d'investisseurs changent-elles la donne?* (2013), http://www.novethic.fr/fileadmin/user_upload/tx_ausynovethicetudes/pdf_complets/Entreprises_controversees_2013_Etude.pdf.
69 Dutch Association of Investors for Sustainable Development (VBDO), 'Responsible Investment, Human Rights and the Extractive Industry', May 2013, http://www.profundo.nl/files/download/VBDO1305.pdf.
70 See for example, Triodos Bank, 'Disputed Territories', April 8, 2014, https://www.triodos.com/en/investment-management/who-we-are/news/newsletter-research/disputed-territories/. See also Armina Ligaya, 'Desert Storm: Why Canadian Fertilizer Firms' Phosphate from Western Sahara is Causing Controversy', *Financial Post Magazine*, February 11, 2014, http://business.financialpost.com/financial-post-magazine/desert-storm-why-canadian-fertilizer-firms-phosphate-from-western-sahara-is-causing-controversy; Meritas, *Shareholder Engagement Activity Report*, Q1/2013, January 1–March 31, 2013, http://www.standardlife.ca/sri/pdf/Engagement_Report-2013Q1.pdf.
71 PotashCorp, 'Phosphate Rock from Western Sahara', August 2014, http://www.wsrw.org/files/dated/2015-07-26/potashcorp_rock_position_aug2014.pdf; PotashCorp, 'Phosphate Rock from Western Sahara', April 2013, http://www.wsrw.org/files/dated/2014-03-25/potashcorp_rock-position_apr2013.pdf; PotashCorp, 'Phosphate Rock from Western Sahara', April 2012, http://www.wsrw.org/files/dated/2013-04-08/potashcorp_rock-position_apr2012.pdf; PotashCorp, 'Phosphate Rock from the Western Sahara', April 2011, http://www.wsrw.org/files/dated/2011-05-15/potashcorp_statement_apr2011.pdf.

Much of the Canadian shareholder engagement vis-à-vis PotashCorp has taken place through the shareholder association SHARE. Canadian investor Desjardins Funds and the SHARE in 2012 expressed concern to PotashCorp vis-à-vis the lack of benefit to the exiled Saharawi population in refugee camps in Algeria.[72] The Canadian investment group NEI, 50% owned by Desjardin Group, is in dialogue with PotashCorp over the matter.[73] Canada's United Church, through SHARE, raised its investment concerns in June 2014.[74]

In 2013, the Swedish government pension fund announced it had blacklisted PotashCorp and the Australian Incitec Pivot:

> The Ethical Council has engaged with both companies since 2010 with the aim of persuading them to cease procurement of phosphate from Western Sahara or to prove that the extractive process complies with the interests and wishes of the Western Saharan people, in accordance with the UN legal counsel's statement of 2002. The Ethical Council has also urged both companies to adopt policies undertaking to refrain from actions that violate international humanitarian law. The Ethical Council concludes that further dialogue with Potash and Incitec Pivot would be to no avail as neither company has indicated an intention to cease procurement of phosphate from Western Sahara in the near future or been able to demonstrate that the extractive process accords with the interests and wishes of the Western Saharan people.[75]

This statement on PotashCorp and Incitec Pivot illustrates a situation where the importer fails to terminate its sourcing from Western Sahara. An exclusion is the last resort for an investor. PotashCorp, Incitec Pivot, Innophos Holdings and Agrium are the main ones in this situation, all of them on new or old long-term purchasing agreements they insist on continuing or renewing.

The most recent of these is Agrium Inc., also from Canada, which entered into a long-term agreement even after the phosphate trade in Western Sahara became a controversial topic for its investors. Agrium signed a large purchase agreement with OCP for Bou Craa rock only recently (2013) and is now under heavy pressure from the same investors, for example being excluded by the government pension fund of Sweden and the bank Folksam.[76]

Coming to an end?

The investor community has shown a remarkable ability to influence positively the behaviour of Western Sahara phosphate importers. Public and private investors, from all corners of the world, have over the last decade engaged in pressure against half a dozen fertilizer companies. Several of the importers have halted the imports, one way or the other. Through that pressure, the fertilizer-dependent country of Australia has more or less ended its decade-long imports from the occupied territory, sourcing its raw materials elsewhere. The remaining companies that have not shown a will to improve observed that hundreds of millions of dollars' worth of shares were sold, with the reputational risk that implies.

These remaining importers are from agricultural nations in North and Latin America, Australasia and Eastern Europe. Australia was the biggest importer in the past; now it only receives a

---

72 Desjardins Funds, 'Bulletin', 3, no. 3 (September 2012), http://www.fondsdesjardins.com/information/bulletin-monde-en-action-2012-t3-en.pdf; SHARE, Shareholder Association for Research & Education, *Shareholder Engagement Activity Report*, Q1/2013, January 1–March 31, 2013, http://www.share.ca/files/Q1_2013_Shareholder_Engagement_Activity_Report_PUBLIC_1.pdf.

73 NEI Investments, 'Ethical Investments, Corporate Engagement Focus List, Update, July 2014', http://www.neiinvestments.com/documents/FocusList/Focus%20List%202014%20July%20Update%20EN.pdf.

74 United Church of Canada, Responsible Investment Update: June 2014', http://www.noodls.com/view/B3629ABB578776679E12989AEEDFACD1D2ED8B42?1793xxx1404476090.

75 WSRW, 'Swedish Government Pension Fund Blacklists Sahara Importers', September 30, 2013, http://www.wsrw.org/a217x2664.

76 AP-Fonden, *Annual Report 2014* (2015), http://www.ap2.se/Global/Etikr%C3%A5det/Arsrapport%202014%20Etikr%C3%A5det%20150409%20SE.pdf;Folksam, *Sustainability Report 2013* (2014), http://media.folksam.se/en/files/2014/05/Folksam-Sustainability-report-2013.pdf.

fraction of what it did. Instead, Canada has taken over as a lead importer. The international investment community must now continue the work in North America. A particular responsibility lies in the hands of the main shareholders in Canada.

Later developments seem to give the importers one less argument to continue sourcing the rock from Sahara. Some companies claim that only phosphate rock from Western Sahara is suitable for the production of some of their products, although this is not regarded as necessarily the case. While Incitec Pivot and others are adamant that they can only depend on the phosphates from Bou Craa, the activity level at the loading dock in Western Sahara is low. In mid-November 2014, the phosphate dock south of El Aaiún reportedly experienced structural damage or failure. That problem seems to have continued for several consecutive months. WSRW has observed that vessel departures from El Aaiún are unusually slow and many vessels are kept waiting to load for weeks on end. In fact, during the first four months of 2015, only five vessels loaded phosphate cargo in Western Sahara. If that trend continues, the total exports of 2015 will be less than half those of 2014. The leading importing companies Lifosa (Lithuania) and Agrium (Canada) in 2014, accounting for 58% of the total imports, had only received one vessel altogether during the first four months of 2015. As the northern hemisphere agricultural season starts from middle of the calendar year, it appears nearly all phosphate supplies must come from other sources. Some importers that have always argued that they could not do without phosphate rock from Western Sahara have now done without it for at least half a year – undercutting their assertion of absolute dependency. The investors have a chance, and the means, to push them to look somewhere else.

Since the 1980s, Australia may have imported as much as 4–5 million tonnes of phosphate rock from Western Sahara, although the exact figure is uncertain. This rock belongs to the Saharawi, both those living as refugees and those living under occupation. The rock could have been the foundation of the establishment of a new state. Regrettably, after four decades of exploitation, the Saharawi last year lost the top layer of their phosphate reserve – the most valuable part. A large volume of that national wealth is spread over farmland and pastures all across Australia, to the Moroccan government's and Australian farmers' benefit.

Even though the large-scale import of this valuable rock into Australia has nearly ended, the phosphorus of Bou Craa is still, and will for a long time to come, be found throughout food products made from Australian soil.

Disclosure statement

No potential conflict of interest was reported by the author.

Index

ab initio treaties 59–61
absolute dependency 136
abuse 1, 38
accountability 32–46
achieving justice 115–16
Act of Free Choice 1969 112
actions by investors 128–30
African Oil Policy Initiative Group 40
African Union 42–4, 108, 113
Africa's last colony 13–16, 32
Agency for the Development of the Southern
    Provinces 20
agri-food system 73, 88
Agrium Inc. 123, 126, 136
algal blooms 75–6, 80
Aminoil Arbitration 56
Amnesty International 45
Annan, Kofi 34, 37
annexation 16, 20–21, 23, 25–7, 29–30, 46, 113–14
AP-Fonden 87, 127–8
apartheid 34–5, 107
APC *see* Australian Phosphate Corporation
appropriation of property 63, 67
Arab Meghreb Union 43
Arab Spring 2011 119
arguing investors 126–8
armed conflict 1–2, 4–5, 33, 42–3, 50–62, 67
armed independence struggle 33
arms race 43
arrival of the future 99–102
assessing risk 74–5
Australian dinner table 120–36
Australian Phosphate Corporation 123
autonomy 4, 6, 37, 43–4, 101

Baker, James 34, 37, 40–41, 109–111
Baker Plans 4, 41, 43, 109
Ban Ki-Moon 16, 110
Bell, J.E. 73
belligerent occupation 54–5
Beni Hassan tribe 2
berm wall 33–4, 43, 53, 108
Big Oil 40
bilateral negotiations 35–6
biological risks 76–81

black marketeering 64
bloodless occupation 54–5, 61
Bloomberg 132
boycott 42
brave era of decolonization 104–5
building independent Western Sahara 89–103;
    conclusion 102–3; introduction 89–90; potential
    of resources 99–102; resource governance policies
    96–9; Saharawi people 93–5; self-determination
    95–6; sovereignty over resources 90–92
Bush, George W. 37–8, 40

calling a halt to imports 135–6
Camp David Agreements 1978 60
Case Concerning East Timor 60
Charter of the United Nations 23, 25, 32, 38, 44–6,
    48, 52, 57–8, 89
Cheney, Dick 40
Christian Super 132–3
Christmas Island 123
civil activism 45–6
civil war 5–6
classification of armed conflict 50–62; belligerent
    occupation 54–5; coercion 55–8; final issues re
    Morocco 61–2; *jus cogens* 58–9; legal
    consequence of coercion 59–61; Morocco in
    Spanish Sahara 51–3
Clinton Global Initiative Conference 2015 42
Clinton, Hillary 42
codifying referendum modalities 37
coercion 54–61; legal consequences of 59–61
Cold War 3
collapse of global oil prices 40
colonialism 2–4, 23, 32–3
combatting terrorism 38, 42–3
Common Fisheries Policy 14
community development agreements 99, 111
compromising phosphorus security 88
confiscation of property 62
conflict and *jus cogens* 59–61
conflict phosphates 120–36; arguing investors
    126–8; Australian imports 123–6; coming to an
    end 135–6; controversial industry 121–2; how
    investors succeed 128–30; introduction 120–21;
    making contact 130–35; massive trade 122–3

INDEX

Congo v Uganda 64
continuing occupation of Sahara 11–31; Africa's last colony 13–16; continuation of taking of Sahara 30–31; pillage made good 26–30; plundering of Sahara 16–21; resources and law 21–6
continuing taking of Sahara 30–31
controversial industry 121–2
Convention of the Sea 14–15, 25, 98
Corell, Hans 4, 25, 39, 42, 62, 94, 118
corporate criminal liability 64–5
corruption 87
cost of phosphate fertilizers 69–88
Covington and Burling 131
credibility mechanism 27
cultural development 38

Dahak, Driss 14
Damanaki, Maria 15–16
Danske Bank 87, 128
de facto administration 39, 113
de jure administration 4, 22
dead zones 8, 80
dealing with natural resources 47–50
declaration of independence 22
decolonization 3, 6, 12–14, 22–3, 32, 37, 52–3, 55, 104–6
deepwater sites 15
defining occupied territory 50–62
denial of self-determination 48
desert impasse 111–12
Desjardin Group 135
destruction of property 62, 64, 67
determination of own destiny 45
determining the future 118–19
Devil's Garden 1
displacement 1, 53
disputed territory 37
dissuasion line 51
divestment strategies 87
DLA Piper 131
Doody, D.G. 85
duress 56–7

East Timor (Portugal/Australia) 25, 104–5
easy way out 131–2
economic development 38
economic integration 43
EEC *see* European Economic Community
enforceability 21
Environmental Protection Agency (US) 79–80
environmental risks 76–81
EPA *see* Environmental Protection Agency (US)
erga omnes requirement 24, 48, 109
Eritrea 44
Esso 40
ethics 120–21, 126, 128, 130
EU *see* European Union
EU–Morocco Fisheries Partnership Agreement 15, 17–19, 30–31

European Economic Community 14, 17
European Union 17–19, 39, 42, 102
eutrophication 80
exile 34, 82
exploitation of natural resources 12, 17, 26–30, 38–42, 47–68

F&C Asset Management 133
failure to seek consent 127–8
Fertilizer Industry Federation of Australia 124
Fertilizers Elimination 124
fiat 104–119
FIFA *see* Fertilizer Industry Federation of Australia
final issues in Morocco's occupation 61–2
financial enrichment 27
Fisheries Jurisdiction 56
fishing 3, 13–16, 29
flag of convenience states 17–18
FLU *see* Front de Libération et de l'Unité
Folksam 133
foreign flag fishing 16–18, 49
FPA *see* EU–Morocco Fisheries Partnership Agreement
Franco, Francisco 33
Freedom House 45
Front de Libération et de l'Unité 55
fundamental ethical rights violation 41, 128
Furness Karumba 132
future of Saharawis 42–6

General Assembly 22–6, 30, 34, 36, 38, 53, 55, 59
Geneva Convention 21, 26, 49–50, 54, 61, 67
genocide 45
geography of Western Sahara 32–4
Geological Survey 2000 40
geopolitical risks 81–3
geostrategic components 39–40
global boycott 42
Global Compact principles (UN) 128
Green March 3, 33, 35–6, 51, 54–5, 57
groundwater 93
guaranteeing local benefit 128
guerrilla war 36, 43
Gulf War 1991 64

Hague Convention 21
halting imports 135–6
hammada 1
hard way out 132–4
Hasana, Salek Baba 5–6
heavy metals 79–80
hidden cost of phosphate fertilizers 69–88; approach 74–5; conclusion 88; implications for stakeholders 83–5; interventions to mitigate/manage risks 85–8; introduction 69–71; typology of phosphorus risks/impacts 75–83; valuing invaluable/uncertain 71–4
historical ownership 2
Hmada, Mariam Halek 6–7

INDEX

Houston Agreement 1997 4, 37
how investors argue 126–8; failure to seek consent
127–8; fundamental ethical norms 128; human
rights norms 128; illegality 128; UN Global
Compact principles 128; violation of
international law 128
human rights norms violation 38, 45, 128
humanitarian law 47–68

ICC *see* International Criminal Court
ICJ *see* International Court of Justice
ICRC *see* International Committee of the Red
Cross
IHL *see* international humanitarian law
illegal exploitation of resources 38–42
illegality 128
Ilmarinen 129
immigration 34, 36, 43
Impact Fertilizers 123, 125
impacts from mine to fork 69–88
impasse 131–5
implications for stakeholders 84–5
importance of phosphorus 69–71
imports coming to an end 135–6
imports to Australia 123–6; Impact Fertilizers 125;
Incitec Pivot (IPL) 124–5; Wesfarmers CSBP
125–6
inalienable right to self-determination 34–6
Incitec Pivot 87, 123–5, 127–9, 135–6
incomplete decolonization 37–8
independence by *fiat* 104–119
independent Western Sahara 1, 22, 89–103
Index Mundi 123
indirect economic consequence of fishing 19
inhabitants' rights 38, 41–2
Innophos Holdings 128, 135
Institute for Advanced Strategic and Political
Studies 40
institutional risks 83
international accountability 32–46; background
32–4; future 42–6; illegality of resource
exploitation 38–42; introduction 32; legal status
34–7; subsequent developments 37–8
international armed conflict by occupation 51–3
International Committee of the Red Cross 53
International Court of Justice 21, 25, 32–3, 35, 38,
43–4, 47–8, 55, 92, 107
International Criminal Court 21–2, 31, 49
international environmental law 64–6
international humanitarian law 8, 12–13, 21–3,
25–6, 47–68; classification of armed conflict
50–62; conclusion 65–8; introduction 47–50;
regulation of natural resources 62–5
international law 20–26, 32, 38, 127–8; violation of
127–8
interventions to mitigate risk 85–8
intrinsic value of ecosystems 72
invaluables 71–4
invasion by Morocco 2–4

investors' actions 128–30
IPL *see* Incitec Pivot
Israeli Wall Advisory Opinion 48, 61

Jaffee, S. 74–5
Jinhui 132
JPMorgan 130
jus cogens 54, 58–61; legal consequences of
conflict 59–61
justice 115–16

KCM *see* Kempen Capital Management
Kempen Capital Management 130
Kerr-McGee 39–41
King Hassan II 33, 35–6
King Mohammad of Morocco 4–5
King Mohammed VI 38, 110, 117
Kosmos Energy Ltd. 15
Kosmos Energy Offshore 41
Kosovo Advisory Opinion 107, 111

lack of valid consent 54–9; coercion 55–8; *jus
cogens* 58–9
land reclamation 1
last colony in Africa 13–16
Law on the Decolonization of Sahara 3
law of occupation 62–5
law in Western Sahara 21–6
leakage 85
legal consequences of coercion 59–61
legal implications of resource exploitation 65–8
legal redress for self-determination 22–3
legal status of Sahara 34–7
legal test for belligerent occupation 54–5
lessons from Timor Leste 104–119
liberated territories 53
liberation 34
lifecycle energy 75–6, 80
Lifosa AB 123, 136
local production economy 17, 27

mackerel 18
Macready, Tim 132–3
Madrid Accords 3, 13–14, 22, 33, 36, 52–62, 65
Maghreb 43, 95–6
making contact 130–35; Mosaic Co. 131–2;
PotashCorp 134–5; Wesfarmers 132–4
making good pillage 21–6
managing risk 74–5, 85–8; interventions 85–8
Manhasset Negotiations 4
mapping supply chain risks 69–88
maritime judicial areas 14–15, 98
market-based risks 76
massive trade 122–3
Matopoulos, A. 73, 87
Mbeki, Thabo 117
mediation 36
military presence 17
MINURSO 23, 34, 38, 66, 108, 110, 116, 129

INDEX

Mission for the Referendum in Western Sahara *see* MINURSO
mitigating risk 85–8
modernization 53
monetizing approaches to impacts 71–2
Moroccan Constitution 44
Morocco–Russia Treaty 2013 15, 17, 29
Morocco's invasion 2–4, 61–2
Mosaic Co. 131–2
Moynihan, Daniel Patrick 36
multi-stakeholder supply chain risks 69–88
Mundy, Jacob 105

National Energy Policy 40
National Office for Petroleum Exploration and Exploitation 39
national question 114–15
National Saharawi Union Party 3
natural resources 11–31, 38–42, 47–68, 89–103; exploitation of 38–42, 47–68; regulation of 62–5; and Saharawi people 93–5; *see also* resources
negative externalities 72
nomadism 32–3, 53
non-renewable resources 32
non-self-governing territory 21–5, 31, 37–9, 48–9, 59–60, 63–7, 105–6, 113–16, 125
non-violent actions 43
Nordea 131

Obama, Barack 38
occupation 8, 11–31, 47–68, 90–91, 101, 108
occupied with referendum 114–15
OCP *see* Office Chérifien des Phosphates
Office Chérifien des Phosphates 15, 42, 54, 81, 121–2, 125, 128, 130–31, 134
Office National des Hydrocarbures et Mines 41, 94
Omar, Abd Alkadar Talch 5
Onarep *see* National Office for Petroleum Exploration and Exploitation
ONHYM *see* Office National des Hydrocarbures et Mines
oppression 1, 38, 43
options for impasse 116–18
Organization of African Unity 36, 43, 108; *see also* African Union
out of the desert 93–5
out of impasse 116–18
ownerless companies 128–30

P for Plunder 2014 122–3
Palestine Wall 30
Palestinian Liberation Organization 60
parallels of Timor and Sahara 112–14
Peace and Security Council 42
peacekeeping missions 34, 36, 38, 106, 108
people of the Sahara 93–5
PetroMaroc 41
PhosBouCraa 14–15, 19, 27, 121–2

phosphate fertilizers 69–88
phosphate mining 13–16
phosphorus supply chain 69–71, 73
pillage 11, 22, 26–30, 62–4, 68, 89–90, 101–2, 105, 111
plebiscite 37
PLO *see* Palestinian Liberation Organization
plundering 2, 16–21
Polisario Front 1–7, 12, 15, 31–7, 42, 44–5, 50–53, 55, 66, 90–96, 109–111
political risks 81–3
Popular Front for the Liberation of Saguia el-Hamra *see* Polisario Front
post-self-determination strategy 102
PotashCorp 87, 127–9, 134–5
potential of Saharawi resources 99–102
precedent of decolonization 105–7
price spikes 19, 84–5, 88
promise of decolonization 105–7
prosecution of war crimes 68
public policy 83
PUNS *see* National Saharawi Union Party
pursuing an ideal 90–92

'question' of Western Sahara 11–31

radical Islam 5–7, 43
RapAgRIsk framework 73–5, 85, 88
receiving stolen goods 64–5
recolonization 22
referendum 34–7, 44, 47–8, 51, 55, 58, 106–114
refugee camps 1–4, 30–31, 33–4, 36, 38, 66, 136
regenerative thermal oxidizer 133
Reguibat tribe 2
regulation of natural resources 62–5
religious prerogatives 44
reparations 20–21
repatriations 34
repression 38, 43
RESC *see* resource-efficient supply chains
resilience 83
resistance 32, 43, 61–2
resolution of Western Sahara issue 1–10
resource curse 82–3, 95
resource governance policies 96–9
resource-efficient supply chains 73–4
resources 1–46; in continuing occupation 11–31; and international accountability 32–46; role of 1–10
restraint 35
return to war 2, 4–9
right to self-determination 11–14, 32–7, 45–6, 90; *see also* self-determination
ripple effect 84
risk assessment 73–4
role of resources 1–10, 89–103; background to conflict 2; building independence 89–103; Morocco's invasion 2–4; return to war 4–9
Rome Statute 1998 49, 64, 68

INDEX

rooting self-determination 89–90
roots of referendum 107–111
Ross, Christopher 110
RTO *see* regenerative thermal oxidizer

SADR *see* Saharawi Arab Democratic Republic
Sahara 'issue' 1–10
Sahara as occupied territory 47–68
Saharawi Arab Democratic Republic 1, 4–5, 15–16, 29–33, 41–3, 90–103, 113–19; Constitution 96–9
Saharawi people 32–4, 37–8, 40–46, 51–5, 57–8, 65–8, 81–3, 89–127, 130–32
Saharawi self-determination 95–6
Saharawi sovereignty 90–92
Said, Mouloud 6
San Leon Morocco Ltd 42
Sand War 1963 2, 7
Santa Cruz Massacre 1991 6, 106
sardines 18
SCI *see* Southern Cross International
Security Council 3–4, 16, 25, 30–33, 35–9, 42–51, 57, 68, 104–119
sedentarization 53
seeking consent 127–8
seismic surveys 15
self-determination 11–17, 22–7, 30–49, 55, 58–61, 89–90, 95–6, 104–119; role of resources 95–6
SHARE 135
Sidate, Mohamed 15–16
social development 38
South African presence 11
Southern Cross International 124
sovereignty over resources 11–13, 23, 25, 30–31, 38, 48, 90–92
Spanish Sahara 51–3
Sparinvest 132
stakeholder implications 83–5
statehood 102–3
states and sovereigns 96–9
status of Western Sahara 47–68
street demonstrations 43
success of investors 128–30
suicide 84
super phosphates 123
supermajor companies 39
supply chain risks 69–88
surveillance 42
sustainability 71
sustaining life 1

tacit agreement 51
taking of Sahara 11–31
territorial integrity 26, 90, 101
TGS-Nopec 40
timeline of legally significant events 51–3
Timor Gap Treaty 1989 24–5, 60, 104–5, 113
Tindouf 1–3, 5, 28, 31, 113
torture 43, 45
TotalFinaElf 39–41

towards a just future 95–6
transshipment 18
Treaty of Rome 1957 14
tribal conflict 2
trilateral agreements 36
trusteeship 62, 65–6
tuna fishing 17–18
Tutwiler, Margaret 40–41
typology of phosphorus supply chain risks 75–83; environmental/biological risks 76–81; institutional risks 83; market-based risks 76; political risks 81–3

ultimatum 51
UN *see* United Nations
UN Food and Agricultural Organization 92, 115–16
UN Global Compact principles 128
uncertainty 71–4
UNCLOS 14–15, 25
UNEP *see* United Nations Environment Programme
UNFAO *see* UN Food and Agricultural Organization
United Nations 3–4, 11–12, 14, 21–3, 26–8, 31–8, 43–57, 68, 104–119
United Nations Environment Programme 79–80
United Nations Mission 3, 23
use of threats 56–7

valuing impacts 71–4; assessing and managing risk 73–4; monetizing approaches 71–2
VCLT *see* Vienna Convention on the Law of Treaties 1969
veto 37
viable local economy 17
Vienna Convention on the Law of Treaties 1969 54–5, 57–61
violation of international law 127–8

Waldheim, Kurt 53
war crimes jurisdiction 22, 49, 64, 67
war on terror 38
warfare 4–9
water pollution 76, 80, 88
way out of impasse 104–119
Weeramantry, Christopher 24
Wesfarmers CSBP 87, 123, 125–6, 128–9, 132–4
Western Sahara Advisory Opinion 26, 31, 47–8, 51, 104–5, 111–12
Western Sahara occupation 11–31
Western Sahara Resource Watch 41, 117–18, 121–7, 132, 136
Western Sahara self-determination 104–119; achieving justice 115–16; consideration of options 116–18; determining the future 118–19; impasse in the desert 111–12; introduction 104–5; occupied with referendum 114–15; parallels of Timor and Sahara 112–14; promise

141

INDEX

of decolonization 105–7; roots of referendum 107–111

World Bank 41, 73

World Resources Institute 80

world War II 43, 46, 56

Yemaá 52–3, 58–9

YouTube 131

Zoellick, Robert 41

CPSIA information can be obtained
at www.ICGtesting.com
Printed in the USA
JSHW011510211219
3107JS00009B/53